Tell Them Something Beautiful

To Karen,
Peace & blessings —

[signature]

Tell Them Something Beautiful

ESSAYS AND EPHEMERA

Samuel D. Rocha

Foreword by Max Lindenman

CASCADE *Books* · Eugene, Oregon

TELL THEM SOMETHING BEAUTIFUL
Essays and Ephemera

Copyright © 2017 Samuel D. Rocha. All rights reserved. Except for brief quotations in critical publications or reviews, no part of this book may be reproduced in any manner without prior written permission from the publisher. Write: Permissions, Wipf and Stock Publishers, 199 W. 8th Ave., Suite 3, Eugene, OR 97401.

Cascade Books
An Imprint of Wipf and Stock Publishers
199 W. 8th Ave., Suite 3
Eugene, OR 97401

www.wipfandstock.com

PAPERBACK ISBN: 978-1-5326-0700-4
HARDCOVER ISBN: 978-1-5326-0702-8
EBOOK ISBN: 978-1-5326-0701-1

Cataloging-in-Publication data:

Names: Rocha, Samuel D.
Title: Tell them something beautiful : essays and ephemera / by Samuel D. Rocha.
Description: Eugene, OR : Cascade Books, 2017 | Includes bibliographical references and index.
Identifiers: ISBN 978-1-5326-0700-4 (paperback) | ISBN 978-1-5326–0702-8 (hardcover) | ISBN 978-1-5326-0701-1 (ebook)
Subjects: LCSH: Mass media and culture. | Politics and culture. | Liberalism. | Culture conflict. | Ethical relativism. | Phenomenology. | Love. | Philosophy & theory of education.
Classification: LCC HM891 R7 2017 (print) | LCC HM891 (ebook)

Manufactured in the U.S.A.   04/18/17

To my parents, Noé and Shirley Rocha, who taught me to be free.

Me gustas cuando callas porque estás como ausente.
Distante y dolorosa como si hubieras muerto.
Una palabra entonces, una sonrisa bastan.
Y estoy alegre, alegre de que no sea cierto.

I like you when you are quiet because it is as though you are absent.
Distant and painful as if you had died.
One word then, one smile is enough.
And I am happy, happy that it is not true.

—Pablo Neruda, "Me Gusta Cuando Callas" ("I Like When You Are Quiet"), *20 Poemas de Amor y Una Canción Desesperada (20 Love Poems and a Song of Despair)*

CONTENTS

FOREWORD

Several years ago, when Sam Rocha and I first began getting acquainted—over Facebook, where both of us shared links to our *Patheos* blog
posts—he mentioned in passing that he was hunting for a new teaching
gig. My mother happens to teach at a major university in New York City, so
I thought, "What the heck. Why not try pulling a string on behalf of a new
friend?"

That very day, I e-mailed her a summary of Sam's qualifications. To
ensure she got as compelling an introduction as possible, I pasted a link to a
YouTube video showing one of Sam's "chapel talks" at Wabash College. The
next morning, I received the following reply:

> I spend all week listening to professors talk. Normally, I'd rather
> cut my own throat than belabor my ears needlessly, but in Sam's
> case I had no choice but to make an exception. He held me
> spellbound. I watched him for ten minutes before I had to dash
> off for dinner, but when I got home I rushed right back to my
> computer and watched the remaining fifty. I'm sorry to say I
> don't know of any openings for philosophy of ed instructors,
> but you may tell Sam for me he is an amazingly gifted speaker.

And so he is. Merely lecturing is beneath Sam; he prefers to deliver
full-blown perorations, emoting, dramatizing, thumping the podium for
emphasis. During moments especially pregnant with pathos, his voice
breaks—not in the dorky NPR fashion, but in the way a voice breaks when
tears are about to flow.

The same theatricality is very much present in the essays that make
up this book. When it comes to persuading readers, Sam's M.O. is to take
them on a ride, aiming his pitch as much at their senses as their intellect. In
place of statistics or syllogism, he delivers anecdote and paradox. He writes
poetry with scholarly jargon, milking terms like "the real," "desire," "order of
love," "nihilism," "givenness," "being," and "excess" for suggestive power that

transcends their descriptive meanings. Demonstrating his ear for rhythm, he punctuates his work with sentence fragments, single-sentence paragraphs, and frequent, darting asides couched between parentheses or em dashes. Whether or not readers find themselves receptive to Sam's ideas, they will certainly come away dazzled, or at least disoriented.

Sam was a musician long before he became a writer or a lecturer, but this sensitivity to form and technique is no mere by-product of that training. His preference for truth rendered beautiful over truth served plain reflects his educational philosophy, which holds that man does not learn through the head alone. As he quotes William James, "If your heart does not want a world of moral reality, your head will assuredly never make you believe in one." This conviction, in turn, reflects Sam's phenomenology: like Jean-Luc Marion, he believes that we humans love even before we think.

For appealing to man the lover, Sam rates showing over telling. The teachers and professors he praises impress him by manifesting their teachings, either through their bearing at the podium, or through the details of their lives. By reciting poetry aloud with eyes closed, ("evidence of a full heart"), Maya Angelou taught him "more truth about the human condition than all the purportedly 'social' science in which I was immersed on campus." The late Wabash College professor Stephen Webb mirrored his own "ethics of excess" in his "Dionysian persona." With his common touch, Pope Francis illustrates the Latin American preference for concrete human reality over ideas. "Papa Francisco," Sam enthuses. "How I love your gangsta ways!"

All this is by way of preparing readers, who may be a little surprised to find themselves attending a performance when they expected to confront an argument. Sam makes plenty of truth claims fit for analysis and debate among colleagues, but his delivery will rope in readers who take a strictly practical interest in the philosophy of education, along with some who wouldn't know phenomenology if it stepped into their path and begged for spare change. After complaining, along with so many others, that Western society has become disenchanted, Sam turns his particular talents to the business of enchanting.

This book divides Sam's writings into four sections respectively titled "Diagnosis and Discontents;" "The *Ordo Amoris*;" "Teaching as Deschooling;" and "Funk Phenomenology." Convenient though this division should prove for readers, it does a slight injustice to Sam's vision, which is very well unified. A more or less devout Roman Catholic, Sam is fed up with the fruits of Descartes and the Enlightenment, most of all secularism and individualism, which have paved the way for the human person's reduction to the functions of producer and consumer. One agent in the evolution of *homo economicus* is the school system, supported by the state and its compulsory-schooling laws. By hooking us on spectacle and distracting us from the real, the media, both old and new, also serve as accomplices in our objectification.

Sam's antidote to these ills is the creation of an *ordo amoris,* or "order of love." St. Augustine coined the phrase in *City of God*, where he supplies it as a pithy definition of virtue. The basis for human relations, from the family to the *polis*, should be nothing less than a good-faith human imitation of divine love. Sam, after Augustine, reads this prescription as theological rather than institutional. "It would change everything by refusing to change anything," he says of the *ordo amoris* in an interview that appears in the appendix. Yet he never rules out the possibility that institutions might change in response to it. "The metaphysics we find at these depths would be very radical indeed," he adds. "They would not resolve into the order we might expect in these days of technocratic economy."

In speaking of divine love, Sam makes it clear that, of all of love's varieties, it was *eros* that created the world and sent Christ to Calvary. This love consists of longing, of God for humankind, and of the Son for the Father. Properly understood, education is "the craft of desire," or an ordering of the soul that inculcates it with a reciprocal longing for God and holiness. The person who devotes herself to this ordering, the teacher, answers a calling no less noble than a priest's.

As he envisions this desire, Sam goes out of his way to make room for the dark and the painful. "To offer true love," he writes, "is to be a tragic lover." Christians will find much of this ground well-trodden, but Sam teases out the implications in a way that might raise eyebrows even among dedicated fans of the Sorrowful Mysteries and Flannery O'Connor. He demands we speak more frankly about the experience of torture, from the victim's point of view as well as the torturer's. He also suggests, as a thought experiment, that we imagine how human persons might better flourish under a cruel dictatorship than they're currently doing in our permissive society.

For Sam, *funk* represents all the harsher and less seemly phenomena of earthly existence. As he explains, the word that lent itself to the musical genre perfected by the likes of George Clinton "literally refers to something vulgar: body odor. Funk is dirty . . . born from the bloody womb of the blues." In Sam's view, reality without blood and vulgarity wouldn't be real. He does not approve so much as he dismisses both approval and disapproval as obstacles to unflinching contemplation, a worthier goal. His harshest term of opprobrium is *sterile*—not because cleanliness is bad, but because it is usually false. And if a worldview or an art object is false, it cannot be beautiful. It is in this germ-free and fraudulent state that Sam finds much of today's Catholic arts and letters.

In pursuit of a funk-and-all approach to studying experience, Sam mediates at length on the gruesome side of fishing and hunting and on taboo subjects like racial pride. "A post-racial era," he writes, "has become a dry-dreamed utopia where a neutered and toothless human identity is the desired norm." He fumes over propagandistic terms, like "diversity" and "relativism," that smear the lens through which we perceive the world. He praises mommy blogs and their comments sections as places where angry and damaged people brave each other's harshest feedback to emerge intact and sometimes enriched.

Nobody should open this book expecting a mouthful of grit. Sam's commitment to funkiness is intellectual (and, of course, musical), but he writes of it in the sunny tone he picked up as a preteen worship leader in the Catholic Church's charismatic movement. One fleeting reference to an episode of clinical depression aside, his autobiographical writing is dominated by wonder at his own blessings—in the form of talent, opportunity, and a variety of fascinating mentors. God has been good to Sam, and Sam is smart enough to know it. For all he may be mesmerized by the funk of the Cross, he can't help sounding more like a man jazzed over the Resurrection.

All of these views Sam spells out in greater depth and detail in his scholarly works, including *A Primer for Philosophy and Education* and *Folk Phenomenology: Education, Study, and the Human Person*. The essays in this book are worth reading not only for their content and style, but also as phenomena in their own right. Composed between 2009 and 2015, and appearing originally in various online Catholic venues, they form a kind of Zapruder film that captures a pivotal moment in the cultural history of the American Church.

Sam describes a tortured relationship with the internet that is fast becoming the norm. When he tells us that people "love to hate" mass shootings like the one that took place in Tucson, Arizona in early 2011, we can agree, having ridden emotional roller coasters following similar crimes in Connecticut, Colorado, Orlando, and other places. When he condemns online political engagement as "a way to escape the boredom of dwelling with others," we can look for confirmation to blogging pioneer Andrew Sullivan, who publicly declared "living-in-the-net" a way of "not-living," and renouncing it "the ultimate detox."

Even before Pope Francis made "the culture of encounter" into one of the keystone themes of his pontificate, Sam was calling on adversaries to drop their guard and connect, despite the danger. As he told the students of Wabash College, "I'd rather have a real, rude, funky-ass friend . . . than a deodorized, thoroughly gentrified so-called 'friend.'" Both Sam and Francis take an eggs-and-omelets approach to spreading the Gospel and building community. Francis prefers a Church that is "bruised, hurting, and dirty" from having "ventured out into the street"; Sam praises the early Church for showing "all the stretch marks of a public experiment, the suffering of compromise and consensus."

Sam's indictment of the American political system and its underlying values places him just ahead of the curve. Writing in 2009 for *Vox Nova* on the failures of liberalism, Sam faced so much blowback from incredulous peers that he was forced to clarify his points in a mock interview with himself. Just three years later, Notre Dame political science professor Patrick Deneen published an essay in *First Things* pronouncing liberalism "unsustainable," for many of the reasons Sam lists. Not long afterward, in his own essay for *America Magazine*, Michael Baxter argued that *We Hold These Truths* author John Courtney Murray had been wrong to place so much confidence in American democracy.

Since then, a group calling itself the Tradinistas has published a manifesto for "a genuine polity animated by Christian socialist principles." The document tags liberalism "the great evil of modern times," and employs words like "eradicate," "abolish" and "erase" to describe the drafters' plans for liberalism's fruits. When it comes to vehemence, these people may leave Sam in the dust, but Sam can still claim over them a hipster's bragging rights: he was knocking liberalism from the left (more or less) before it became cool.

On the subject of racial identity and its growing importance in American politics and culture, Sam sees clearly enough to feel ambivalent. He recognizes real value in watering our roots, divisive though this can be. "The realities produced by the fiction of race are more beautiful than most of us realize," he writes, while warning that "racial pride is always too few steps removed from ethnic cleansing." Anyone who's observed the adoption of intersectional jabberwocky as the lingua franca of editorial writing, and the simultaneous rise to relevance of the Alt-Right, must admit that any postracial utopia is a long way distant.

This isn't to say that Sam is always prescient. He declares an end to the culture wars with a little more glee than the situation warrants. So pleased is Sam to hear the last of the old squares that he fails to note that his own side lost, or that the victors might claim among their spoils the power to curtail Christians' freedom of conscience. His insistence that the Church's "cultural and aesthetic anthropology" will ensure its enduring influence sounds far too optimistic. Chartres and Frodo may pluck the right strings with the "recovering Catholics" of Sam's acquaintance, but who can say what impression they'll make on second- or third-generation "nones"?

True, Sam did name Donald Trump as "the president America deserves" years before Trump secured the GOP nomination. But the meaning Sam assigned to a hypothetical Trump presidency is nowhere near as rich as the significance that Trump's actual candidacy seems to bear. For Sam, Trump is simply a Frankenstein's monster of American consumerism, the *homo economicus* evolved to perfection. In fact, Trump supporters are investing their votes with their profound frustrations against an unresponsive political class and—irony notwithstanding—the global economic elite. In politics, no figure comes drenched more lavishly in funk than a populist, so I wish against reason that Sam could have predicted the Trump phenomenon in all its dreadful glory.

This seems the right place for me, as editor, to say a few words about my relationship to the text. I'm not a philosopher or an educator, much less a philosopher of education, so my appreciation for the scholarly side of Sam's work is distant, at best. But many of Sam's "discontents" I understand intimately, since they also happen to be my own. Having blogged for Patheos since 2011, I've witnessed firsthand the way social media overstimulate us, trick us into half-intimacies, and ensnare us, as political animals, in an endless series of moral panics.

More atomized than ever, and more dependent on technology for the maintenance of our identities, we do seem to be facing a civilizational crisis. If Sam is right that liberalism brought us to this point, it will soon hand us all over to a decidedly illiberal form of populism or collectivism. As of this writing, I spend most of my reflective moments careening from depression to nostalgia to stark terror.

To a point, Sam shares this pessimism and even ennobles it. He compares himself, a *Tejano* in Canada writing in the twenty-first century, to St. Augustine, who wrote at the dawn of the fifth century, even as the hooves of the Vandal armies were thundering straight for Hippo. But, as I said earlier, it is simply not in Sam's nature to look for too long on the dark side of anything, even impending civilizational collapse. Sam the aesthete sees too much beauty in mortality and suffering. Such beauty would be invisible to Sam unless he were seeing through eyes graced with the theological virtue of hope. Only armed with hope could he speak of an unchanging human nature that will forever love first—and desire God, the source of all love.

In *Spe Salvi*, his encyclical on hope, Pope Emeritus Benedict XVI writes that relief carvings marking the sarcophagi of early Christians often depicted Christ holding a philosopher's staff. In those days, explains Benedict, the philosopher was no inmate of an ivory tower, but a "teacher in the essential art: the art of being authentically human—the art of living and dying." In every piece in this book, Sam, both teacher and philosopher of the old school, strives to impart these secrets. The more I read, the more I feel my frazzled heart struggling to calm down so that Sam can tell it something beautiful.

Max Lindenman
Phoenix, Arizona
September 20, 2016

INTRODUCTION
The Fleeting Agave

THE AGAVE PLANT IS a perennial, but each rosette flowers only once. Some forms of agave are called "century plants" because they were thought to flower once every hundred years. After gestating for so long, the flower stays in bloom for only a few weeks. Agave plants require little water and are often cultivated and transplanted for their decorative effects. Their nectar can be fermented into *pulque*—the ancient spiritual drink of the Mexicas and Navajos—distilled into raw mescal or tequila.

Beauty is what we share. Everyone is dying. This is what keeps us alive. Suffering suffers all fools. Anything is "beautiful" that can last at these depths. Anything that reveals the ultimate concealment, which can only be glimpsed through darkness and shadow, operates according to the logic of beauty. The Cross is a necessary and sufficient condition for the Resurrection just as nothing is the metaphysical antecedent to Creation. Like the agave, these mysteries are perennials that flower only once, slowly, and always expire too soon.

I do not know where I should be buried, but I know exactly what kind of funeral I will have. The former prevents temporal nostalgia. The latter provides theological stability in the form of a deep erotic longing, a nostalgia for nostalgia, a desire for Desire that locates me in the art of ritual and tradition. Both are distinctly beautiful, both sustain me, but both are anchored in a future grave and a hope for what might be beyond.

In the summer of 2000, I attended a large charismatic Catholic youth conference in Alexandria, Louisiana. During the height of the Saturday night pentecostal prayer and worship service, on a large convention center floor, a middle-aged woman pulled me aside to tell me that she had a vision that God told her to share with me. We had never met before and would never meet again. She saw me sitting at the head of a barge and beating a drum, with rowers pulling the oars to the rhythm I pounded out. She didn't

1

offer any interpretation; she left it for me to puzzle over, which I have spent the past sixteen years doing.

At first, I took her vision to predict I would become some kind of leader. At the time, I was still wondering whether I might be called to holy orders, which sounded a lot better than captaining a slave ship. Today, as a married father of three, I'm still trying to figure out what her dream might prefigure for my ultimate vocation. I have taken up playing the drum set, and when, as a writer and teacher, I struggle to bend words to my purposes, I remember how Flaubert compared language to "a cracked kettle on which we beat out tunes for bears to dance to."

But more and more, when I teach or sit down to write, I feel a bit like a balding barber. I am gaining mastery over my craft as I leave behind any urgent personal need for its benefits. This is not to say I've solved the big puzzles about the universe, eternity, and my own place in them, much less outgrown the need for answers. But I think I've reached a stage where the urgency has died down. One wants sometimes to tempt fate by calling that the beginning of insight, but even the small flashes of clarity I've gained are probably illusions. After all, it is hard to be clear about things that are not already clear in their bare manifestation. In any case, clarity may be less important now than honesty.

Honesty comes with its own warning labels. It can easily slip into a tell-all insincerity. Those who tell all (or "tell it like it is") are often acting from motives more complex than a simple love for truth. They are like the criminal who wants to be caught or the suffering person who craves release in the form of death. Truth can be told in such a way as to conceal or even falsify itself.

By contrast, beauty—the dreamer's overworked go-to savior—does live up to its press, I've found, though it wears thin sometimes. The reality of beauty lasts when everything else evaporates, runs dry, or goes rancid. Even the desperate call of the beaten-down sage has a beauty to be found where fear and loving anchor corruption and hypocrisy.

Like so many others before me, I found my way into the life of the mind, the study of truth and beauty, as an antidote to the daily irritations of life, period. From first through twelfth grade, I cycled through ten different schools. I got made fun of a lot; in the hope of preventing future abuse, I told a lot of lies. Slowly, I realized that the resources for fighting back were not physical or social but intellectual. From there I learned, in an intentional way, to treat my religious formation as an intellectual compass and heritage, and—after a lot of hard work—a skill set.

This is a sketch. None of it happens the way you tell it in books and letters, but you get an idea, an impression. The days when I had to worry about bullies are long past, but now I find myself facing a more grown-up set of concerns. Observing the panicky mood overtaking politics and society—a mood born from an awareness of impending collapse—I feel as though I am sitting in the middle of an absurd parade.

Augustine had worse things than absurdity to distract him. He wrote his *Confessions* in the midst of desperation. Christendom in Hippo, his diocese, along with the rest of North Africa, would soon fall to the Vandals, never to regenerate. Plato composed his *Republic* after his teacher, Socrates, had been executed, and after all of Athens had gone into a steep decline. The Apostles and earliest Christians watched one year melt into another with no Kingdom of God in sight, and with the Romans clamping down ever tighter, Nero making Herod look positively tolerant by comparison.

We've grown accustomed to this absence, to this absurd immanence, but we've lost the robust hope of the Apostles, the Church Fathers, and the ancients. In our primitive way, we expect our messiahs to return in our own lifetimes—tomorrow, if it's not too much trouble. In their absence, we create false ones to adore, and construct palaces from the ether of our expectations. The "We" I speak of here is not limited to Catholics, or even Christians. Something about the present global condition blinds us to the fact that the longer we have to wait on promises, the longer we have something to look forward to.

Most of the essays gathered in this book were written for Roman Catholic readers in the United States during the full double term of President Obama. By addressing so specific a readership, I do not mean to be provincial. This is not an apology in either sense of the word. The readership of any given book is made up of whoever reads it, whatever their reason may be. Regardless of the author's identity or the publishers' marketing strategy—or the academy's shallow expectations—anyone who decides that this book has something valuable to say is more than welcome to listen. Its audience is general while the author is particular, and the dialectical negation between the two creates a universal.

Speaking of universals, I love the modern university for all its faults. I wrote this book within the walls and halls of four universities: Ohio State University, Wabash College, the University of North Dakota, and the University of British Columbia. When I first set foot on a college campus, I knew I was walking on sacred ground. It was a Mount Sinai experience. I am occasionally reminded of that sacredness and feel it anew. It is not a substitute for the Church in my case, though it is for so many whether they realize it or not. For me it is value added and I'm grateful for it. I sense that, along with the deeper and more primal influences, it has had a role on shaping me and the views I set forth in this book.

The art of criticism is to focus and hit your mark, even at a dire cost to yourself. Like a quarterback who exchanges a deep post route for a concussion, you hold your ground until you don't need to anymore and hope you timed your pass well. Eight years ago, when I began writing the entries that comprise this anthology, I had a lot more experience playing football than I had as a social critic. I winged it, attacking problems as I noticed them. But gradually, as a sense of purpose took hold, I found my aim improving. I began sounding to myself less like some thirty-year-old last Roman, and—more authentically—like a confused product of the age I was critiquing who had, despite himself, some hopeful thoughts to offer for the future.

Of course, a single mind may not be the most reliable judge of its own efforts, especially when those efforts were made over a period of several years. Readers' mileage may vary.

Between, yes, but most of all directly within the lines of this book, appears a fuller and better-integrated representation of my life than I have ever set down before, or expect to do at any time in the foreseeable future. Under normal circumstances, I am used to being only one thing at a time, whether that thing be musician, teacher, or social critic. But here, to my astonishment, I see myself being all of these things in a single volume—and also a father, a son, a husband, a Latino, a *Tejano*, a philosopher, and, of course, a writer. For me, the greatest challenges as well as the greatest rewards, come from examining the ways each unit relates to and regulates the others.

Whatever thematic coherence can be found in these notes is largely the work of Max Lindenman, the book's editor. Max is a writer's writer and an intellectual in that word's broadest and truest sense. He stood by this project from the earliest stages of planning, and I count him among my steadiest and dearest mentors and friends. I also thank my many online readers, whom I sometimes address directly as the medium encourages. Having a significant readership outside of my academic field is something I hope to never take for granted.

Special thanks should also go to those who published the entries selected for this book. These brave souls include Michael Deem, the founder of *Vox Nova*; Matthew Schmitz, deputy editor at *First Things*; Elizabeth Scalia, who preceded me as editor at *Patheos Catholic*; Andrew Haines and David Mills, editors at *Ethika Politika*; and Chris Spinks and the entire staff at Wipf and Stock. I am also deeply indebted to friend, colleague, and artist Larry Green who allowed me to use his artwork in this book, my sister, Ana Maria Rocha, who made the cover art, and Natalie Atoniello, for her able assistance as copy editor. I finally want to acknowledge the encouragement of a specifically theological sort given me by my colleague Andre Mazawi; the example of ritual and discipline set by Eduardo Duarte, especially in his book, *Being and Learning*; and my debt to Jorge Lucero for his sense of accidental and "easy" art.

This book is editorial in construction, theological in vision, ritualized in slow and steady gestation—and a total accident, with the happy addition of images that *show* what I can only *say*. Its completion is a testament to the influence these people hold over me. Whatever distinctions exist between research, scholarship, and other forms of writing—including blogging and other vulgarities—these people have blurred those lines for me. This blurring gave me the self-confidence I needed to continue.

As always, I thank my wife Anne and three children, Tomas, Gabriel, and Sofia, for the countless sacrifices they make in the name of my intellectual pursuits. In a special way I extend my love and appreciation to my parents to whom this book is dedicated. All of its errors remain my own.

PART I

DISCONTENTS AND DIAGNOSIS

Tell Them Something Beautiful

FRUSTRATED AT REALIZING THAT my endless think-piece jeremiads against the news cycle served only to perpetuate it, I asked myself, "What should I write; what should I tell people?"

By now I am familiar with this question. It is the question I ask myself as a father, teacher, friend. What should I say? Literally, what words and meanings should I attempt to speak and convey?

In the past, I held fast to the idea that I should speak the truth, which seemed like an irreproachable goal. But I'm starting to see this ideal as a veil for epistemological arrogance. The honest pursuit of truth is worthy enough, but the ideal of speaking it in some pure form distorts that pursuit into something selfish, a means of self-affirmation that does violence to listeners. It may even do violence to the truth. A truth told in conceit is uniquely false.

Truth-speaking, even when the truths spoken are beyond dispute, is impoverished unless it pays deference to beauty. Truth spoken with total disregard for beauty is rendered sterile. Sterile truth cannot bear fruit. It cannot love. Even these "truths" I have spoken here are null and void if they are not perceived as sufficiently beautiful.

Take my attacks on the news. The nauseating effect that the news has on me is real and bespeaks a truth about the world we live in. But to say so in purely bilious language would only aggravate the bitterness and cynicism that the media produce in their consumers. The oppressed would then become his own stomach-turning oppressor.

I must re-evaluate my approach. I cannot simply tell the truth. After all, I hardly know it. Instead, I must strive to offer an alternative, a suggestion that exposes the false dilemma of sterile truth-speaking and limp tolerance. My answer must pierce the façades of those secret twins, fundamentalism and relativism.

Responding to this question, "What should I tell them," I suggested this to myself: *"Tell them something beautiful."*

Instead of speaking the truth, pure and simple, speak beautifully. Beyond sterile data and information, offer the truth that can only be known through love and loving.

I hope I can take my own advice and think of beautiful things to tell you. If I cannot then I must remain silent, which can be very beautiful. Very beautiful indeed.

June 15, 2010
Vox Nova

Cranky, with No Solutions

While discussing politics, I am used to being described in such terms as "cynical," "pessimistic," "negative," "disgruntled," and the like. My politics might be best classified as *cranky*.

That being the case, I often find myself fielding the question "What solutions do you have?" "It's just too easy to just sit there, complain, and point out shortcomings," my shrewd interrogators remind me. "What can you offer by way of a positive alternative?"

As soon as I respond with nothing or with too little (which is usually the case), I find myself caught in their trap. My whole critique now stinks of futility, of unproductive and toxic crankiness. I am exposed for the crank that I am.

I wonder about this. If definite and workable solutions represent the bar, then maybe it's been set too high. After all, solution-worship often backfires—especially when the diagnosis turns out to have been off, even by a few degrees, in the first place. It seems odd that we refuse to begin thinking critically until we know exactly where that thinking will lead in the long run.

For instance, I have neither the knowledge nor the skill necessary for fixing cars. I don't even have that much interest in learning. But if clouds of black smoke are billowing from beneath the hood of my car while something in there pops and pings, do I not get to decide that there must be a serious problem? If the engine flat-out refuses to turn over, do I lack the credentials to accuse my car of not functioning?

This kind of reasoning, the kind that says that one should always have positive solutions, makes as much sense as telling sick people to stop complaining unless they're able to prescribe themselves a cure. What if they have cancer or AIDS? Should cancer researchers stop telling us how terrible cancer is, in graphic detail, until they find a cure? Should doctors stop diagnosing illness they lack remedies for?

The definitive feature of a good critique is not the shortness of the path it offers to solutions but the presence of sound ideas and observations. A *good* critique is very specific about its discontent. "I hate Mexico" is the beginning of a rant. "I hate Mexico because of the following reasons substantiated in the following ways" could represent the beginning of a sound argument.

Even when big ideas are lacking, there is still value in being told that something is broken when it is in fact broken, or even when it *might* be broken. If one of my tires happens to be leaking air, I would like to be told. I would never say, "Don't give me all that negativity unless you have some real solutions!" Even if my source knows no more about cars than I do, there is still real benefit in learning that my tire is about to go flat.

Never are we so adamant in our demands for solutions than when the critique we face is not to our liking. Then, all of a sudden, we become defensive and place extra burdens on the critic. If the critic can't deliver, we feel justified in dismissing the critique. That way, even if everything else is broken, our ego remains intact.

Critics without solutions deserve our ear. We should engage with and listen to what they have to say and have the courage to determine how much of the truth they're telling.

In the end, we might find ourselves living in something closer to reality and agonistic (not antagonistic) charity.

April 22, 2009
Vox Nova

The Media Watch Us Die and Love to Talk About It

I just got back from eating lunch at MOYS, my regular Chinese spot across the street. I enjoy their tea and most of their food, but I don't care for the stream of network news running through the otherwise serene dining area. Today I couldn't help but notice, and become quite interested in, the endless reports about swine flu. The reporters were marketing their news beyond the confines of their medium, reminding me that I could follow everything online, and even get updates on my cell phone (if I had one). Behind their predictions of a pandemic was an almost euphoric buzz. Free of charge, they threw in the scoop on a string of notable murders, so on and so forth.

Here is my point: the media loves to watch us—and help us watch others—die, suffer, and kill. During the political season they love to help us hate each other in the name of discharging the duties of citizenship. By straining their news through the sickliest reaches of the human imagination, the media offer us the worst that the human condition can produce.

Through their good offices, we spend our mornings, lunchtimes, evenings, and much of the time in between feeding on each other. Unlike the games in the Roman circus, which would divert and stupefy the public on a semi-regular basis, we are *always* plugged into the bloody games of news and TV. It is no wonder then that we have so little time to live and love and be still. To dwell.

We cannot resist the glowing, rectangular coliseums of the popular media screens. Sometimes we can't help seizing sword or trident and joining in the blood sport ourselves. Makes you wonder how *anyone* survives.

April 27, 2009
Vox Nova

The Spectacle and the Real

The mass shooting that took place last Saturday in Tucson, Arizona, was real. Of the event itself, we can know nothing. We only know *about* it, but we cannot truly know it. We can project meaning onto the event by way of trying to create *something*—perhaps something meaningful, cathartic, or something that will cure our boredom for an hour or two—but that something will not be reality. It will be a spectacle.

Those who have known death, real death, know that it is not spectacular; nothing is more mundane. Tragedy is not a spectacle; it is a part of real life. We only disfigure tragedy into spectacle in the hope of escaping the real and distorting truth into something extravagantly false. We end up falling in love with our creations and desiring spectacular things instead of real ones.

From watching the news, we can learn only what is marketable as spectacular novelty. Those who know its real origins know that it is the ordinary, distorted and embellished, tarted up through spectacle, with spurious meaning.

As many polite lies might be uttered—lies of sympathy and remorse—we all know the basic truth: We love the spectacle. We love these events. We may say that we hate them, but we hate them amorously. We love to hate them. By fattening the public on these confections spun from emotional extremes, the media fatten themselves. For some, this fantasy has replaced reality completely, and reversing that substitution could have real dangers. Some addicts will kill anyone who threatens to kill their buzz.

Our certainty that we can see these unreal events blinds us to the fact that we're sitting in a theater, absorbed in productions staged for the benefit of nation-state politics and global conglomerates. This is the new global order.

Political spectacle is the *status quo*. It is the norm, not the exception. It is the most reliable vehicle for success: in politics, whoever stages the better spectacle wins.

A dose of reality would jolt the social order into the chaos of the real. It is not strange or crazy for strange and crazy things to happen in a culture that feasts on the spectacle, a culture where real food is the exception, where "reality" is a television genre, where the ordinary is insufficient.

I will not comment on the Tucson mass shootings themselves, because I do not know them. I only know *about* them. But I do know that I desire less than the spectacle. I desire the sufficiency of reality, the simplicity of beauty, the ordinary love that knows nothing more than how to be excessive in and of itself.

The sign of ideology is the spectacle. The sign of truth is the real. One is an idol, made and loved by a culture that, in its blindness, mistakes it for real, as some shiny new thing: an opportunity for making money, for feeling better about ourselves, for justifying our misery. The other is an icon, mysterious and fleeting, visible mainly to children—the ones who know better than to pretend to know what they do not, and cannot, know.

> And so, whoever makes himself as little as this little child is the greatest in the kingdom of Heaven. (Matthew 18:4)

January 10, 2011
Vox Nova

Politics and Boredom

In the previous entry, I tried to demonstrate that the news is a spectacle: a distortion of and—for some—an escape from reality. A few insightful commentators disagreed that absorption in spectacle is peculiar to our culture; on the contrary, they argue, it's a universal human trait. I concede that this point has some merit, but the case shouldn't be overstated. Some societies place a higher premium on spectacle than others, and the differences are far from trivial.

The mass murder carried out in Tucson is being objectified to an unusual degree, together with all the players—the victims, including Representative Giffords, and Jared Lee Loughner, the alleged shooter. But I cannot deny how thoroughly it captures my imagination. From all those who participate in making the news—even minor players like bloggers—it seems to demand a response. I can't keep my mind off it, try as I might.

I have tried to pin down why I feel moved to write about spectacle and, addressing the more fundamental question, why politics is so effective at creating it. Politics, it seems, can take just about anything and turn it into news; it's the force driving the infamous 24-hour news cycle. At length, I have reached the following conclusion: *in our (anti)culture, politics is a palliative cure for boredom.*

I suspect that many people gorge themselves on media coverage, including online commentary, in the hope of filling the void of modern boredom. If you're a reader, you may object to this. You may protest that your reasons for spending your time and thoughts here are high-minded and worthy. You may in fact lead a busy life, with more responsibilities than free time. But (as I ask myself first and foremost): What is boredom but loneliness, alienation, lovelessness, and the desire for something to occupy our time in a way that puts those stark realities at a distance? What is boredom but not quite feeling at home in the place where we are?

At the basic, descriptive level, I log into *Vox Nova*, other websites, and my personal e-mail accounts because I am not doing anything else. This is obvious, but it points to the descriptive fact that when we are here, we are not elsewhere. Depending on where elsewhere might be, we can begin to see how—and perhaps why—this place is not a place at all: it is an anti-place, a site of virtual reality that exempts us from the real. Virtual reality seems particularly oriented towards the spectacle. No wonder politics proliferate online.

But I also suspect that much of the online futzing around that many people (myself included) dignify with righteous-sounding names like "political activism," "ministry," "advocacy," "scholarship," among others, is really just a way to kill time—a way to escape the boredom of dwelling with others in real communities, real streets, real rooms, real daydreams, real conversations about real things. Real prayer.

This can't be the total truth. There must be more to political commentary and discourse than the objectifying effects of the spectacle. But if I am honest with myself, I also know that boredom is not irrelevant here. I spend too much time escaping boredom online. (Am I doing it now? Is this a cathartic way to keep on doing it without feeling guilty?)

Am I dulling my brain with news in preference to calling a friend or a relative, or perhaps sharing a cup of coffee and random conversations that include genuine questions about real things? Is this what I—what we—are really doing here?

As a thought experiment, imagine for a moment that the entire spectacle of politics is simply an attempt to escape the boredom of modern life: a life that has more to *do* than ever, but less and less to *be*. Less room for Being. What would this (re)vision of politics mean? What effect would it have on how we see and interpret our daily lives and the spectacle of politics that saturates it? And, finally, how many of these experimental thoughts get close to the truth?

I fear to say it and I have little idea of what to do about it but, at least for the moment, I must admit that the more I am here, writing about the news, the less I am elsewhere: with my family, my students, myself, a stranger, with God. And these various elsewheres are much more important, not to mention valuable and beautiful. But the reality of it all makes it ordinary and dull. So instead of facing the real and living God, I make an idol of spectacle.

Embrace the absence; God is there!

January 13, 2011
Vox Nova

Live Free and Die

Libertines, everywhere. We have conservative libertines, liberal libertines, secular libertines, and religious libertines. We have reactionary libertines, sexual libertines, social libertines, cannabis libertines, economic libertines, and anarchist libertines. Groupie communitarian libertines, solo individualistic libertines, populist proletariat libertines, and ironic aristocrat libertines. Indigenous sovereignty libertines, nativist isolationist libertines, border-crossing pragmatic libertines, and starry-eyed lovely libertines. Intellectual libertines and anti-intellectual libertines, influential and non-influential libertines, modernist and post-modernist libertines.

Liberty and freedom have imprisoned us, swallowed us whole.

I'm a libertine, too. I am trying to free myself of libertinism. I think we all need to liberate ourselves from the ideology of liberty. Emancipation from the shackles of freedom fantasies, that's what we need. It's a little more complicated than that in the fine print, but hopefully you get the general idea.

That's why I don't understand the United States Conference of Catholic Bishops' Fortnight for Freedom very well. Joanne McPortland has written a thoughtful post on the messy implications of taking religious freedom to its logical conclusion. She also notes how the first version of the Fortnight was fueled largely by Republican and conservative energy, running high on election politics. But we need not ignore versions of this coming from the other side with the same frequency.

Some American icons of libertinism are especially absurd. For instance: "*Live Free or Die.*" This gem of a saying implies that there is a choice between living free and dying. Of course, it seems to be using the word "die" to suggest a sort of existential death, an unwilled living death like a zombie's. But it should be obvious that this choice is an illusion, a false binary. If you live free, you are not excepted from death. There is no immortality, no transcendence, within this libertine exhortation. Live free, if you wish, if you can, whatever that means, and await your death. You will never be free from your mortality. Libertinism offers no exit from the morbid beauty of life.

"Don't tread on me," a close cousin of this slogan, is even more childish and revealing.

I'm not a scholar of history, but the obvious reading of these words suggests that the person objecting to being trod upon is a poisonous snake. If you tread on me, I'll bite and maybe even kill you. It is something like the more aggressive version of "Live Free or Die"—"Let me live free or *you'll* die." Unlike the first saying, this one has real logic behind it, and the logic serves to illustrate the aesthetics of libertinism. It is a system of aesthetics that prizes poisonous and cranky isolation and pushes its agenda with thinly-veiled threats. It is coiled and fanged and serpentine. Sour yellow. Pissy.

The left may not employ these particular images and slogans, but all things considered, their version of libertinism is no better. If anything, its insistence on cloaking itself in pious altruism makes it even more sickening. In fact, I prefer this sneering libertinism to the dreamy sanctimony of the John Lennon-esque sort.

Libertines, all of them. All of *us*.

June 25, 2013
Patheos

"Liberalism is a Bunch of Lies": Limbaugh is Right About Being Wrong

While listening to 610 AM radio this afternoon, I caught the recap from Rush Limbaugh's first hour. He summed it up this way: "Liberalism is a bunch of lies." And truth be told, I agree.

The problem is that both major United States political parties are decidedly committed to liberalism. Their programs may vary in certain respects. On one side are pre- and anti-Rawlsian classical liberals, along with libertarians of varying stripes. On the other are social democratic progressives of all kinds that seem to take seriously the corrective points of John Rawls' *Theory of Justice* or, in some cases, the writings of Karl Marx. But make no mistake: *There are no conservatives out there today.*

Many will accuse me of word-switching, but these two very simple summaries of liberalism and conservatism should suffice to prove that I'm operating in good faith.

Liberalism refers to the collection of ideas that gave rise to the Enlightenment, whose socio-political climax was the birth of the modern nation-state. These ideas emerged from a hard-won fatigue with religious conflicts and a mistrust for the divine right of kings. From the seventeenth through the nineteenth centuries, they found their champions in notables like John Locke and John Stuart Mill. Liberal articles of faith come in the form of two myths: (1) secularism, or the notion that the state should be neutral in matters of faith; and (2) the notion that the autonomous individual represents the basic unit of value in the body politic.

Conservatism is not the mere converse of this view. It is not a pure resistance to change. Instead, it articulates two independent views of its own: (1) the existence of a divine will or natural law—some ontic primordiality— as the ineluctable, fundamental source of any authority; and (2) the notion that the person cannot be reduced to anything but personhood; the whole cannot be reduced to its parts. It traces its historical roots to the critique of the Enlightenment and the Enlightenment's political consequences, most vividly, of course, the French Revolution.

Chapter eight of First Samuel glaringly contrasts the liberal and conservative mindsets. In the relevant passage, the people of Israel petition God for a king, to God's confusion, not to say annoyance. Boiled down, Israel's argument goes: *Everyone else is doing it!* God, of course, appoints Saul to be their king. But the King of Israel isn't thrilled about it.

Here God comes off looking like a radical conservative. It is not so much that God is resistant to change—after all, God is the very essence of change—but, rather, that the God and king of Israel finds the sudden and pressing need for the trappings of worldly nationhood to be silly and perhaps even dangerous.

So too with the Age of Reason and Enlightenment. Burke's opposition to liberalism, like the earlier warnings from Pascal and others, has nothing to do with nostalgia for holy war or a Luddite-like dread of technological innovation. Instead, these critics articulate a legitimate fear of jumping out of the frying pan and into the fire. As their readers know well, these thinkers come up with alternatives that involve destroying the frying pan from within—re-imagining the state apparatus itself, from the ground up.

When Limbaugh asserts, "Liberalism is a bunch of lies," I agree with him wholeheartedly. The neutral, secular state is a lie. The atomistic individual and the corresponding notions of autonomy and rights are all lies. These lies have seduced self-styled conservatives almost to the same degree that they have self-styled liberals. These lies have survived despite the corrective update offered to liberalism by Rawls (and much more recently, Charles Mills) in the past century. Together, they constitute a powerful mythology that seems impossible to overcome at this point.

Because it must negotiate the appearance of impossibility, the authentically conservative imagination is much more radical—and subversive—than the one of *status quo* liberalism. To imagine conservatively is not to resist change, but to reconsider the false wisdom that Satan can cast out Satan, and to recognize that programs based on the myths of secularism and individual autonomy have no hope of reversing liberalism's effects.

Rush Limbaugh ranks among liberalism's biggest dupes. Without realizing it, he believes many, if not all, of its defining lies. If he has an axe to grind, it's against proportions and degrees of liberalism. Worst of all, Limbaugh, like so many others, seems unaware of liberalism's history, or for that matter conservatism's. In professing liberal articles of faith dating back to the Age of Reason and Enlightenment reaction against it (which is more complicated historically, but has not been born out in full by implication), Democrats and Republicans are all liberals alike.

Even stranger than Limbaugh's obvious confusion is the occasional confusion on the same issues by people in the Church, who, with a much richer intellectual heritage to tap, really ought to know better. Nonetheless, given the choice, I would take true conservatism in a heartbeat. I style myself a postmodern conservative of sorts, which, to my mind, makes me a better conservative than Rush Limbaugh, who is no conservative at all.

November 23, 2009
Vox Nova

Don't Forget: Liberalism is Bad

Q: What is liberalism?

A: Liberalism is the product of the modern Age of Reason and Enlightenment that, in fruitful secular opposition to monarchism, created the political apparatus we know as the secular nation-state. This of course doesn't mean that liberals are against religion per se, none of the classical liberals were, but it does mean that a liberal's sense of social order is strictly and strategically secular, by strict necessity.

Q: Why is that bad, would you rather have kings or despots?

A: We would all like a perfect king and would equally dislike a despot, but this is all beside the point. Liberalism has a king too, you know. The liberal king is the autonomous individual. This new king rules in a more complex way than the kings of the past, but the individual's claims to autarky are just as false as the Bourbon claim to rule by divine right.

As Catholics, we desire the reign of God. So, in a very real way, we should feel very strange in a secular nation-state or a monarchy where supreme authority belongs to anyone other than God.

Q: Okay, so who are the liberals?

A: Anyone who accepts the secular nation-state and its king, the autonomous individual. In the USA, this would include almost every politician in both major parties.

Q: Are you saying that Republicans and other self-professed "conservatives" are really liberals?

A: Yes, that is exactly what I am saying. Look at the genealogies of both parties. They all come from liberalism; the apple cannot fall far from the tree. Look at the hierarchy of their beliefs: everything in both party platforms rests on a belief in the autonomous individual. They *must* be liberal. In many ways, they are more, not less, liberal than the self-proclaimed "liberals," who often carry collectivist critiques of liberalism in their traditions.

Q: Are the liberals who vote Democrat liberal in the same sense?

A: Yes. Their party came into being during the same historical moment as the GOP, and they share similar beliefs in a secular nation-state and autonomous individual, though they may buy into liberalism's characteristic secularism more strongly than Republicans.

Q: Why is a belief in an autonomous individual bad?

A: Because individuals don't exist. In order for there to be a truly autonomous individual the world could not be as it is. Individualism is an isolating and alienating concept foreign to the reality of human persons. Our species desires *communio* and love. For individualism to have any basis in reality, God would have to die, as the death of God from Hegel to Nietzsche reveals.

Q: So what is the alternative to this liberal king, the autonomous individual?

A: The human person. The referential being that exists only insofar as it is loved. These persons can have thoughts and desires that belong to them psychologically, but such things are never beyond the order of love—the *ordo amoris*. That order of love is the center of a true politics for the person. It is the alternative to the nihilism of liberal individualism.

Q: What are liberalism's more practical defects?

A: Well, liberalism evolved during the Enlightenment, which committed itself to installing secularism as a new religion. One immediate, and apparently positive, effect was tolerance for a wider range of religious expression. But over the long run, secularism has had a more nefarious effect: it became a religion in its own right. In practice, this means that you're free to believe anything you want so long as you don't really believe it, and to live out your beliefs provided your life doesn't go against the grain approved by secularism, the one true faith.

Q: What's wrong with that?
A: We are in effect prevented from believing in a way that goes beyond the secular idea that individual freedom is the end all-be all. This idea manages to be a terrible form of both relativism *and* fundamentalism.

Q: But hasn't the secular nation-state pre-empted a great deal of religious violence and warfare, like the Holy Wars and Crusades?
A: Yes—at the cost of encouraging the most devastating wars that the world has ever seen: those fought between nation-states for mainly secular reasons. Meanwhile, as 9/11 and other terrorist attacks demonstrated, secularism doesn't immunize the nation-state from Holy War so much as place it on the receiving end. Plus, the historical record of "religious violence" is uncompelling, as William Cavanaugh convincingly argues in *The Myth of Religious Violence*.

Q: And what is the alternative?
A: A true community of persons who live a religion of love that demands respect for the personhood—the referential relationality—of each person as a non-negotiable principle of political order. In simpler terms, the alternative to secular individualism is to live as a human family.

Q: That sounds utopian. Are you some kind of hippie, talking about world peace and harmony?
A: No. Human families are tragic, not utopian. They are not perfect. But they seem to understand that there are no individuals that exist in total isolation. They also seem to grasp that nothing can be neutral. No mediator can be perfectly objective; everyone has a vested interest insofar as everyone desires love and community. The brilliance of the human family as a body politic is that families live within the flux of uncertainty and vulnerability, not in some sterile place outside it. They cannot pretend to escape from the order of love—even when they hate it, their hatred presupposes love. A politic that analogizes itself to this familial order will always strike closer to

the truth than one that is trying to imitate an isolated creature—as Shelley shows us so vividly.

Q: So bottom-line it: Why is liberalism bad again?

A: In no particular order: Liberalism is bad because it cannot move beyond its own historical ties to the modern Age of Reason and Enlightenment. It lacks the imagination to think outside its favored political form, a nation-state ruled by some arrangement of autonomous individuals who enjoy the freedom to believe so long as they believe in a secular way. Liberalism is bad because it conceives of us as individuals, not persons. Liberalism is bad because it monopolizes religious belief under the mediation of a state-approved secularism. Liberalism is bad because it is at the heart of every major political aberration we find on both sides of the aisle. Liberalism is bad because it paved the way for both world wars. Liberalism is bad because we know that the politics of the day are corrupt on both sides and liberalism is the motor that keeps those politics alive. Liberalism is bad because it prevents us from truly believing in the reign of God. Liberalism is bad because it prevents us from aspiring to become a human family governed by an order of love. Liberalism is bad because it prevents us from *being*.

Don't forget: Liberalism is bad. Far, far worse than bad, actually.

December 20, 2009
Vox Nova

On the Dangers of Liberal Society

Section I

As the saying goes, "You catch more flies with honey than vinegar." In other words, honey's sweetness is instrumental in forging an effective fly-trap.

In a similar way, it might be that other seemingly sweet, innocent, and good things can serve as instrumental "honey" for purposes that are other than sweet or innocent. This thesis may seem obvious, but its implications are not as obvious when one surveys the political scene.

Many times, when I begin to think in these terms, people remind me that my freedom to question and express dissent suggests that my pessimism is ill founded. And, of course, this is a reasonable and in some respects helpful reminder. The fact that I feel confident enough to declare strong disagreement without fear of repercussions is certainly sweet. Nonetheless, I wonder: Is it sweet or is it *sweet*? In other words, could it be the case that the hallmark freedom we enjoy in liberal societies, including the US, is, or at least could become, a means of appeasing or even oppressing the populace? Is it a people-trap?

In many cases, I think it is clearly a trap. For example, when the idea of compulsory school attendance—under the name of the "free" common school—was first transplanted to the USA from its native Prussia, critics considered it a radical intrusion on civic and custodial freedom. There were many holdouts; the last of them, in the state of Mississippi, waited until 1916 to give in. Today, even school choice advocates and reformers agree that school attendance is a perfectly normal thing for the state to compel, since only a schooled populace can execute the responsibilities of a free citizenry.

This is just one case where freedom has proven a rather elusive ideal while simultaneously eroding silently. It erodes as its definition changes, and as we are peddled new types of "freedom" that in many cases serve as the bait, to be switched with forms of repression. Religious freedom, for instance, changes with every generation.

The greatest marketing slogans of liberal society, liberty and freedom, might be the very things that oppress us most. More effective than killing or jailing people is allowing them to behave as they like while reminding them that their freedom to do so depends on maintaining some form of the *status quo*. Do not be misled: whether it is violent or benevolent, oppression is oppression.

As the saying goes, "You get more peasants with freedom . . ."

June 15, 2009
Vox Nova

Section II

In the first section, I claimed that freedom or liberty—or whatever you would like to call the thing that liberal societies claim as a hallmark feature—is not desirable on its own merits. I claimed that freedom can serve as an intoxicating sedative that stifles human flourishing; I suggested that it is the real opiate of the masses whether peddled by Church or State. At the risk of following one cliché with another, I am pointing out how liberty can work like the water that boils the unsuspecting frog to death slowly. In short, liberty is not benevolent—an obvious but oft forgotten truth.

To the casual student of politics, this might cause shock, or even alarm. If liberty is unhealthy, does it follow that illiberalism can be healthy? Does fascism, for example, offer us a rare opportunity to exist in something like a

Hobbesian state of nature, with the strong lording it to their hearts' content over the weak? Without making a case for fascism outright, and perhaps offending those who have suffered personally under the heel of fascist rulers or military juntas, I think it's worth exploring, as a thought experiment, how living in the midst of salient injustice and illiberality might cause the human person to flourish in ways unknown to the person who lives in apparent freedom.

Some may find the idea cheaply provocative, but I maintain it has value. We rarely see movies glorifying the human spirit's ability to thrive in the midst of plenty. No, instead we like to see underdogs, slumdogs, and other pitiable, caninesque creatures show their mettle in adversity.

Could it be that these cinematic heroes are not only extraordinary fictions, but in fact depict traits that emerge as a general rule under dire conditions? Instead of praising those who survive or rise out of oppression as heroic individuals, should we pity non-oppressed people because they have no opportunity to try? Can one be oppressed by the absence of oppression?

In this speculative view, liberal societies and their comforts become shackles that prevent us from encountering the brute force of life and death, pain and suffering, and, of course, the love only born from hardship. It turns an ironically tragic but beautiful light on the very places we long to escape from. This is no real consolation, but its reality is an aporia to consider nonetheless.

With the exception of anarchy, no political form would expose people to these brute forces. If fascism can look like the theoretical solution to widespread discontent, or the realization of a dream, what does that say about liberalism? Can too much freedom and security sap our ability to live at the height of our powers, powers that only acquire their musculature through trials of some consequence?

June 17, 2009
Vox Nova

Section III

Let me be clear about my project: Speculating about the potential benefits of living under tyranny is a cowardly and self-indulgent thing. To be sure, I have neither the intention nor the desire to bring about an end to liberalism as a vulgar political experiment. That would take far more courage than I possess. My only goal in conducting this thought experiment is to test the limits of possibility—even of my own thought.

But speculation can sometimes lead us out into the real. "Plenty" seems to be a rather normatively phrased human desire, often elevated to the level of virtue. We desire to be full, not hungry. Yet, hunger (metaphorically speaking) keeps us, well . . . hungry, restless, and so on.

Human societies seem to cycle through oppression, revolution, and oppression at regular intervals. In these cycles, the second oppressor is usually dressed in the garments of a liberator, a populist, a champion of democracy, ourselves or people like us, and so on.

For that reason, this false liberator is hard to distinguish from the Gandhis of the world. The first oppressor, however, is clearly who she really is and, while we may have good reason to fear her, at least we know when she is around.

The virtue of fascism is its honesty. That is not to say that fascists do not lie, indeed they do. But their lies are lies. In a liberal society it is hard work—and counterintuitive work—to spot lies because they come on a silver spoon covered with honey. The lies of fascism at least give themselves away when pressed, which is why it must oppress all freedom, especially creative, religious, and intellectual freedoms.

But, as I said in my first post, "You get more flies . . ." I also wonder what it means to say "Keep your friends close and your enemies closer," even if it means that we are required to take up Zarathustra's advice to love our enemies and hate our friends.

June, 20, 2009
Vox Nova

Donald J. Trump: The President We Deserve

Newt Gingrich has come and gone. I thought he might offer something valuable in the way of immigration reform. But, alas, he seems to have backed off, adding counterproductive provisos along with more counterbalancing nonsense. Oh well.

Since becoming disillusioned, I've been searching for my next candidate.

Listening to him promote his new book, *Time to Get Tough: Making America #1 Again*, on the radio last night, I began to regret Donald Trump's dropping out of the GOP primary discussion so quickly.

Thankfully, this morning I received some wonderful news: Trump is considering running as third-party candidate! Here is the perfect Christmas gift for the United States of America: a president we deserve. I mean every last word of that sentence.

During the secular Christmas season, which begins on Black Friday, we see what this country is made of. We unite in the sacred ritual of shopping. We attend the new, modern cathedral: the shopping mall. Some go on pilgrimage, others hold vigil services outside, still others create their own alternative observances—"Small Business Saturday," sponsored by American Express.

Surely, if the USA is going to be *numero uno* again, we MUST go shopping. We consume more than any other nation in the world. The others are catching up quickly and we must rise to defend our title.

The only really despicable sin in the American catechism is the sin of poverty. It is a sin to be poor, especially for those who make no firm purpose of amendment to become rich.

Donald Trump will surely teach us how to shop, how to consume, how to be true Americans. This is why America is struggling: we are not as rich as we need to be. Trump understands this. By his bankruptcies we will be saved.

I understand that some people vote for a presidential candidate who represents an aspirational vision of what our country could and perhaps should be. We like to elect people who make us feel as though we are headed somewhere better. I think it's time to stop this madness: it is high time to elect a president who shows us where we are now, who we are today, what we have become up to this point. It is time for a national selfie, no filter.

It is time to elect a president in touch with our truest national self.

No one I can think of fits this description better than Donald J. Trump. To elect Trump is to look in the mirror and face the reality of what this country is all about.

During the secular Christmas season, we like to pretend that we are a Christian nation and also that we are a democratic, pluralistic nation. We compete over territory that is already fixed and set. Everyone secretly knows what we *really* are: we are a nation where, no matter who you are, no matter what you look like, no matter what you believe or disbelieve, money is power. Get rich and everything else will take care of itself.

That's why we stay engaged in wars: to force the military-industrial complex to go shopping.

That is why we have these huge, so-called "public" institutions like schools and jails and other places where people sit in cells, observed by surveillance cameras, being herded like cattle at feeding time into cafeterias: they create very particular economic demands. By teaching people to value themselves and others for their pocket books and tennis shoes, these institutions train future shoppers. Trump embodies the sacred consumer virtues that saturate and sanctify our collective psyche. If we want someone who will really represent Americans for who they are truly are, then we must elect Donald Trump.

He's the president we deserve.

December 12, 2011
Vox Nova

The Culture Wars Are Over

It began when a bright, cheeky, occasionally rabble-rousing group of students I befriended at Wabash College found themselves running low on intellectual ammo. Their publication, *The Wabash Commentary*, toed the conservative line in the culture wars; it pushed a counter-revolution to regain ground lost in the tumult of the 1960s and 1970s. Of course, at Wabash, an all-male liberal arts college founded in 1832, the mood and sense of what was possible always ran a decade and a half behind the rest of the country. I consider this proclivity for the unfashionable to be one of the school's greatest strengths.

As an early millennial, I was regarded as a senior-ranking generation member by these kids born in the late 1980s and early 1990s. On this particular occasion, after our ritual lunch of bad sushi, I stood in line to pay my bill as the editor told me about his latest and greatest idea for an article. It was one of those "What's the matter with kids these days?" things.

"The culture wars are over," I said.

My reply surprised even me. It seemed so harsh. A year would pass before I came to believe those words. Even more time had to pass before I began the task of thinking seriously through the implications.

*

I've grown to appreciate the practical virtue of patience. The art of being patient. Work takes patience. Time. The painstaking dwelling in the deliberation of a creative process. Creativity isn't always slow. It can strike right away. Sometimes an essay—or even a book—just falls out, uninvited. It's pushy and won't let you sleep or play with your kids.

I wrote my dissertation in under six months. A total surprise. Sometimes a melody will just escape from my fingers without the slightest notice or effort. Improvisation. Poetry starts leaking, so I place a bucket under it and try to catch some stanzas before the tap goes dry again. Pure folly. These fleeting moments of creativity are not so rare, but they are incomplete. Only one small part of the process.

I used to kid myself that I could create a respectable body of work from these random moments. Writing, music, teaching. I used to wait around or stall until inspiration came. Waiting to catch the Holy Ghost. Or try and force it. But there's a lot of life in the stuff that doesn't come right away. There are things worth waiting for. And, many times, as hard as it is to admit, the instantaneous art fades just as quickly as it arrives. Plus, the quick stuff almost always needs the slow attention of editing and practicing and so on. Even when inspiration flows, elegance and taste oftentimes begin to emerge only after a long process of fine-tuning.

I'm not a patient person. At least that's the persona I adopt when advertising myself.

*

Once in a class where I was invited to give a lecture on the philosophical significance of the life of Malcolm X, I began by drawing a distinction between action and reaction. The activist commits herself to the first, the reactionary settles for the second.

Activism, real activism, takes work and study. Creativity. Homework. Martin Luther King Jr. read more than a few books. Malcolm X, too. And Lincoln. Far too many of today's so-called activists are really just reactionaries. If they do read books, they don't read any good ones. Maybe most are just clowns, the lowest breed of reactionary: the reactionary who peddles cheap derivation reactions.

This distinction is kin to another one. Philosophy vs. philosophers. There is a difference between the history of philosophy and the philosophy of history. The former is primarily about philosophers, *their* work and ideas. The latter is about philosophy: the work of having an idea, a *personal* one. Primary literature is philosophy. Secondary literature is philosophery, or something like that. You know what I mean.

It is easy (and often profitable) to be a reactionary. Find just about anything, or nothing at all, and make a fuss. Then come the reactions to the reactions. There are better and worse reactions, but all of them are secondary, tertiary, or whatever comes after that. Activism requires more than a reaction. It demands the formulation of something original. Many have confused activists with reactionaries and vice-versa, but separating the two reveals a stark and palpable difference.

Blogs seem to be a reactionary medium, either by definition, or thanks to the acquired habits of bloggers. We react. Constantly. News cycles spew out current events as fast as we can forget them. We try to stay relevant—or generate attention and keyword hits—by appealing to what is new or popular. But I suspect that blogging has more to offer than that. Maybe we have something slow and patient to make from time to time.

*

For Catholics, cultural warfare is both familiar and foreign. I don't think I need to waste any time explaining what I mean by that. Those of you who live in the United States and read blogs drink in the paradox every day. If you're here now, reading this, chances are good you're looking for trouble. I am too. Whenever I tell myself these rumbles are more of an acquired taste than a native one, I recall Augustine's *City of God*, and think: Never mind.

Over the course of this long culture war, the Church has taken many sides, often at the same time, and it's unlikely to quit the field or form ranks behind a single banner any time soon. Matching Church doctrine to pre-fab ideologies is just too difficult. Catholic social teaching was built for this stuff, right? At the very least it's useful for culture warring.

War is useful as a metaphor for its binaries more than its bellicosity. War divides things into mutually exclusive sides. Even a war on binaries does that. Thankfully, perhaps, most cultural warriors hold our attention precisely because they are able to shatter any illusion of calm or unity. The Church sometimes fills this role, too, I think.

A certain breed of iconoclast was born to engage in cultural warfare, and can be found on any side, so long as there's action. These battlers don't change with the season. They are sanctimonious, without the sanctimony. Unlike reactionaries, they have something authentic about them.

*

"The culture wars are over"—that's what I said to my student and friend a year and a half ago. I recalled these words last Christmas. I was incensed yet again, this time over a bad book introduced to me on Christmas Eve. A book I found offensive and all wrong. I typed out a scathing, detailed, devastating, line-by-line rebuttal in my mind, with my head still resting on my pillow. On Christmas, I was tired from staying up reading and losing sleep while blowing up the author in my head. But I was also tired, heavy-hearted. Once again, I had become part of the problem about which I complained. I was tired of the problem, this senseless cultural war I'd been fighting in all my life.

I still believe in deconstructing things. But there's another way. Sneakier. More compelling. Better taste. Simpler, even. Fewer apologetics and how-to books and blog posts about how we need fewer apologetics and how-to books. More stories and memories. Slower. A little bit weird. Rigor. Not boring but unafraid of tedium, detail, and hard work. Openness to surprise. Religious without forcing it.

One of the first things the New Evangelization needs to do is extract the expression "New Evangelization" from its vocabulary. All easy and quick routes and words and convenient audiences and echo chambers can be toxic to the good news that lives inside the Gospel.

Some people work very hard to convey lesser realities. The rest of us might try following their lead. The culture wars have become easy and rote. They belong to a recent past that has mostly abandoned us. Disenchanted, we long for and must begin once again a more tedious task: the labor of love.

December 28, 2012
Patheos

Those Immune to Violence Arm and Disarm

My late Tio Manino (short for Marcelino) had a bottle of Presidente brandy beside his recliner. He was well into his eighties, past his drinking prime, so I asked what it was for. He replied that with break-ins and robberies and murders becoming so commonplace in his neighborhood—and with senior citizens like himself targeted most often—he had made it the basis of a self-defense strategy. If a thug entered his small trailer home he'd tell him there was nothing of value to be stolen. Then he'd invite the criminal to take a seat and have a drink. *Una copita.* Then another one. And three or four more. And one after that.

"Once he's good and drunk," my Tio said, with dark mischief in his eyes, as he reached under the recliner with his large, wrinkled hand, "I'll cut his neck with THIS!" He produced a three-foot *machete*, sharp and terrifying, like something out of a Coen Brothers film. Real.

*

The night before my grandmother's funeral, after the rosary and visitation, a second cousin I never knew was shot to death at a party. We mourned my grandmother deeply; regarding the cousin, everyone sighed and shook their heads, looking disappointed and a little embarrassed. "His poor mother," they all said.

When you drive the streets of their neighborhood in Pharr, Texas, it's common to see shattered glass sprayed across the pavement. Broken car windows. Signs of a break-in or a shooting or both. All my great-uncles, like my grandfather, were armed in three ways or another. They were born and raised on a horse ranch, where guns were essential tools. I will inherit my great-grandfather Crecencio Rocha's lever-action 30-30 Winchester—"the gun that won the West." I've shot it before. I took a white-tailed doe's life with it, in some woods close to Brady Lake in Brady, Texas.

There's a big difference between hunting and self-defense. I don't hunt anymore, but I think I'd like to start again. In hunting, the gun can be either a tool for sport, like an expensive tennis racket, or a tool for work, like a tractor. Tools can be lethal, but it's their ultimate purpose that brings them credit or discredit. Although I am not well acquainted with hunting for pure sport, I know that hunters of either class are like athletes or farmers: they usually take good care of their tools.

This distinction holds for self-defense, too.

*

Most people who buy guns and pay to shoot at targets at gun ranges while swaddled in goggles and earplugs, and who enroll in classes to qualify for permits and so on—let's be honest: these people don't really need guns. They don't hunt and are rarely in danger of their lives. They are not rural farmers tip-toeing out into the dark in their underwear, squinting, carrying the twelve-gauge they normally use for bird hunting, firing into the air to warn the kid trying to steal starter-fluid for his meth lab, and then shooting again towards the noise, half hoping they kill the sonofabitch, half praying he gets away safe but never comes back.

These valiant gun lovers don't generally live in places where shootings occur on a weekly basis; where violence and crime, motivated by poverty and desperation, lower the cost of human life without the media's taking any particular interest; where the schools are guarded like the prisons that they are; and where clubs and discos, despite employing bouncers who pat down and wand patrons as a general rule, still have bi-monthly shootings in the parking lot.

No, the people who are arming themselves these days to assert their Second Amendment rights in response to moral panics sold them courtesy of the NRA and Fox News—these are not people in imminent danger. Whenever violence erupts in their quiet and privileged communities, the media swoop in and we mourn for the victims—as we should when the exception becomes the norm. Or is it the other way around?

Their neighbors, living next to them or a bit deeper into the trendy, hip side of the city, away from the ghetto or the barrio—these pious mirror images beating their anti-war war drums on Twitter and calling for a ban on all guns—are not so different. In deference to principles formed mainly in ignorance, they would never hunt. They don't worry much about self-defense because, like their separated brethren, the gun lovers, they know they're not in any real danger.

They claim to adore Zapata and Guevara and X and other brave martyrs of the left. They claim to hate the military-industrial complex, but they don't have the slightest problem letting the very same nation-state disarm its public. They don't know much, actually, and the pleasure they take in Quentin Tarantino's stylized bloodshed doesn't jibe with their gleeful finger-wagging against the violence reported by the news media.

These sanctimonious gun-banning yuppies and college students are just as insulated as their right-wing counterparts. Sure, they might not all live in suburbia, they might think they are worldly and multicultural and progressive, but they forget that though Martin Luther King Jr. preached non-violent civil resistance, his bodyguards were packing heat. Assault weapons, even. They also seem to forget that their beloved, humane president has knowingly and willingly made use of assault weapons. Drones are assault weapons, right? Where are the calls for a ban on drones? Where is the mourning of the innocent children in the Middle East?

Both sides that arm or disarm in the hope of preventing future violence, miss the present and past reality: violence is ubiquitous and has been for some time. Guns have been here forever, many of them owned by people who got them for hunting or self-defense. The anti-gun absolutists are the come-latelies to the scene, only they don't seem to realize it.

We harbor the largest, most aggressive, and active military in human history. How do we end violence? *Really*? Is that even a serious question?

Neither side seems willing to acknowledge what is really going on right now. We're just lashing out at anything that moves. When guns are unlikely to be put to proper use, buying them is silly and dangerous. Stupid. Banning them for those who, like my relatives, (sometimes tragically) need to use them is equally outrageous.

*

What is the difference between a thug who straps a Glock to his hip and a nation that stockpiles nuclear weapons? There are some differences. But the similarities are just as salient. After 9/11 we went to war. Why? Because we needed to. We needed to vent. We punched a hole in the wall. An Iraqi catharsis.

Right now on the home front, things are not so different. The shootings of kids in cold blood, now enshrined in a sub-genre called "school violence" and given 24-hour media coverage, weigh on us all. As they should. Prayer, questions, doubt, terror, melancholy, paranoia: all of it makes sense. Show respect for the living and the dead.

Insisting that we either need more guns or can prevent the recurrence of such ghastly events by banning guns, is just a wounded projection of the fact that we are already immersed in violence. Every day. Physical and mental and spiritual violence.

Maybe we can guarantee safety in the places we are not ashamed to look at or afraid to live in. The schools that seem so pristine and innocent. The twin middle-class paradises of suburbia and Hipster Town. The pleasant fantasies realized at a safe distance from rural anxiety and urban pain— and international terror. Maybe the places far from where our sensational news items originate, the unreal place whence I am writing, where reality television reminds us of the alligator-killing exceptions out *there*, in the wild—maybe these places can be secured. But any such victory would be pitifully narrow. It would result in nothing more substantial than a peaceful Potemkin village. A mere illusion. A sterile illusion.

I don't have any solutions because I remain unconvinced that we have truly understood the problem—gun advocates and apologists alike be damned.

December 19, 2012
Patheos

Limits and Dangers of Ideology: Against Diversity

> What difference does it make to the dead, the orphans, and the homeless, whether the mad destruction is wrought under the name of totalitarianism or the holy name of liberty and democracy? —Gandhi[1]

There is little doubt: in many places, especially higher education, "diversity" has become what Gandhi called a "holy name." Too many holy names make up an ideology.

Ideology is part of the human condition, but it functions in various ways. When settled on in advance, ideology acts as a screen that prevents each party in a dispute from knowing and understanding the other. It serves

1. Gandhi, *Non-Violence in Peace and War*, 1:142.

as an excuse to consume the other before she is given to me. It distorts and reshapes the other according to my own horizon of possibility. This function of ideology, *ideology-in-advance*, sanitizes and deodorizes the world with a fragrance I can control and live with. There is no room for death or dying in this world—no space for real life, as there is no oxygen or warmth.

No, there are only numbers, objects, lists, casualties, quotas, and statistics to be sacrificed to our ideology-in-advance. Like a butcher, ideology-in-advance quarters and measures the world and the person. As passionate as we may become and as pure as our ideology may seem, even an ideology of love, compassion, democracy, diversity, multiculturalism, or what have you, when used in advance, is not innocent.

We can never escape ideology completely, but neither should everything be political. Rather, ideology should only emerge after our encounter with the world and the person. The excessive and overwhelming nature of the world and real people should make the ideas we endorse afterward tremble with uncertainty and humility. Our ideology should always remain an *ideology-to-come*: never quite decided; always suspended; rooted in the truth.

Martin Luther King Jr.'s priceless work has been reduced to dreamy slogans and Gandhi has been domesticated into a nice, rather thin, old man. But their place in history was fixed, not only by what they did, but also by the work they left to be done, in the opportunities they bequeathed to their successors and critics. It is false to think that either one of them, or any other of the notable humanitarians of the past century, was a multiculturalist, if by that term we mean someone who accepts that strange cocktail of ethical and cultural relativism mixed with absurdly postmodernist notions of reality. No, quite the contrary, each of them burned with a religious sense of love. Neither the l-o-v-e word sold in bulk by other ideologues nor its connotation, they believed deeply in its phenomenological veracity, only known in the flesh of suffering.

There is nothing tolerant about Zapata's claim "*La tierra pertenece a quien la trabaja,*" "The earth belongs to the person who works it." There is nothing relativistic about Paulo Freire's fight for the oppressed. These activists' claims are truth claims that are non-negotiable, which is what gives reason and substance to their activism and rebellion. There is something amiss when Marxist revolution is cast as relativistic. Even Derrida's deconstruction and Foucault's genealogies were not meant to instill a new language for demagogy or colonization. In every case I've mentioned there is a strong spirit of righteous intolerance towards objective evils in the world: hate, genocide, racism, xenophobia, sexism, to name only a few. The greatest opposition and source of intolerance seems to be the dehumanization of the person into a mere object or resource—the transformation of the *homo sapiens* into the *homo economicus*.

The problem, as I see and experience it, is that the language of activists and critical theorists has been reduced to slogans deployed to promote the diversity business. At the educational, business, and civic level, a reputation for being "diverse" bestows tangible benefits to the corporate entity. Those in charge often need my Mexican identity to cleanse their hands and sanitize their institution, and to help immunize them from infection by the virulent label of "racist." And they pay. But my identity is not for sale; I am not reducible to a billboard, regardless of how many have been abandoned to the shell of pure identity.

The surest sign that an idea is ideological appears when the interrogation of its keywords, or preferred language, is interpreted to be evil, or at least morally suspect. So be it. As Gandhi reminds us, it makes no difference to the oppressed what we call an ideology. Oppression can come under many different nomenclatures, including "diversity" and even "love." That is why deconstruction and critical insight must always remain under erasure and reconstruction.

Whenever we settle on a nostrum like diversity, democracy, or what have you, we lose the essence of its meaning—the *being* of meaning. Radically pluralistic ideas are not relativistic or patronizing, and yet they are never decided once and for all. They thrive in the flux, they are in constant motion, they are spoiled by being still. Even if we were to exchange names we would still miss the point, which is to remain nameless, undecided, yet dogmatically committed to something concrete and worthwhile beyond the immediate. This can only be accomplished if we suspend our ideology-in-advance and convert it into an ideology-to-come.

The restlessness of ideology-to-come reminds us of the flesh of matter. The numbers, statistics, good causes, and other things that were once persons before ideology-in-advance cleansed them, once more take on flesh. They become more than posters and slogans bragging about how many poor and colored folk they have collected, all for the sake of appearing not racist or anti-racist.

Suspending our ideology preserves people as real, bleeding persons to be loved. Ideology-in-advance remains once we have fooled ourselves into thinking that we've been healed. We find salvation in the wounds instead.

May 1, 2009
Vox Nova

Fear of Generosity

If you ask for an opinion on something controversial, like abortion or war, in intimate and full confidence, the answer you get will differ vastly from the one you would get in a public forum. Understandably so—there are real liabilities to being open and honest. Anyone who has told the unvarnished truth too many times in public has been punished for it.

Excuses aside, there is still a serious problem: in place of sincere but measured conversation and dialogue, we assume postures directed at repelling attackers and holding ground. Sometimes they work; they may even help us to gain ground. But the gains and losses come and go. Long after the former are celebrated and the latter mourned, the fear of generosity remains. It is combat's most enduring legacy.

I've heard it said many times: "I think X view, which is contrary to my own, has some merit, and I might even consider adopting it, but the other side is using X to find an opening to muscle their way in." The slippery slope fallacy has its own logic, but that logic is much more emotional than truthful. The mere thought of conceding ground or extending goodwill to opponents has the power to terrify and calcify.

I am sure that I am guilty of this defensiveness, too, in ways I am presently blind to. But, somehow, in spite of myself and my defenses, I've managed to meet communists who love to play golf, Republicans who volunteer every week at the local food pantry, Democrats who care for ungrateful foster children, atheists who love the religious arts, theists who skip church, and other human anomalies. From direct and extended contact with real radical feminists prepared to fight for legal abortion and real Christian fundamentalists prepared to fight against it, I can say, with no reservations, that each person holds a real portion of the truth.

In fact, I'd bet there are few areas of controversy where any side, no matter how crazy it may sound, operates purely out of malice or bad intentions. Sure, false consciousness plagues us all, and blind spots forever abound, but when it comes to what people intend, I am not so sure that goodwill has abandoned the field.

Of course, as Ivan Illich reminds us, the road to hell is paved with good intentions.

Conversation depends on generosity, the willingness to assume that an interlocutor is speaking in good faith and operating with good intentions. If we cannot be generous, we cannot communicate. There is no conversation between ungenerous combatants. We can't even fight and we don't—we repeat the same, tired refrains to people who already agree with us and give angry gotcha replies to the ones who venture into our territory.

The same is true in other forms of combat: find a great competitor in war or sport and you will find someone who has respect for the most contemptible of opponents.

Hatred, in its purest form, can be a form of reverence.

Nowadays, we don't know how to hate. We hate like kindergartners. We call people names and convince ourselves that they are really, really, *really* bad and naughty. We don't take the time or effort to be generous and hate properly.

There is a great deal of money to be made and attention to be gained by casting things in polemical binaries. These binaries are as mutually beneficial as they are exclusive. To have a healthy rivalry, you need to create mirror opposites, with points and counterpoints, each side caricaturing the other perfectly. There is no room for "Perhaps," "It depends," "Maybe," "It seems," and "Could you give me an example of what you're talking about?"

Some contend that this represents a failure in argument and discourse. I disagree. I think it is garden-variety fear. Knowing the stakes, and the possibility that we might be taken advantage of or misinterpreted, see our words abused and our intentions distorted, we avoid argument altogether. Terrified, we've created fortresses and castles to guard against generosity.

To be generous is to risk—to risk being hurt or, even worse, being wrong to some degree.

But there is another risk in generosity, in the offering that precedes the gift: the risk of love.

This is what the fear of being generous conceals, I think: the greater despair that desires love so much, it avoids and runs from it at all costs.

What we need is healing, and that won't come so easily or so fast. I don't know where to begin except to note that generosity begins in trust and all the Hallmark clichés.

Perhaps we might begin by considering the predicament and dwelling in its shadow before we run at the next plastic solution. I think we often seek solutions before fully understanding the scope of the catastrophe. Or maybe we should quit considering so damn much and just go ahead and show some generosity, risks be damned. This will require courage, and light.

May 14, 2014
Patheos

Ideologies of Food: A Reply to Webb

At six this morning, I was butchering three large catfish, one of them well over twenty pounds. I filled a small cooler with fillets. We ate catfish for dinner last night and we will eat catfish again (and again). Tonight, and for lunch tomorrow.

Catching fish—especially big ones—is thrilling. Cleaning them isn't. I recall my nausea-filled regret that Sunday evening in adolescence when I shot nine rabbits—a personal record—and had to clean them all, each one stinking, with their delicate summer fur sticking to me and my knife. I don't hunt rabbits anymore.

Back to the catfish: Unlike other fish, catfish bleed thick, red blood that clots and sticks to your hands. It is very hard to kill them mercifully, since it's nearly impossible to determine, as *rigor mortis* sets in, whether they're dead or alive. There is very little romance in cleaning a fish—even less in cleaning a whole mess of them.

Catch-and-release is the luxury of those who fish for pure, self-indulgent sport: it marries the reward of the catch to the absolution that comes with a safe release. Fishing for food is very different. Sure, you get the rush of the catch, but you also face the responsibility and labor of harvesting, storing, cooking, sharing in a plentiful catch.

To put it crudely, the superior airs assumed by catch-and-release fisherman come from their ass-backwards and self-deluded thinking. No matter how expensive and delicate your tackle is, no matter how noble and enlightened your intentions, at the end of the day you are still exploiting fish as objects for cheap—that is to say shallow, not inexpensive—pleasure, and ducking the responsibilities, not to mention the gore, involved in food-making.

Catch-and-release fishing is quintessentially liberal: the bloodless violence, justified by a pious creed of tolerance, mutual respect, and compromise that conceals an objectifying disenchantment. Like the fly-fishing snob who only photographs his pristine catch, the liberal is a closet predator who insults his prey by refusing to eat it outright. By living out the delusion that they are not predators at all, or at least belong to a better class of predator, both end up consuming more voraciously than ever.

Those who hunt and fish for food, especially because they *need* the food, see and experience something about the tragic beauty of nature that the self-righteous, liberal "sportsman" is blind to.

I am not trying to argue that one ought to fish or hunt or even eat meat. But those who hunt and fish for sport, without the responsibility of food-making, are wrong to moralize or act uppity. And, of course, those who make food from their prey should do so with a sense of reverence for the life they take and blood they spill.

This view I hold explains some part of why I am in concert with the spirit of the latest article by my colleague and dear friend, Stephen Webb, "Against the Gourmands: In Praise of Fast Food as a Form of Fasting," which appears in the issue on food and flourishing in *The Other Journal.* Webb has been involved with the topic of food and theology for some time. A more careful look at his thoughts can be found in his books, *Good Eating* and *God and Dogs.*

Here, Webb is happy to display a sense of conservatism so tortured as to be effectively liberal—even progressive. A conservative, one would think, would be skeptical of change, certainly of the drastic changes to the ways we eat. Wendell Berry is deeply conservative in this way. Webb is not.

Instead, Webb declares himself "a supporter of free markets and an optimist (for the most part) about technology." This leads him to wax optimistic about corporate food production to the futuristic extreme of "in vitro" and "cultured" meat products. It seems today's self-proclaimed conservatives don't care about conserving much except the free market, free and willy-nilly liberal as can be.

Tortured conservatism aside, Webb's biggest mistake is to speak of food without recourse to the phenomenological experience of food and eating. (*Babette's Feast* and fried catfish both immediately come to mind.) And what about the body? Surely we are not cars that run on fuel, surely our bodies are not combustion engines. For Webb, there is little difference. He invokes platitude after platitude about this thing called "food" to the point of making the laughable claim that, since the only non-utilitarian meal is the Eucharist, we might as well eat McDonald's the rest of the time.

But at least Webb writes in an irreverent tone. With high piety weighing down so much of the contemporary discourse on food, this counts as a saving grace. When Webb critiques William Cavanaugh, Michael Pollan, and their ilk from a capitalist point of view, I may disagree with his formal analysis, but I am grateful to Webb for jolting awake the irony latent in the ways we now think and practice eating, fishing, and the rest.

In the end, by showing how the market co-opts *everything*—including the socially conscious, fair trade, free range, all-natural-no-preservatives, community-garden types—Webb eventually defeats his own argument for capitalism and vindicates Cavanaugh's objections to it. This is precisely what is wrong with capitalism, and there is no way to fix it.

To cleanse free markets from the influence of sin, as Webb proposes, will never work.

Socialism will never do, only a departure from modernity itself, a second Enlightenment, an Age of Re-Enchantment.

As I see it, the deeper point goes back to where I began: there is a liberal ideology of consumption that hates to acknowledge itself as an enabler of predation. A deep-seated self-hatred and deception lurks in and around the righteousness of fair trade coffee shops, fly fishing boutiques, and organic food specialty stores.

Webb, in his unapologetically capitalist spirit, tells us what the more pious, in-vogue types surely won't admit: in real life, there is no catch-and-release. There will always be tragedy and blood—even at Holy Communion.

A bloodless, sterilized world of secularism, individualism, and nation-states, born from the liberal womb of modernity is a toxic, disenchanting ideology that hides its absent core: nihilism.

Almost time to go fishing again. After all, it is *the* Gospel sport.

August 8, 2011
Vox Nova

The Splenda of Truth: Remarks on Relativism

Those most upset by and concerned about relativism usually claim the goal of preserving truth. If this is the case, then it would make sense to clarify for the record what relativism is and is not. Otherwise, there is something amiss and asymmetrical about the whole situation.

Sadly, I often observe this messy lack of symmetry in discussions among anti-relativists. In fact, one of the most relativistic aspects of today's discussions about relativism is the use of the term "relativism" with very little effort made on anyone's part to define what, exactly, the term is meant to describe and show.

Relativism, in anti-relativist circles, has become something like a code word for, "This is very, very bad; it encourages all the things we don't like about the world and is becoming very influential; you should be scared and angry and use it, negatively, to convince people that you are on our side, the good side."

Maybe it is useful for some people to use the word "relativism" that way. A pep rally jeer. An anti-mascot. (Cheerleader: "Relativism?" Crowd: "No! HELL no!") The fun of rally cries notwithstanding, this usage cannot make the necessary claims to support the judgment that relativism is so very bad in the first place, or even in the last place.

There are a lot of relativistic anti-relativists out there.

*

The quick argument from authority, at least among Catholics, involves citing Benedict XVI's well-known formulation "the dictatorship of relativism." By quoting it recently, Pope Francis has raised its stock.

On close examination, however, it becomes apparent that both of these claims refer to something very specific. The popes are not using the term carelessly. In many ways, their use of the term—especially Francis's effort to be faithful to Benedict's original usage and intention—is a good model of how to be a serious anti-relativist.

On its own, in isolation, Benedict's logic would go something like this: (major premise) Dictatorship is bad; (minor premise) Relativism has established a dictatorship; (conclusion) Relativism is bad. This sort of circular logic does no justice to the claims Benedict made in his final homily as a cardinal:

> We are building a dictatorship of relativism that does not recognize anything as definitive and whose ultimate goal consists solely of one's own ego and desires.[2]

Though Francis used the term in a slightly different context, he demonstrates that he understands its original meaning:

> But there is another form of poverty! It is the spiritual poverty of our time, which afflicts the so-called richer countries particularly seriously. It is what my much-loved predecessor, Benedict XVI, called the "tyranny of relativism," which makes everyone his own criterion and endangers the coexistence of peoples. And that brings me to a second reason for my name. Francis of Assisi tells us we should work to build peace. But there is no true peace without truth! There cannot be true peace if everyone is his own criterion, if everyone can always claim exclusively his own rights, without at the same time caring for the good of others, of everyone, on the basis of the nature that unites every human being on this earth.[3]

2. Homily of his eminence Card. Joseph Ratizinger, Dean of the College of Cardinals, Vatican Basilica, Monday, 18 April 2005. Retrieved from http://www.vatican.va/gpII/documents/homily-pro-eligendo-pontifice_20050418_en.html on February 11, 2017.

3. Audience with the diplomatic corps accredited to the Holy See, address of Pope Francis, Sala Regia, Friday, 22 March 2013. Retrieved from http://w2.vatican.va/content/francesco/en/speeches/2013/march/documents/papa-francesco_20130322_corpo-diplomatico.html on February 11, 2017.

What kind of relativism are Benedict and Francis referring to? It would seem that they are speaking about a very general, but quite real, kind of egoism, rooted in pride and ending, ultimately, in a fundamental ontological disorder. In technical philosophical terms, this could describe any number of specific positions, but it is an apt way to think about all major schools of thought within modernity and beyond.

Most of all, when captured within a politically salient tradition, it seems to refer most directly to western liberalism, libertarianism, and all the liberty-based logics of social order that have proliferated over the past four hundred years or so.

In one sense, the relativism noted by our present and past popes is very generic, so generic that it could simply be called "sin," but it is also specifically oriented against the thinking behind the politics of early, mid, and late modernity: the individualist state-neutrality of liberalism. We should expect, then, to find other relativists than the so-called liberals of the left. The liberals of the right, today's so-called conservatives, often invoke an identical relativism of the type that Benedict and Francis condemned.

The liberalism of relativism can be found everywhere within the US political context. It is found as commonly among self-professed conservatives as among self-professed liberals, though only a few sharp-eyed observers seem to take any notice.

*

When I think of the word "relativism," without an appeal to authority, papal or otherwise, I think of its most obvious reference. Something about relatives and relations between them.

Relativism, in ordinary language, seems to point to the characteristic of being dependent on something else in order to be true. My relatives, the people I am related to, are the people I depend on, in a very literal way, in order to exist. Declaring something to be relative, then, suggests no more than the following: What something is depends on its relation to something else in order to be what it is.

Not only is this idea harmless, it also seems to be true. Could it be the case that relativism, rather than denying all truth, is instead descriptive of an important truth?

Maybe. It depends.

*

Most people who invoke the term "relativism" by making statements like "It's all relative" inflect it to make a claim both stark and normative.

They seem to be saying that, since things cannot be the case outside of their relations, then everything hangs on these fragile relations, and nothing has integrity in itself.

Relativism, under this formulation, is one step away from nihilism.

Not that this claim need be offensive, nor should it be dismissed automatically as false. It can be used to make some claims that lead to the obnoxious sort of relativism that many anti-relativists, myself included, abhor. But it can also be parsed out in other ways.

Here are three different, but related, popular forms of relativism:

1. Metaphysical relativism. This is the view that the world itself, the reality of all things, is relative and therefore cannot exist with any objective sense of integrity. To be a metaphysical relativist is, ultimately, to question the very reality of one's sensations, and to critique all things beyond them for existing outside that relation. No one can set the boundary of what is real or not real—no one, that is, except a singular, intending ego that refuses to recognize the real.

2. Moral relativism. This is the view, often based on metaphysical relativism, that, since moral duties, obligations, and just deserts are relative and not based in a comprehensive account of morality, nothing can establish a universal ethics. It all just depends. (Some call this view consequentialism, but they do injustice to the consequentialist tradition in ethics. Moral relativism is more radical and would deny the systematic claims of rule utilitarianism, to cite one example, as relative.) Moral relativism also argues that moral codes or systems cannot be judged except in relation to themselves in their social and historical context.

3. Cultural relativism. This view is usually based on the previous two views. It claims that peoples and their ways of life are relative to the relations and experiences that define them, not to any outside, and therefore unrelated, view of the matter. Therefore, cultural relativism claims that a culture or cultural practice cannot be judged according to the relative speculation of another culture. A certain kind of multiculturalism, an outgrowth of a certain kind of cultural anthropology, is based on this view.

Memorizing these forms of relativism will do no good. The point is to use this taxonomy to understand what, for some people, relativism is about.

It is important to acknowledge that each of these forms of relativism has something significant to say about reality, morals, and culture. It is also important to recognize that these generic positions do not offer a perfect understanding of what someone who believes in relativism really thinks.

Furthermore, many people who hold these beliefs do so without knowing what to call them and how to understand them. And I am not sure that they are mutually inclusive, they seem like they should be, but who knows.

*

Relativism thrives in two places: (1) in the form of shallow ideas popular with the US public at large, often passed on through schools and television and making their way into undergraduate classrooms everywhere (and also among a few unthinking dimwit professors who haven't read a book since the 1970s); and (2) among perennially worried and angry anti-relativists, many of them Catholic, and many to be found online and on talk radio, who want you to think that relativism writ large is everywhere, saturating politics and ideology, especially amongst those rancid and sour lefty academics.

I cannot speak for all of academia, but I can speak for a couple hundred or so academics and, of course, for myself. Many of us may lean leftward, at one angle or another, but none of us is a relativist. Not one. The farther left our politics, the harder a stand against relativism we're likely to take. Whenever a colleague's offhand remark has left me in doubt, a few questions sufficed to establish that relativism played no part in shaping the person's worldview.

Among hard scientists and mathematicians, I've routinely observed that anything resembling relativism, especially metaphysical relativism, is received with total disdain.

*

A recent statistical study involving 3,000 analytical philosophers revealed the following points of consensus:

- Non-skeptical realism about the external world
- Scientific realism about theoretical entities
- Atheism
- Belief in a priori knowledge
- Switching on the trolley problem (intervening so that 1 person dies instead of 5)

The first two bullet points declare an unsurprising and obvious note of solidarity between Catholics and atheists (and most reasonable people): we're not inclined to doubt the reality of the external world, nor the reality of theoretical things, like concepts.

In fact, it is not absurd to claim that the atheist point of view requires a stronger aversion to relativism than the religious one. Indeed, in certain important respects, Catholics may, in fact, be more prone to relativism than atheists.

*

In the 1990s, the late feminist political philosopher Susan Moller Okin published a provocative essay asking the question "Is Multiculturalism Bad for Women?" She demonstrated the incompatibility of the multiculturalist position that endorses cultural relativism and the feminist position that defends the notion that women are the moral equivalent of men. This argument, which stirred up great controversy, revealed another incompatibility between feminism and moral relativism.

As a purely anecdotal note, of all the feminist theorists and academics I know, not one subscribes to relativism. Add to that the prophetic Black intellectual tradition and, again, I know of zero relativists, past or present, in intellectual circles.

*

Pragmatism is a form of relativism, you say? I think Richard Rorty came very close, but his book of essays *Philosophy and Social Hope* shows some clears signs that he managed not to go all the way. From the works of C. S. Peirce, William James, and John Dewey, there isn't a relativistic idea to be counted.

And what of postmodernism and poststructuralism? If you're talking of the serious variety, the kind that bred the theological turn in French phenomenology, then you will find a radical sense of relationality or subjectivism, but you won't find any easy relativism.

The real relativists, it seems, are the ones Benedict and Francis warned us about: Those of us who hold on to our pride and egoism and try to remake the world in our own image.

*

In the end, I think that relativism, in its worst and most terrible sense, is intellectual laziness. That many non-intellectuals are relativists today tends to indict the rampant anti-intellectualism that has become the norm. This dumbed-down relativism gets away with mislabeling itself because stupidity these days so often passes for sanity.

The world of relativism is a flat and tidy idea within which there is no need to take things seriously or to understand them with any depth or rigor. This is a world that can put up with our culture, and vice-versa.

The few relativists of this lazy sort known personally to me are all employed at schools and colleges of education—and, as I said earlier, among arts and humanities folks who have been living under a peace-and-love rock for thirty years. In administrative and bureaucratic centers and offices that often spew soft and silly ideas about schooling, teaching, and the professoriate, you will find relativists, too. And, also, among pseudo-intellectual journalists and talking heads in the media.

But these are rare. Loud, but very rare in real life. The rest of us, I think, are pretty much non-skeptical realists in our day-to-day life, at least when it comes to the basic stuff.

Relativism of the kind I've outlined—reality-denying, morality-free, rubber-stamping beliefs and practices from all cultural traditions—is not going to eat you alive and kill your family and unite with all the other bad pet terms and ideas to roast your puppies alive to the tune of Kumbaya. It is a paper tiger, a hologram. No one of any real importance runs around preaching the gospel of relativism, not as that gospel is commonly misunderstood.

Relativism of the sort that Benedict and Francis warn us against, however, is not rare at all.

*

The lazy kind of relativism is a quick, low-calorie substitute for real work of telling the truth. A diet pill. It spares those who take it from having to deal with the real thing. For those who define their positions against this relativism (and all its works and empty promises), relativism has become a buzzword, an equally cheap substitute for real intellectual engagement.

Look, Kumbaya relativism was dead on arrival and took some time to decompose. Benedict's and Francis's relativism has been around since the Fall. It shows up in a thousand places under a thousand names, and shows no sign of disappearing anytime soon.

Thundering against either relativism, making either one into a philosophical bogeyman, only goes to show how little we understand of what is really dangerous out there, namely, scientism and materialism.

The truth is not hard to see, if you are willing to treat it with respect and remember that there is more to the truth than getting all the details right. The battle over relativism that rages and foams in the Catholic ghetto often ends up distorting the truth as much as relativism itself. And, like the production quality of EWTN, this sort of display only shows the world how lame we often are.

Thank God for my lame and blind and borderline crazy Church! A place for Peter, Paul, and Mary Magdalene. We've always been a collection of misfits and odd ducks. A few show flashes of brilliance, but many more show flashes of knuckleheadness and downright perversity. But we have our riches, too. We have a story and a testimony and a light that is meant for better things than blowing up straw-made relativists. We are supposed to light up the world, even when the light shines darkly.

The real thing. Not a substitute. Not a handy-dandy vocabulary list compiled to separate naughty from nice. Just the truth, shown in beauty and brokenness and love.

The truth is that Christianity is not, first and foremost, a system of metaphysics or ethics, or a cultural anthropology. Next to what Christianity actually is, all these things are petty, defensive. Christianity, in all its fullness, is a mystery and a sacrament. Our call is not to be objectivists or absolutists or fundamentalists, or the converse.

We are called to be holy.

January 25, 2014
Patheos

Reality and the Virtual: Relativity is not Relativism

Now that we've named some terms and established a range of possible ways those terms can be used, we can hazard the next step.

This next step is sorely missing from our public conversation nowadays. We talk about the surface so poorly that we often distort it out of all recognition. This begs for a sounder surface, one with more clarity and nuance. But it also confines discussion to that surface as, again and again, we cycle through basic disagreements while kidding ourselves that we're having a far deeper and more interesting conversation than we really are.

At best, these limits postpone addressing the really interesting stuff. At worst, they banish these in-depth conversations beyond the realm of possibility.

That academics have sometimes abused these conversations is a vast understatement. But in some instances the academy has outdone itself, hosting fruitful conversations where the groundwork was properly laid, allowing participants to plumb deeper. I've experienced some of this and profited from the experience.

*

Was Albert Einstein a relativist? The answer depends on what you're really asking.

Two of Einstein's great scientific theories were about relativity. The first, Special Relativity, had a narrower focus than the second, General Relativity. Special Relativity involved the effects on time accounting for the speed of light. General Relativity dealt with much more general and fundamental questions about temporality at larger scale. It addressed the same question as the first theory, but in a way unbound by constant motion at a constant rate. It was followed by astronomical observations and calculations meant to empirically test its validity.

Both theories have held up so far. But the implications were not all pleasing to the theorist. Some indirect results of his research on relativity, including nuclear weapons and quantum mechanics, caused Einstein a great deal of apprehension.

*

Anyone who wants to understand the physical world needs to use the simple fact of relativity to do it. Thomas Kuhn has perhaps offered the most radical theory about the relativity of science in a way that approaches something like relativism or subjectivism. But there is something instructive about acknowledging the obvious fact that we experience the world *relative* to a number of variables, interactions, and reactions.

Nothing is the case in a vacuum, as far as we know, including vacuums.

Anyone who would easily dismiss "relativity" because the word has a family resemblance to "relativism" is, quite simply, nutty.

More importantly, anyone who erects a barricade against an ideology of relativism by ignoring the insights of the physical sciences—and the simple fact of the relativity of empirical observation, induction and deduction—is being cheap and easy about the *truth* of relativity.

*

Einstein first worked out his theories in daydreams and his conceptual imagination. Then he put them into mathematical and logical notation, with very specific and absolute claims to follow. Then came the tests, especially the eclipse photos, with strict parameters and measurements.

His meticulousness shows the delicate balance between the relativity of the world and the truth of relativity. These are not contradictory claims.

It is possible to say "X is relative to Y" and, simultaneously, to make the claim that *the previous claim*—"X is relative to Y"—is true. That being so, it would make sense to say, "The truth is relative." This is not a claim meant to abolish truth; rather, it's a claim about how the truth functions. It is, you might say, a *description* of the truth.

If anyone tried to claim that the truth was *not* relative in the same way, using the terms as I used them above, that skeptic would be denying the truth of relativity.

This may sound circular and petty. It is also a vexing but essential aspect of relativism that gets left out of our discussions because, I think, we are so busy doing the preliminary work on the surface.

*

In my very limited and perhaps naïve way, I understand quantum physics to be unique in the following sense: When big and slow things (like humans) try to observe small and fast things (like subatomic particles), fundamental problems arise in the relation between observer and observed. The difference in scale assigns them to radically different conditions of temporality.

It is not that they exist in different worlds. Rather, a deficiency is built into the ability of one world to observe the other, and to describe the observations accurately. Theology, which deals with God, has always struck me as a more radical version of quantum physics. This is why I am neither a physicist nor a theologian. The problems of scale confound me.

Relative to dogs, we smell almost nothing, or at least very little. Is smell relative? Sure, in one sense. But in another sense, it is an objective truth that smell functions in this relative way between two different noses.

*

The problem, as far as I can tell, with confusing the truth of relativity with the various ideologies of relativism, is that the former is rigorous and the latter is not. But perhaps there is a more serious difference between them. One is a real aspect of reality itself, confirmed by the natural sciences; the other is an abstraction, a mere virtual fabrication. A guess.

There is nothing wrong with guessing. Einstein was guessing when he started. A good guess is often better than a bad conclusion. But I think we've allowed all this relativism business—both the hippy-dippy, feel-good, it's-okay-to-be-yourself nonsense *and* its counterpoint, the relativism-is-going-to-end-the-world moral panic—to become almost purely ideological and virtual, barely tethered to precious concrete reality.

*

In the meantime, we might do more serious and honest work, unmotivated by ideology or fear, to understand the way that relativity functions as a part of the truth of the way the universe works, and to see how far it can extend into other cases. We might then measure those cases, in proper proportion and scale, and use the measurements to help regulate our feelings about relativism.

There is a sense in which things can and must be relative without abolishing the truth that governs those relations.

Most of all, we should carefully address the task of distinguishing between what is real from what is virtual—and then, perhaps, between virtual reality and the reality of the virtual. But that's a project for another day.

*

Ironclad truth. That's what we need, right? That'll keep the kids Catholic and preserve them from the infectious and rampant relativism they are being fed by the monstrous media and those slimy academics. Right? Am I the only one who listens to Catholic radio?

This predictable drivel is nonsense, packaged to sell bad books, like NFL commercials selling merchandise after the Super Bowl. (Your team just won! Buy a shitty T-shirt and a cap!) That's the goal behind lots of this relativism talk, make no mistake. If it's partly true, it's mostly false, and foreign to truth in all its delicate beauty.

We live in constant fear of mystery, which transcends subjectivity and objectivity and all other dualisms and binaries. When we try to construct a theory of truth (or Natural Law) that has no seams or holes, we are obeying the same knee-jerk reaction that leads us to reject the truth we know in Christ. Christ didn't do his work in arguments, theorems, or experiments, and I don't believe this choice resulted from any oversight on his part. His decision to confuse people by telling stories and performing acts of love and mercy was a deliberate one.

Some might say that Christ should have been more objective about things, and others will surely say that he should have been more subjective about things. Either way, to treat the Gospel as a lapse in messianic judgment is to miss the point that Catholicism is not a school of thought. Sure, it has produced many ideas and theories, as well as a culture suffused, but we should never mistake its truth for some petty or provincial idea of the truth.

January 28, 2014
Patheos

PART II

THE *ORDO AMORIS*

Certainty? Uncertainty? Love!

When it comes to certainty, I have a scattered heart and mind. I won't say that I am uncertain about certainty, because that's cliché. Besides, I'm too uncertain to speak with such certainty. But I am quite certain about this *particular* uncertainty. I don't have a rating for certainty, religious or otherwise. (Is any kind of certainty *not* religious?)

For starters, I constantly run into the same problem: I don't know what people mean by the term "certainty." It's usually loaded. The sides taken are predictable, as are the reactions that follow.

In philosophical circles, the term "certainty" is a hint one drops in order to identify oneself as a particular type of philosopher. It has very much the same meaning in religious circles. When a dose of politics is added, things can get nasty and confusing. Another pissing match. By the end of it all, I usually end up convinced (certain, even!) that everyone is using the term "certainty" in different ways, and are united only by their uncertainty about what they are really trying to say.

This is unfortunate, not to mention unnecessary. I believe that "certainty" can be described and understood to refer to something both universal and crucial to human experience. The term "certainty," in ordinary language, attempts to show what happens when someone is convinced of something all the way down. Down to the bones, to the marrow. To the root.

This sense of certainty differs from other versions that dwell on its logical rigors. For the positivist and the scientist, certainty is about the head, not the heart. For me, it's about both, with an emphasis on the heart. I am absolutely certain that nobody becomes certain without the uncertainties of intuition, sentiment, and emotion. As William James put it in *The Will to Believe*, "If your heart does not want a world of moral reality, your head will assuredly never make you believe in one."

It is this emotional dimension of certainty that makes it so difficult to deal with. When people argue for or against certainty they are really speaking of convictions that go beyond rational argument and logical reasoning. Each holds the meaning of their own personal certainty close to the chest, along with their other deep-seated beliefs. In his *Confessions*, Augustine shows us the simultaneous juxtaposition of certainty and doubt in a majestic and moving way.

Here, for whatever it's worth, is how I *feel* about certainty:

For me, "certainty" describes how I'm able to believe the things I believe, even when I don't understand them, but especially when I think I do. Certainty is the absolute feeling I get in my gut and my bones, the literal heartache that sears and sizzles just beneath my ribs, the absolute beauty of a moment, a thought, or a thing—a blue note. I am certain when I am in love, when I desire something, especially when I miss someone. When I mourn. The heart of certainty is the inexhaustible desire for love, for God. The merciless, constant, driving rhythm that keeps me alive. Of this I am absolutely, totally certain.

Yet this certainty makes me profoundly uncertain. It fills me with doubt, questions, insecurities. Despair. In turn, this uncertainty also makes me deliriously *happy—overjoyed*, as Stevie Wonder put it.

Because my certainty causes me to feel alive, yearning for touch and for love—because of all of this and more—I am uncertain about what it means, where it comes from, who I am, whether it is real or not, what will come of it all. And philosophy only makes things worse.

I also know that some of the things I am most certain of are also the objects of my deepest (though usually unconscious) doubts. My certainty that I am loved conceals the possibility that I am alone, unloved, hated. Abandoned to my own self-loathing. When I emphasize this or that certainty, I am squelching the doubts that assault it whenever my head hits the pillow. If I can rest easy, then perhaps my certainty is too cheap or shallow. The psychic secret of certainty is uncertainty. Anything worth believing in comes infected with doubt.

It is important to be certain and uncertain, to be in and out of love; to feel the warm, safe embrace of being secure and the empty, shameful alienation of being insecure. When we are naked, this is a time when we can experience intimacy *and* abuse. The vulnerable, naked body can be a lover or a lynching victim—or both.

Certainty and uncertainty are like nakedness. They find their way into my greatest conviction, my most cherished belief that conceals my deepest fear and doubt: the love of God.

August 8, 2011
Vox Nova

Postmodern Theology and Jean-Luc Marion

Preface

I would like to spend some time describing Jean-Luc Marion's postmodern approach to theology. I also want to say something we—or at least those who study these things—all know: "postmodern" is a thorny and ugly word that has been mangled by postmodernism's supporters as well as its detractors. Please don't dismiss it out of hand.

If Marion needs any orthodox "street cred," know that Franciscan University of Steubenville, believed by many to be very orthodox, dedicated last year's conference on Christian philosophy to his work. Steven Lewis, an FUS professor of English and local leader in Communion and Liberation, hardly a champion of heterodoxy, is the translator of Marion's most recent book, *The Erotic Phenomenon*.

Let me begin here, briefly, by citing a passage from David Tracy's foreword to Marion's book *God Without Being*, which I find very descriptive:

> One classic modern theological strategy wants to correlate the claims of reason and the disclosures of revelation. The other strategy believes that reason functions best in theology by developing rigorous concepts and categories to clarify theology's sole foundation in revelation. On this second view, since revelation alone is theology's foundation, any attempt at correlation is at best a category mistake—at worst, an attempt to domesticate the reality of God by means of reason and being. As the title *God Without Being* suggests, Professor Marion embraces the second, revelation based strategy for Christian theology.[1]

I will resume by laying out Marion's genealogical argument against being, which is rooted in the history of the phenomenological concept of givenness—surprisingly begun in analytic, not continental, philosophy— and the earlier error of the Cartesian *cogito*. From there I will explain the useful distinction of the idol and the icon that he uses to make his argument for a *God Without Being*.

June 10, 2009
Vox Nova

Being and Givenness

As I noted earlier, "postmodern" is a misnomer for the core of Marion's thought. I would say that "postmodern" more aptly describes the *effect* of his thought on theology than its substance.

When we look to Marion's conceptual foundations, we find that he is a phenomenologist through and through. This is hardly surprising since, after all, we would have no entry for what most call "postmodernism" without

---

1. Marion, *God Without Being*, x.

phenomenology. It is here, within phenomenological discourse, that Marion offers an interesting and rather straightforward historical analysis of the phenomenological concept of givenness that takes us to that famous student of Brentano's: Alexius Meinong.

Marion traces the concept of givenness to the turn of the nineteenth and twentieth centuries, when the very notion of being came under intense scrutiny. This scrutiny took many forms, but its clearest elucidation is to be found in Meinong's *Theory of Objects*. In this theory, Meinong distinguishes between existence (e.g., mountains) and subsistence (e.g., $1+1=2$), and the corresponding poles of non-existence (e.g., golden mountains) and non-subsistence (e.g., $1+1=5$). Because the objects in these categories can be given, Meinong does not deny that they have being.

What Marion didn't mention, but which I cannot resist adding, is that Meinong's *Theory of Objects* sparked over a decade of discourse over metaphysics that proved as fundamental to analytic philosophy as Frege's earlier breakthroughs in logic. Meinong's debates with Bertrand Russell present the most detailed paper trail. The most compelling and grand effect of this line of reasoning is the analytic proof that, within language, the principle of contradiction is weakened by negative existentials.

How does this add up to givenness and the erosion of being? Meinong and Russell were unable to draw a serious line on what has no being for the very reason that, insofar as a thing gives itself, it must be an object (i.e., a source of being). Their successors haven't had much luck drawing that line, either.

In this fashion, being becomes accountable to givenness. In other words, being only refers to the possibility of being given; givenness becomes the condition for the possibility of being. For the standard of givenness, Marion supplies this maxim: "Everything that shows itself must give itself."

Marion also says: "We cannot confuse 'the beings' with 'being.'"[2]

He means that we need not lapse into denial of "the beings"—the things that are given. But we must reject the notion that "being" is the horizon or limit of ontology. Marion is very direct when he says, "Givenness is beyond the reach of being, it is beyond being."

We can rest assured that Marion is not asserting the nonexistence of God in his book *God Without Being*. Existence is only descriptive of "the beings," the things that are given. Instead, Marion challenges us to abandon being as the ontological limit of God and consider the givenness of God in revelation, because, once again, "Everything that shows itself must give itself."

---

2. These two quotes come from my notes taken during his keynote, "The History of Giveness" at the 2008 Conference on Christian Philosophy at Franciscan University of Steubenville.

In the next section, I will examine Marion's critique of Descartes's *ego cogito* and his advocacy for a return to the *ego amans*.

June 12, 2009
Vox Nova

From Ego Cogito to Ego Amans

Marion's critique of being is rooted not only in the history of givenness, but also in his own critique of modernity for neglecting the person as a lover. He traces this neglect back to Descartes's *cogito*, the blueprint for the modern conception of the human person.

Marion began as a Cartesian scholar and translator, so this critique is crucial for understanding his thought in general, specifically, how his critique of being led him toward postmodern theology.

In *The Erotic Phenomenon*, Marion notes that in the original Latin of Descartes's *Meditations* the *ego* is described as excluding love. Duc de Luynes, Descartes's first translator from Latin into French, added, "which loves, which hates" to the opening of Descartes's Third Meditation.

Though Descartes never intended such a revision, it found favor with Marion, who exhorts us to take it seriously. In Marion's view, we must see ourselves "as the *cogitans* that thinks insofar as it first loves, in short as the lover (*ego amans*) . . . substituting for the *ego cogito*, which does not love." Marion goes on to write, "It will be necessary, then, to take up the *Meditations* from the starting point of the fact that I love even before being because I am not, except insofar as I experience love, and experience it as a logic."[3]

In short, Marion challenges the ontological structure of the widely accepted, and distinctly modern, *cogito* and argues that we do not exist because we think. We are given prior to being. We give before we think. We love first.

Marion's philosophical move from *ego cogito* to *ego amans* in *The Erotic Phenomenon* follows his earlier, theological point about God without being. We will return to that in the next section, but here it is in short: Once we abandon the inferior category of being, we can locate God within the intimacy of love as an iconic gift.

June 16, 2009
Vox Nova

3. Marion, *The Erotic Phenomenon*, 8.

Marion and the Theological Turn

The development of phenomenology has always been pregnant with theological implications, but Emmanuel Levinas was the first to deliver them fully and without apologies. This is an oversimplification, of course: at least three of Husserl's students—Scheler, Von Hildebrand, and Heidegger—also had theological interests. But it does seem fair to observe that, since the 1990s, when Levinas' work first made its impact on the Anglosphere, French continental thought has been leading phenomenology and the theological turn. At the very head of this turn has been the seminal, contemporary voice of Jean-Luc Marion.

Strangely enough, neither the academy nor the general culture showed much awareness of this turn toward theology as the new millennium approached. Compared with the wildly celebrated Cornel West, Jacques Derrida, and Michel Foucault, Levinas and Marion have remained obscure, though in some ways this obscurity has worked to their advantage.

This contrast is fraught with irony. West's impact on postcolonial and critical race theory is primarily the fruit of radical black *theology* (especially James Cone). In the latter part of their careers, both Derrida and Foucault developed an interest in things Christian. Jean-Francois Lytoard's final posthumous book is a poetic meditation on Augustine's *Confessions*.

Nonetheless, postmodern thought has largely been reticent, if not hostile, when it comes to admitting that this turn to theology—particularly Christian, Catholic theology—is inevitable, given the project of critiquing the liberal, secular Enlightenment and the modern age it has shaped from the Age of Reason onward.

But this reticence may not withstand the pressures of our age. As polemics between theism and atheism have reached a new (bookselling) high, this "theological turn" has begun to spill outside the confines of phenomenological discourse and into the culture at large.

Particularly in Europe, the Marxist-atheist philosopher Slavoj Žižek has introduced serious theological considerations into the critical discourse. Celebrity has given Žižek advantages as a pitchman that previous phenomenologists, including Marion, lacked. You can see this in his most recent book, *The Monstrosity of Christ*, which features theologian John Milbank *en contra*. In his excellent introduction, editor Creston Davis sees this theological turn as one exceeding the limits of postmodernism.

Just how effectively Žižek's endorsement can serve theology remains to be seen. Žižek's atheism may yet sanitize theological discussion beyond all recognition, or worse, render it sterile, stripping his work, in the public eye, of its seriousness and reducing the man himself to an enigmatic spectacle.

But regarding Marion, there is no question: despite his engagement with and impact upon postmodern thought, his devout Catholicism makes him too orthodox a figure to blaze a trail for theology. Only now that a heterodox spokesman has appeared can secular culture pay serious attention and sell Žižek over and over, in the very capitalistic machine he rails against.

Let me be clear: I welcome Žižek's role in steering this current theological turn. But I am also unwilling to find it altogether fascinating or noble, since this turn has been in progress long before Žižek appeared to give it his seal of approval—it relies on ancient texts, after all. And it's a sad sign of these times that the slightest flicker of interest in the divine makes for such startling news that observers seek explanations in the backing of superstar scholars.

In the entry to follow, I will extend my examination by commenting on the effects that this theological turn might have in phenomenology, postmodernism, and the culture at large, particularly within the Church. In particular, I will focus on the possible end of the "God taboo," and a general reconsideration of Eucharistic theology and devotion.

June 19, 2009
Vox Nova

Marion and the Theological Turn, continued

In the previous section, I noted the impact of postmodern theology on the "theological turn" now at large in the general culture, and especially visible since Slavoj Žižek's "materialist theology" has begun attracting attention. In this post I will focus on two potential effects of this turn.

1. *The end of the "God taboo."* In our secularized culture, there is a pervasive fear of God, one much less wholesome than the fear described by St. Paul in his letter to the Philippians. Even speaking God's name aloud seems to raise a general alarm. Shackled by political correctness, trussed by an ideology that prescribes bland, undifferentiated goodwill, we feel constrained to take as non-polarizing a view as possible where God and faith are concerned. Sadly, this taboo is on sale in the same emporia as postmodern philosophy. In a strange twist of fate, the very thing, postmodernism, that seems so well positioned to fight positivist fundamentalisms, has become infected by a rather positivist approach to speaking about God, or more exactly, to keeping silent on God.

By exempting God from serious public discourse, this taboo has also emptied the moral and theological imagination. Better to drain God of his power than risk being seen as an agent of the Inquisition, the guy who gathered the kindling for the Smithfield fires.

Postmodern theology and this theological turn have the potential to serve as antidotes. Not that we should expect a final cure, but we may finally feel free to talk again. Whenever I attend secular academic conferences, I can make use of Žižek's cultural cachet to introduce theology; conversely, at Catholic academic conferences, I can use Marion's reputation as a shoehorn for postmodernism. Does this sound too pat? Perhaps it is, but I maintain that theology's new relevance in spheres outside theology departments will steadily chip away at the taboos of both secular and religious fundamentalism, which sounds like a beautiful thing to me.

2. *A reconsideration of Eucharistic theology and devotion.* The Catholic pastoral understanding of the sacraments has been deeply inscribed by a *Roman* Catholic sensibility. This sensibility is based on an Aristotelian worldview inherited from Thomas Aquinas. The Roman Church favors the empiricist-tinged Latin meaning of *sacramentum* (sign) over the Greek *mysterion* (mystery) in understanding the sacraments in general and, more specifically, in the doctrine of tran*substantiation*, steeped in Aristotle's substance-versus-accident distinction.

A postmodern approach to theology would require a new understanding that, to my mind, would lead us closer to the tradition of the Greek Church and a new preference for the legacy of John over Peter (or Aquinas). This approach would describe the Eucharist, not as substance or accident, but as saturated phenomenon: God giving himself in excess.

June 22, 2009
Vox Nova

Marion and Benedictine Caritas

Once again, as I grope toward my conclusions regarding Marion and postmodern theology, I feel the need to interrupt the anticipated order of this series to address a connection that has deeply affected me. In the previous interlude, I focused on the somewhat recent theological turn in phenomenology and philosophy in general. Today I want to note something even more contemporary and prescient: Pope Benedict XVI's most recent encyclical, *Caritas in Veritate*.

To be clear, I have no knowledge of any connection—academic, personal, or otherwise—between the pope and Jean-Luc Marion. Yet I would argue that, given their shared affinity for Augustine and deep reflections on the subject of love, a broad family resemblance between their viewpoints should come as no great shock. Key passages from Benedict's recent encyclical reveal a striking similarity between his notion of *caritas* and Marion's *erotic phenomenon*. This similarity justifies some speculation on a common ontological underpinning that orders the relationship between charity and truth.

Much has been made, and will be made for some time to come, of this new encyclical's implications for our understanding of politics, economic policy, and social arrangements in general. Given the document's importance, we would be short-sighted to overlook the basis for this social teaching, which is none other than Benedict's clear and fresh theology of charity.

Benedict opens by stating: "Charity in truth . . . is the principal driving force behind the authentic development of every person and of all humanity."[4] To place his geopolitical insight before his theology of charity would be to read and understand him backwards—which would result in a misreading and a misunderstanding.

In his first encyclical, *Deus Caritas Est*, Benedict brings *eros* back into full view without apology, citing Christ as his authority. *Eros,* as the desire of the Son for the Father, becomes a starting point that wipes away the prudish taboos that demoted *eros* to a subordinate place beneath *agape* and *philia*.

Benedict doesn't belabor this point at any length. Finding the best word for understanding what God-Who-is-Love is, is not his chief aim. Rather than lead us into distracting debates by insisting on *eros*, Benedict retains the general Latin term *caritas*.

But Benedict does note the delicate relationship between *caritas* and *veritate*, which calls to mind the relationship of shape to color described by Plato's *Meno*. Marion would describe the same relationship as erotic. In the distinction and unity between them, we find a clear statement on both the ontological order of that relationship, rooted in the fact that God is Love, and the intelligibility of revelation rooted in the Truth.

The takeaway here is the similarity between the ontology of love—an ontology that overcomes the firstness of being—with which Marion pushed back against modernity, and the view of love propounded by Benedict in his

4. Encyclical letter *Caritas in Veritate* of the Supreme Pontiff Benedict XVI. Retrieved from http://w2.vatican.va/content/benedict-xvi/en/encyclicals/documents/hf_ben-xvi_enc_20090629_caritas-in-veritate.html on February 11, 2017.

latest encyclical. The fact that Benedict has been teaching the same theology of charity throughout his pontificate should only encourage us further to take notice.

A more detailed comparison will follow in the next section.

July 12, 2009
Vox Nova

Marion and Benedictine Caritas, continued

At the center of Benedict's theology of charity is an ontological contention that is also central to Marion's postmodern theology. Both demand of Catholics: What does it means to (re)think theology under the sole and sufficient terms of love?

Rather than answer that question, I will try to describe it in useful detail. In doing so, I will cite the places in his most recent encyclical where Benedict elucidates ideas that fit Marion's erotic ontology.

To begin with, here is the opening passage from *Caritas in Veritate*:

> For the Church, instructed by the Gospel, charity is everything because, as Saint John teaches (cf. 1 4:8, 16) and as I recalled in my first Encyclical Letter, "God is love" (*Deus Caritas Est*): everything has its origin in God's love, everything is shaped by it, everything is directed towards it.[5]

Here we find a striking ontological declaration: ". . . charity is everything because . . . everything has its origin in God's love . . ." This is very close to the claim Marion makes in *The Erotic Phenomenon*: "I love even before being because I am not, except insofar as I experience love, and experience it as a logic."[6]

Love's primordial originality as emphasized in Benedict's theology and Marion's phenomenology presents a robust alternative to the modern pre-eminence of reason and rationality. The alternative is not irrational, but it confirms the dynamic flux between love and truth. In that flux, we find that love is not merely revealed in truth, but that love bestows on truth its originary credibility—a credibility that truth cannot give in return to love. In other words, truth becomes instrumental to revelation as a lamp is to sight, but it is not the source of the vision.

Benedict explains:

5. Ibid.
6. Marion, *The Erotic Phenomenon*, 8.

Truth needs to be sought, found and expressed within the "economy" of charity, but charity in its turn needs to be understood,
confirmed and practiced in the light of truth. In this way, not
only do we do a service to charity enlightened by truth, but we
also help give credibility to truth, demonstrating its persuasive
and authenticating power in the practical setting of social living.

Thus, while love, or *caritas,* can be found in the light of truth, it retains
its ontological originality. Benedict goes on to put the ontological priority of
caritas into more concrete terms. Not only does love pre-exist truth, it also
transcends justice:

Charity goes beyond justice, because to love is to give, to offer what is "mine" to the other; but it never lacks justice, which
prompts us to give the other what is "his," what is due to him by
reason of his being or his acting. I cannot "give" what is mine
to the other, without first giving him what pertains to him in
justice. If we love others with charity, then first of all we are just
towards them. . . . On the one hand, charity demands justice:
recognition and respect for the legitimate rights of individuals
and peoples. It strives to build the earthly city according to law
and justice. On the other hand, charity transcends justice and
completes it in the logic of giving and forgiving.

If we recall Marion's idea that we experience love "as a logic," we see
that the logic of giving and forgiving is of a single kind. Moreover, we find
that Marion's phenomenological reduction to givenness is affirmed in Benedict's own discussion of giving. As with truth, we find that justice and charity are not simply put into a relationship: their complex relations are ordered
by a distinct ontology.

This ontology—an erotic ontology, an ontology of charity—lies at
the very heart of Benedict's developing theology and Marion's developing
phenomenology.

August 24, 2009
Vox Nova

Marion and Charles Taylor[7]

As we have seen, in *The Erotic Phenomenon,* Jean-Luc Marion critically notes
that, in the original Latin of Descartes's *Meditations,* the *ego* is described

---

7. This is an early version of my chapter on the human person in *Folk Phenomenology.*

without love. Marion exhorts us to see ourselves "as the *cogitans* that thinks insofar as it first loves, in short as the lover (*ego amans*) . . . substituting for the *ego cogito*, which does not love."[8]

This challenges the ontological implication of Descartes's *cogito* and affirms Augustine's claim: *Nemo est qui non amet*—There is no one who does not love; she who would not love is nothing; without love, *I* am nothing. In other words, I do not think and therefore exist, as Descartes would have it—I love and therefore exist and think and love again (and again and again . . .).

Marion's position *contra* Descartes also takes the form of a question and answer. He asks, "Why is love thrown to the wind, why is it refused an erotic rationality . . ." Then he answers his own question:

> The answer is not hidden far away: because love is defined as a passion, and therefore as a derivative modality, indeed as an option to the "subject." . . . And, in fact, we think of ourselves most of the time as just such an ego, a being who cogitates orderable and measurable objects, so that we no longer look upon our erotic events except as incalculable and disordered accidents happily marginalized, indeed optional . . . [9]

Earlier in the book, Marion makes this striking statement:

> The result of these failed efforts is that ordinary people, or, put another way, all those who love without knowing what love wants to say, or what it wants of them, or above all how to survive it—that is to say, you and I first and foremost—believe themselves condemned to feed on scraps: desperate sentimentalism of popular prose, the frustrated pornography of the idol industry, or the shapeless ideology of that boastful asphyxiation known as "self-actualization." Thus philosophy keeps quiet, and in this silence love fades away.[10]

For Marion, this silence of philosophy is neither a disciplinary silence in academia nor a problematic gap in philosophy's history. It is instead a failure of *philo-sophia*, the love of wisdom. It is the silence of love alienated from itself, the divorce of *eros* from its passion fruit, love. In Marion's work, this strange *philo*-sophical forgetting of love is even more fundamental, and even more prescient, than the neglect of being noted by Heidegger in *Being*

---

8. Marion, *The Erotic Phenomenon*, 8.

9. Ibid., 6.

10. Ibid., 2.

and Time. In this abandonment of love we find a critical question about the constitution of the subject in and by the modern world.

In Charles Taylor's *A Secular Age*, we find a striking similarity to Marion's *Erotic Phenomenon*, whose English translation appeared the same year (2007). In his geneaologies, Focault argues that societies acquire shape not through the application of brute force, but through biopower, a subtler force expressed through the gradual formation of custom and convention. Taylor agrees. He describes the secular age as one in which "disciplinary society" built a "new model of the human being." In his review of the book, Peter Gordon writes:

> With the rise of the disciplinary society Taylor also sees a change in the very conception of human being. The older conception of the self as embedded in a holistic but differentiated natural-social-theological order slowly gave way to a "disembedded" selfhood understood to be ontologically prior to and independent of its surroundings. The realist conception of the world as the bearer of intrinsic meanings to which we must conform was supplanted by the notion that the only orders we must acknowledge are those we construct for ourselves. The social imaginary no longer envisioned as an interdependent system working in concert but a dispersal of atomistic individuals only to themselves and only contingently responsive to those around them.[11]

This new human being that Taylor sees as the signature of the secular age's disciplinary society is strikingly similar to the Cartesian *ego cogito* critiqued by Marion. Taylor calls it "the buffered self." This "buffered self' replaced the "porous self" during the Age of Reason and Enlightenment ushered in by Descartes, Locke, Rousseau and Kant. Gordon describes Taylor's "buffered self" as one that is "assertive, rationalistic and stakes a claim to autarky that shuts down its experience of intimacy even in relation to its own bodily passions."

In striking similarity to the dialectic of Descartes's *ego cogito* vs. de Luynes' *ego amans* that we find in Marion, Taylor's contrast of the buffered and porous selves brings out the tragic elements of this tragic lover—elements that, for Taylor, come cloaked in religious mysticism. He writes:

> Living in a disenchanted world, the buffered self is no longer open, vulnerable to a world of spirits and forces which cross the boundary of the mind, indeed, negate the very idea of there being a secure boundary. The fears, anxieties, even terrors that belong to the porous self are behind it. This sense of

11. Gordon, "Place of the Sacred," 661–62.

self-possession, of a secure inner mental realm, is all stronger, if in addition to disenchanting the world, we have also taken the anthropocentric turn and no longer even draw upon the power of God.[12]

The description of the dispossessed porous self as something fearful, anxious, and even terrorized adds an extra layer of tragic meaning and mystery to Marion's *ego amans*. Wed to an amorous *ego,* a porous self will know, in the deep ontological sense of existential intimacy—*connaître* or *conocer,* as opposed to *savoir* or *saber*—that to offer true love is to be a tragic lover. Such a self will reject the nihilism of liberal individualism and plunge headlong into the flux of relations in the life-world, come what may.

October 12, 2009
Vox Nova

The Sovereign Lover, the Reign of Love, and the *Ordo Amoris*

I often write myself into a narrow space between liberalism and something else. What this something else consists of is the big question. In addressing it, I want to continue to defend the dialectic I have introduced. I can think of no better defense than a thorough explication of the alternative as I envision it. My explication may prove too thin to convert hearts, but it will have to do for a start.

Ronald King, one of the most frequent commentators at *Vox Nova,* submitted a critique of my work that succeeded in stunning me. He rejected the notion that, as Catholics, we should desire the Reign of God. I maintain that the Reign of God is exactly what we ought to desire, especially given liberalism as an alternative. It is nothing more or less than the "something else" that eludes precise description.

But first I must clarify something fundamental to this ongoing theme. A vast gulf separates what is desired from what actually is. As everyone past a certain age knows, it is much easier to desire true love than to find oneself at the receiving end of it. Still, even when unrealized, our desires frame our sense of what is possible. Without the desire for employment, for example, the possibility of getting a job is nonexistent.

For the same reason, I persist in believing that we ought to broaden our political appetite and imagination. Far too many people desire the status

12. Ibid., 662.

quo, namely, liberalism and all its trappings. This consensus effectively ne-gates the possibility of anything else—even the existence of God.

It is my view that we must connect with our appetite for something still unrealized. We cannot let liberalism, or whatever else we take as the horizon of political possibility, monopolize our sense of what is beautiful, true, and possible.

Ronald King has a point that presenting the Reign of God as an alter-native to existing political arrangements smells like an opening for religious repression. If that is what I wanted, then I would be a dangerous fanatic. But this is not at all the vision I intend to convey.

What if this theocracy—this Reign of God—were the reign of the mysterious God Who is Love? What if, in other words, fully informed by the theological challenges to knowing God on one hand, and the need for a good and just social order on the other, we were to discover that seeking the Reign of God was the least problematic of political ideologies, and a big improvement over liberalism? Maybe believing Aristotle when he called democracy the "best among the worst" has effectively blocked the "best of the best" from our imagination.

What would this politics be like? Well, it would seem to be a postmod-ern monarchy where the Sovereign is a lover. It would be a kingdom where the reign of the Sovereign would feel like the reign of love. Consequently, the entire social order would be held accountable to the *ordo amoris*, the order of love.

This is a sketchy recipe for the meal that I think we should learn to crave, but it is my belief that if we were truly to desire the Reign of God, we might begin to imagine and expect anew what politics should and could be like. The implications of such broadened imaginings go well beyond the political. They also raise eschatological questions of the now *and* the not-yet, the here *and* the to-come, of the Kingdom of God itself.

Aren't these the living waters we should dive into?

January 6, 2010
Vox Nova

Imagining Serious Presidential Change

The First Poor President

Lately, I've been moved to write on the impoverishment of our political imagination and the need to begin imagining politics anew. Lacking in these exhortations are specific examples of what I imagine. In this entry, I would like to introduce a radical impossibility: the first poor U.S. president.

Toni Morrison declared Bill Clinton the first black president, a declaration that appears to have been both corrected and vindicated by the election of Barack Obama, a literal black man. But we would be doing an injustice to our history and politics by defining our presidents, first and foremost, by their race. Each and every one of them can be defined even more basically as rich. Some of them got rich in their own lifetimes and others inherited their riches from previous generations. Either way, make no mistake, we have not had a poor president.

A few may have bordered on not-rich (Lincoln comes to mind), but never has a president experienced poverty as defined by the standards of his time, much less elected to remain poor out of principle, in the manner of a mendicant friar.

From Andrew Jackson to Sarah Palin and Barack Obama, populists have always preferred candidates who rose to wealth from the middle; that none of these candidates has ever returned to poverty after leaving it makes no difference to their boosters. But imagine that a vow of poverty were a prerequisite to becoming president. Candidates would promise, upon election, to sell all they possessed and donate it to the poor, never to reclaim it. Not until completing their term(s) of office would they be permitted to resume the business of amassing money and property.

Alongside this radical ideal, racial milestones look bland and routine. *So what* if we have a blind or transgender or Muslim or albino president? Many of you must be rolling your eyes at the sheer implausibility of this idea, and for good reason. After all, the politics of the day make it highly unlikely that such a requirement will ever be adopted. That's my whole point. Yet for the imaginative and faithful Roman Catholic, a poor chief executive shouldn't seem that strange. We have the pope, after all.

Critics will recite the long history of papal venality and corruption by way of proving that popes can't be poor in any meaningful sense. But though the Church has been burdened with its share of self-indulgent pontiffs, it's also been blessed with some who lived under a vow of poverty. Comparing the short list of poor popes with the blank list of poor US presidents rescues this type of speculation from the realm of pure fantasy. The possibility of poor leaders may be remote, but remote is not the same thing as unreal.

So instead of trying to figure out how we push token people "of color" into office, we might up the ante and begin to imagine a politics that sees the politician as a true public servant, one who must renounce all worldly goods in exchange for the power to decide who gets what. Now this would be serious change. By training our imaginations to think and feel it as something possible, we take the first step toward making it a reality.

October 27, 2009
Vox Nova

The First Rich President

Because the United States has never had a poor president, she has never known a president who was truly rich. Though I define poverty, like most people, in terms of dollars and cents, my notion of "richness" falls well outside the common definition. When I speak of a rich president, I mean a president overflowing with love.

This love-filled president would be even more radical and strange than the previously imagined poor president. The rich president would be called to surrender more than his possessions or comforts. He would have to be willing to surrender his life.

Like the Roman pontiff with his Swiss Guard, the President of the United States requires a corps of armed protectors in the form of the Secret Service. Like Louis XIII's musketeers, immortalized by Dumas *père*, the president's security detail esteems it the highest honor to lay down their lives in order to protect their leader. But to give one's life in the richest way, I would think, means doing so out of a love closer, in its purity, to a mother's than a musketeer's.

As it stands, our presidents claim the title of public servant but remain unwilling to render the service they require from publicly funded guards. It seems to me that the first rich president would be the president who would make this sacrifice willingly and out of love. Even if circumstances never demanded his self-immolation, he would have to demonstrate both the desire and ability prior to accepting his party's nomination.

The figure of the leader as human sacrifice isn't wholly without precedent, even in American politics. Populist sentiments run highest in support of military figures. From Jackson to McCain, the image of a president who would suffer physical injury in service to the nation has proven compelling to voters.

But this brings us back to the question of poverty. In the current cultural climate, being poor is almost worse than being dead. Since the housing bubble burst, we've seen a rash of post-bankruptcy suicides, evidence of the pocketbook's morbid vitality. So we might ask, if a president full of love—a rich president, as we've decided—would give his life, why would he not begin by giving away his money? In this economic age, where every human life carries a price tag, a willing surrender of assets should impress the nation as the ultimate sacrifice.

If the skeptical public needs proof that the president will reciprocate the devotion shown him by a publicly-funded militia, his renunciation of all worldly goods for the benefit of the poor should close the deal. Thus, in this world we've imagined, we find that the first poor president is the same person as the first rich president: a president full of love who cannot serve while holding an ace up his sleeve.

This political imagination isn't seeking a nice president, or a kind president, or a populist underdog we can feel good about. Instead, it is searching for a lover—a true lover. A lover who does not simply declare love, but who loves in advance. This is the president we should learn to desire.

And even now, as the drought of such possibilities parches the public throat, we should strive to slake that thirst by envisioning a politics of love. After all, this desire reaches beyond the polls. This is a desire for a God-to-come who is here, with and in us, right now.

October 28, 2009
Vox Nova

In Defense of Torture

Yes, there's some shock value in this title. Torture is wrong, you must be thinking. End of story. Any inquiry into its purposes and meaning only opens the door to it. Torture, you may want to say, is indefensible, all the time. No matter what. The Catholic Church seems to agree. So why even speak of it, much less defend it? All right-thinking people should quarantine such a perverse thought once and for all.

The answer I have is theological. We adore a tortured Christ. This is not to say that the torture of Jesus somehow justifies the torture of others. But it is an inescapable fact that the breaking of the Christ's Body and the spilling of his Precious Blood are necessary conditions for our faith and its sacred mysteries. Since no less a being than God suffered an undignified and painful death, we should not turn away from the reality of torture when it occurs in the present day. To close our imaginations to torture completely would mean forgetting the gruesome means of our salvation.

Beginning with our duty to recall Christ's own torture, we must enter into a serious discussion of what it means when people torture one another.

It will force us to grapple with the overwhelming excess of the Incarnation, of which the Passion forms an inseparable part.

We are often quick, too quick, to say how depraved torture talk is. I often suspect that people offer these sorts of indictments for fear of being seen as potential torturers. But such sweeping inhibitions blunt the edge of dialogue and turn it into something puritanical. The more we prove the purity of our intentions to ourselves and each other, the harder it becomes for us to battle with the enemy.

Among Catholics, abolitionist views on torture are too self-consciously heroic. Those who oppose torture seem to relish the cut-and-dried state of the issue. The few Catholics who defend torture tend to take a cut-and-dried approach to abortion; approving torture, in their case, is a rare instance of flexibility. Both sides fight with vigor, immune, in their heroism, to persuasion by the other side, because, after all, they can name God as an ally.

Is this schema too stark? Too melodramatic? Maybe, but it serves to make the point that neither side bothers to investigate the actual process of torture, much less enter into the mystery of the experiences of torturer and victim. What does it mean to inflict pain on a person, to kill a person, perhaps even eat a person? What does it mean to be on the receiving end of such brutality?

Given the bloodlessness of our daily lives, such inquiries seem prurient and ugly. But without fully appreciating the meaning and mystery of human suffering, we can't begin to appreciate divine suffering. Our peace and safety comes at the price of wisdom. Though none of us should want to inflict torture, much less experience it, our lives will be sterile—flesh with no blood, fibers without liquids—unless we stretch our imagination to include it.

We need torture. By this I mean that we should talk, write, pray, and think about it in ways that plumb as deeply as we can. I do not think that we should torture people for any reason—although we often and inevitably do—but we should also never forget that we are complicit, somehow or other, in the torture of our fellows where it does occur, and in the suffering of Christ.

Both consequentialist arguments in favor of torture and Catechism entries against it distract us from the sacred flesh of the matter: We need the Cross in order to get the Eucharist, and we need the Eucharist in order to gain eternal life.

Of course we should never torture, but that is all beside the point. The real point is that we should never consign speaking and thinking of torture to the realm of taboo while we rest on our laurels. Whenever the matter of torture arises, we should open our minds to it, especially when the victim is Christ, a saviour who never loses his wounds.

May 5, 2009
Vox Nova

The Danger of the Imagination

More and more, glowing rectangles tell us what to think, feel, and believe. I am staring at one right now. Under this dictatorial regime, it is hard to be still or silent, much less to exercise the imagination. Even when we manage to imagine something, we are forbidden to take our imaginings seriously. We must treat them as fictional, divorced from reality.

The life's blood of that cesspool we call "politics" has by now congealed into a giant scab. We dare not pick at it lest warm blood flow and remind us that we are dealing with living flesh. We would then have to confront the fact that the stakes in every election involve the fate of human persons— real, living persons, who cannot profit from the fetishes of individualism or self-sufficiency.

Imagination threatens that tranquility. It possesses the potential to melt the ice of our secular, modern, liberal society and—rather than re- store to the reign of the Inquisition—make all things new, again and again, through the magic of conversion. Unleashed, imagination could force us into the perpetual conversion that resides in the world, not the cramped spaces normally set aside for the convert.

Most of all, by using our imagination, we run the risk of confronting *the* image, the *imagus Dei*. God's image does not belong to us. It is not a thing we can ever hope to possess in significant rational proportions. In its sheer excess, we find our cup overflowing with the wine of life and death, revelation and mystery.

But this is too hazardous an experiment to undertake outside the boundaries set by language, grammar, prose, and thought. Certainly the political arena is no fit place for imagining. For all we claim to want, we only really want what we have. By simply existing, imagination puts us in constant attentive fear of the relief of the possible.

October 8, 2009
Vox Nova

Economics and the Imagination

Economics and the Political Imagination

I find economics very difficult to understand. In using the term "economics," I am not limiting myself to the academic discipline. Instead, I am referring to the ways people in the modern world think and feel about money and capital in relation to themselves and their neighbors.

In many ways, I find it easier to think about a generic economy, about transactions that establish relationships between people and the things they care about. There is no doubt that many economists understand "economics" in this way, but there is something about the stranglehold that economics in the monetary sense seems to have over the political imagination that both confuses and frustrates me.

I appreciate the need to survive. If "economics" referred strictly to ways of living and surviving, then my objections would be beside the point. But the term "economics" seems to have acquired some value added that goes far beyond the primal need to survive or even to flourish. As Bill Clinton via James Carville reminded us, "It's the economy, stupid." The driving questions of politics nowadays, on both sides of the aisle, are all economic.

There's a logic to this. Money is, after all, a powerful means. What becomes problematic is when money becomes more than merely instrumental. Whenever means become ends, values become disfigured and inverted. Whenever economic well-being is elevated to an end in itself, all human persons—and with them, all of creation—are demoted to the means that serve it. The darkest perversion occurs when an entire culture comes to believe that financial abundance *per se* represents the fullest realization of the good life.

Think about the constant tug-of-war between capitalism and socialism. All too often, both sides fall back on purely economic arguments. Though both parties seem to want more than money—though they define freedom differently, they agree on it as their goal—they lack the vocabulary for addressing any concerns other than economic ones. What if they were to rediscover what they want to use money for and treat *it*, not money, as the highest good?

I suspect one reason that economics so dominates the modern political imagination is because the cycle of modernity itself represents a transition from the Age of Science to the Age of Economics, that is, from the Age of Reason to the Age of Money. After the secular dethroned the sacred, claiming to act in the name of reason, economics dethroned reason by proclaiming itself the end of reason. The distance from the sacred, if anything, increased. As of this writing, we are two gods removed from God.

With our political imagination decoupled from its primal, sacred engine we are left with cheap and unhealthful substitutes. Whoever dares propose to restore the original would be lucky to escape with his life, never mind winning a primary.

This is where a Catholic vision of politics should threaten the status quo. It is a vision that draws its sustenance not only from disembodied ideals, but from actual history. Or it could be, at any rate, if the present Catholic political imagination weren't so thoroughly colonized by economics as an end in itself.

May 15, 2010
Vox Nova

Economics and the Vocational Imagination

So, tell me, son, what do you want to be when you grow up? This question may not be a new one, but its meaning has surely evolved over time. At its heart is the question of what one is and who one might become. This, as I see it, is the vocational question: the question of what and who I am called to *be*.

There is a longstanding tradition of equating what and who one *is* with what one *does*. In its most basic form, this need not pose any problems. Real benefits can be gained from viewing one's job as an element of personal identity as well as a set of responsibilities or a source of income. In Spanish, the phrase *hacer las cosas bien*, which means to do things well, or right, elevates a job well done to the realm of the good and the beautiful. A vocation, then, is more than a means of earning a paycheck; it is an opportunity to become an artist, a creator. This view can extend to everything involved in being a person, in practicing the arts of life and love.

But few people these days conceive of the person-at-work as any kind of artist. The new view can perhaps best be understood through satire like Scott Adams's comic strip *Dilbert*, the movie *Office Space*, and the current American adaptation of *The Office*. All of these cultural artifacts affirm the view that most work nowadays is banal.

While working among Mexican welders and steel cutters, I observed that workers from different generations approached their tasks differently. Whereas older tradesmen took the time to *hacer las cosas bien*, and also met or exceeded their daily quotas easily, the younger ones got the job done good enough, with no other attachment to their work, artistic or otherwise. In their view, time was money, and the pay was what counted.

Of course earning the means with which to provide for one's welfare should be one of the chief rewards of any vocation. No sane person would dispute that. But, as I elaborated earlier, there does come a point when a vocation's economic function becomes its primary or sole meaning. When money and capital become the ends, the meaning of the vocational question "What am I *called* to be," changes, and not for the better. The vocational imagination is impoverished, and the order of love that makes the relational person the end of a true vocation is lost. The person is called from nowhere to be a slave to money and capital, leading to the same empty abyss.

May 18, 2010
Vox Nova

Economics and the Educational Imagination

The etymology of the word "education," the Latin verb *educere,* denotes a process by which something is led outward. The history of pedagogy reveals dramatic changes in how this drawing-out has taken place. Whereas schooling has existed in many different forms throughout human history, the past two centuries, since schooling in the Western world became compulsory, reveal the triumph of a distinct vision of schooling's means and ends.

This complicated evolution has both beautiful and ugly aspects. Beyond dispute, however, is the absolute dominance which modern ideas of schooling enjoy over the educational imagination—the imaginary of what to draw out of the human person and how to do it. To boot, this educational imaginary has become the captive of macro- and microeconomics.

In its macro form, schooling has become a tool of nation-states to promote their own self-interest. Among these, economic self-interest reigns supreme. This explains why, at the national level, we emphasize subjects like reading, math, and science—a curriculum for the head that leaves very little time for the heart, and none at all for the soul.

In its micro form, schooling has become a pathway to responsible jobs that offer purely economic rewards. In fact, many of these jobs are toxic for persons, but their monetary rewards make them even more desirable than others that might enrich the holder's life and the lives of others.

The very idea of learning as the chief end of pedagogy ignores the person who is constituted by the knowledge selected for the curriculum. Education's original form as a way of becoming has given way to a method for getting informed, all for the sake of gaining access to money and capital, the economic cycle needed for a nation.

Here, again, we see the inversion of values that has distorted our life-ways into money-ways. Economics drives the engine of modern-day schooling and, since so few recognize the difference between schooling and education, it too has captured the near-total imagination of educational possibility, including the possibility of what education might aspire to become.

For a good example, consider that teacher education—the pathway to gaining the credentials for teaching in public schools—consists almost solely of methods for instructing students; it gives no attention to the meaning and history of education or schooling. For an even more basic example, consider how common sense now holds that you get an education by going to school, and you go to school in order to get something—namely, a career and a paycheck.

May 19, 2010
Vox Nova

Economics and the Existential Imagination

So far, I have named three areas where we find an inversion of the order between money or capital and the welfare of the human person: politics, work, and education. In every instance, this inversion is fairly new, a byproduct of the philosophy that many call neoliberalism, which converts the autonomous individual from a seeker of reason to a seeker of material wealth and social standing.

The *ego cogito* of Descartes has now been replaced by the *homo economicus* of Wall Street. The rational man of liberalism has become the economic man of neoliberalism.

These changes insert a genealogical distance between ourselves and the kind of person that Jean-Luc Marion describes as the *ego amans*, the person as lover who begets reason. Charles Taylor describes the same shift as one from a "porous self" to a "buffered self." Taylor and Marion both miss the next genealogical and anthropological step in the alienation and disenchantment of the person: the evolution of the *homo economicus,* or the person as consumer and producer, which now seems to approach the total surrender of the human person to posthuman nihilism.

Neither money nor capital are new, but the order governing relations between them and the human person—not to mention God—has lately become disordered to an especially disturbing degree.

Take the idea of a profession. Once upon a time, every profession was ordered toward some good. Medicine served the good of health; law the good of justice; academia the good of truth; art the good of beauty, and so on. This was the norm for most of human history, including most of modernity.

Liberalism was conceived out of the desire for the goods deriving from the development of human rationality. Nowadays, however, we have "professionals" who serve only the false good of self-interest. Overseeing and holding persons accountable to this false good, we have a class of professional managers, who profess nothing since they also must do as they are told.

We operate under a definition of the *self* that reflects individualism on economic steroids. The existential imagination is so monopolized by economic concerns that we begin to think of ourselves as producers and consumers first and foremost.

Even less wholesome than the autonomous individual self, the economic self, born from the womb of modern, secular liberalism, inverts the meaning of existence into a travesty of living that is really closer to dying—a death-as-life anticipated by Tolstoy in *The Death of Ivan Ilych*.

One escape from neoliberalism's conquest of the existential imagination can be found in the Catholic Church. In the tragic Catholic view, the human person is a sacred end in him or herself. But the Church teaches that this human person is no individual designed to float about in isolation. Instead, each of us is called by God to *communio*.

In these relations we find powerful antidotes to the economic enslavement of our times: the embrace of poverty, the love of enemy, and the death to self.

May 28, 2010
Vox Nova

Epilogue: "Death to Self" as a Catholic Post-Humanism

Writing critical genealogies is not hard work. Most people willing to see things as they are can sense the disenchantment and alienation surrounding them. If not, then, as I suggested earlier, they have Tolstoy and Mike Judge to remind them. Now begins the search for answers.

Phenomenology, psychoanalysis, postmodernism, genuine conservatism, and many other critical traditions of thought have made similar assessments of our times. What they have failed to do is to offer a realizable alternative—an alternative that won't serve to maim reality further. In designing their utopias and dystopias, they cannot help but be infected by the very era they are attempting to deconstruct. They cannot imagine an enchanted world because their own horizons are thoroughly disenchanted.

Lacking any serious alternatives, whoever would heal the wounds of modernity is left with less than nothing.

Truth be told, I can only think of one plausible alternative with any record of substance: the Christian Gospel.

Just beneath the posture typical of critical discourse—indignation over injustice combined with an inability to rectify it—lurks the Gospel, pregnant with dark truth. This dark truth is *that we must die in order to live.* Dying must precede living. God himself, in the person of Jesus, demonstrated this. His life-through-death is now a model.

Here we find a more radical alternative than all the critical claims that modern times have produced, a Christian post-humanism that rejects both the rational, self-enclosed individual *and* the irrational, all-consuming economic man. It rejects both the end of autonomy—the naïve idea of self-determination—*and* the end of economic power. It rejects both the modern notion of "God" as an optional add-on to humankind *and* the pre-modern "God" as an idol carved, arrogantly, in humankind's image. In place of all these, it offers the person as lover, the mad *eros* of the Cross, and the erotic power of unselfish love.

Humanism and liberalism will always fail because they cannot avoid being anthropocentric. They will always love the human first and foremost. They are fundamentally *self*ish. They deny the truth of *theosis* and *kenosis*.

The call to love in the Gospel reveals that we can only realize our greatest hopes under a new order, the order of love—love both divine and worldly. This is not the affectionate, hippy-love we have become accustomed to. This love comes in dark shades of death that bring true life.

The end of this age of economics—the inevitable successor to the previous age of the secular individual—might come through a widening acceptance of this Gospel truth:

> In all truth I tell you, unless a wheat grain falls into the earth and dies, it remains only a single grain; but if it dies it yields a rich harvest. Anyone who loves his life loses it; anyone who hates his life in this world will keep it for eternal life. (John 12:24–25)

May 31, 2010
Vox Nova

PART III

TEACHING AS DESCHOOLING

Teaching as Deschooling

Two terms describe the rarest, most anarchic and apophatic approaches to schooling. One is "unschooling," the other "deschooling." The former was coined by John Holt, one of the leading voices in the Youth Rights movement of the 1960s and 1970s. Though the movement has mostly been forgotten, the term "unschooling" remains popular among radical home educators. "Deschooling" comes from Ivan Illich's book *Deschooling Society*, published in 1971. This term is less generally known. Where it is known, it is often misunderstood, partly because Illich himself resisted defining it precisely.

At first, Illich's proposal in *Deschooling Society* seems straightforward. His opening chapter is titled "Why We Must Disestablish the School." However, later in that chapter, he writes, "Not only education but social reality itself has become schooled."[1] Illich's interests, then, go far beyond educational reform. He takes aim at the present institutionalized state of social reality. His program calls for nothing short of total transformation.

If one reads Illich's other works, there is a remarkable consistency to his message, regardless of the topic. On medicine, water, cities, language, third world development, technology, and more, Illich—a Roman Catholic priest—strikes out against everything he sees as objectifying the human person into a creature he dubs "Promethean man." No wonder his notion of deschooling was almost wholly misunderstood in its time and is unpopular these days, when it is remembered at all. No amount of external or technical change could satisfy his call for deschooling.

Teaching precedes schooling, anthropologically and metaphysically. Humans relied on teachers long before schools existed. Even before civilization brought humans into permanent settlements where schools could emerge, teachers were at work. The person of wisdom, the parent, the exemplar—all of these and more are embedded into the Socratic and rabbinic models of the teacher. Socrates taught Plato long before Plato founded his Academy. Jesus taught in the synagogue, yes, but he also taught on the mount and the sea. Even on the Cross, Christ taught the thief. As an art, teaching is so ancient as to be pre-institutional, if it is not positively anti-institutional. The teacher who dares to teach, the professor who risks a profession, the master who shows more than she tells—over such figures, no school has any power, much less a monopoly.

Teaching, then, is a form of deschooling insofar as it is an act whose roots go deeper than those of the institutional school. The misplaced assumption that to critique the school is to insult the teacher could not be

---

1. Illich, *Deschooling Society*, 2.

further from the truth. In fact, this assumption, which shackles teaching to schooling, offers the greatest insult to teaching because it puts the teacher under the arbitrary authority of the school and the nation-state. Even death cannot rob a teacher of her power, wisdom, and grace.

Teachers today sometimes seem unaware of the subversive potential of their vocation. It may appear that teaching is lost, but this absence is possible only within a schooled vision of teaching. Among professional teachers, the deeper and more ancient roots of their vocation have not wholly vanished from sight. Many teachers, both those who quit the profession as conscientious objectors and those who hang on doggedly, know the voice that calls them to teach comes from a deeper and more intimate place than the school bell. The law of the teacher is the same law to which Martin Luther King Jr. appealed when he gave his national lesson in Washington, DC. This is the law written on the heart of the person, the inviolable law that so many schools and nations fear and seek to control.

Ivan Illich's definition of deschooling did not include proposals for a program by which deschooling might be realized. This absence left many readers dissatisfied. Illich had in some respect abandoned deschooling by the 1990s, but he failed to realize that the teacher is a deschooler by nature. Schooling is not a necessary condition for education, but teachers are. The instrumental treatment of teachers as mere technicians shows that the schooling-industrial complex of today understands the danger of teaching. No wonder teachers require so many handlers, administrators, tedious textbooks, and tests. These disciplinary schooling devices are first implemented against the teacher before, in a perverse cycle of violence, the teacher is forced to use them against the student.

The economic questions of teacher pay and unions are mostly distractions, obscuring the difficult truth that the ontological status of the teacher is the real stake in today's game. If we allow teaching to be reduced to a mere profession, we have already lost the argument. For the corporate state school to thrive, the teacher's deschooling potential must be destroyed, and for this reason deschooling may be as simple as restoring the art of teaching to what it is and will always be: the love of wisdom. Yes, my claim is that teaching as deschooling is nothing more or less than the restoration of the practice of philosophy as a way of life and a preparation for death to the vocation of teaching.

January 25, 2015
Ethika Politika

The Schooling Consensus

Even in the polarized United States, everyone agrees that schools are in sorry shape. This observation takes a variety of forms, depending on whether it issues from left or right, reformists or radicals, restorationists or revolutionaries. But the common ground is real, and its existence might prove a rare opportunity for bridge-building.

The left champions public schools as services that add value to a democratic society much as roads and libraries do. In this view, public schools have failed by becoming the tools of private interests. Public-school curricula, they tell us, are infected with a pro-Christian bias and, paradoxically, a worshipful attitude toward the US nation-state.

The right seeks alternatives to public schools, in the forms of private academies or charter schools, because it believes public delivery methods restrict students' intellectual growth and waste public funds. Public schools are inefficient because they are gummed up by bureaucracy. They kowtow to local interests and the state. Their curricula are infected by political correctness, which manifests itself in biases against Christianity and American exceptionalism.

There are more radical positions, of course, that reject the school altogether, or would at least transplant it to the home or other unconventional settings. Radicals believe more strongly than anyone that today's schools are in a bad way. But unlike reformists on both left and right, radicals do not see schools as failures. Schools, the radicals say, are quite successful at doing exactly what they were created to do, namely, divide a nation into neat and predictable binaries and cultivate ovine characteristics in future citizens. We do not need to reform schools, in the radical view; we need to destroy them.

Opposition to Common Core emerged almost as soon as the policy was introduced. Like No Child Left Behind and Race to the Top, it was a bipartisan effort—and so is its opposition. Traditional proponents of classical schooling models hate Common Core every bit as much as Marxists and anarchists do. This I know because I work closely with members of all camps: leftist and anarchist educational scholars and theorists, classical liberals, and Catholic conservatives, among others. Each group accuses the others of supporting these recent policies, or at least of feeling sympathy for some part of the reasoning behind them. They would love to hold their ideological foes responsible. But such recriminations are misplaced. For once, these ancient enemies are in fact allies.

Those who support the status quo model of compulsory schooling—regulation by standardized tests based on nonsensical standards, administration by arbitrary rules cooked up in a crockpot of social-scientific studies with a three-year shelf life—do so mainly out of ignorance or resignation, not because they approve of schools. For most people, schools are the most reliable routes to miserable jobs and money available, so why rock the bank?

Revolution begins with dissatisfaction. A true consensus is always already present in a dissensus widespread enough to enter conventional wisdom. Perhaps this is why politicians say next to nothing about schools, except to camouflage their defects with Hallmark-card platitudes about education. The general public does not understand what schools are here to do, where they came from, and why we decided to make people attend them for twelve consecutive years under penalty of law. There is blame enough to go around several times over. We've lost our way, or perhaps we've found our way into a dissent that is long overdue.

The decay of schooling even seeps into colleges and universities. Ask any thoughtful academic for the prognosis of her profession and home institution and her reply will invariably be grim. The schooling consensus replicates itself across the humanities, which explains why atheistic analytic philosophy departments and leftist cultural studies faculties feel just as threatened as religious studies scholars and theologians. Academics sometimes like to think that the other side is profiting from their own side's subjugation, but in truth, this monstrous philistinism respects neither persons nor parties.

In the fine arts, the panic is pitched even higher. School killed jazz, some people say. Who knows? What seems clear is that the school of today is no longer the school of yesterday, the school that, whether public or private, functioned as a civic institution, fulfilling both disciplinary and protective social purposes. Today's school is indifferent and even allergic to the civic model; in scope and purpose, schooling is becoming less and less political and more and more economic. Like prisons, schools are run for profit. They are barrels of fish waiting for a quick-buck artist to show up with a spear, under a national mandate.

This new economic school is a threat to all. It is a monster with teeth and appetite enough not to care whom it devours next. We may not agree on the purpose or the proper shape of education, much less the political questions of what a society is and should be, but I think that we all agree that schooling today is lost. To salvage any part of it, we must subject its most basic assumptions to a ruthless scrutiny.

This is a weak basis for consensus, to be sure, but it is a start. From here, we might begin searching for a path forward that would help schools more than it harms them. If nothing else, this schooling consensus might serve as a modest experiment in trusting our own fate to another's good will.

January 21, 2015
Ethika Politika

The Tests Have Failed

When I was studying in a Texas high school during George W. Bush's tenure as governor, students from all over the state had to sit for a standardized test called the Texas Assessment of Academic Skills. We called it the TAAS test. The aggregate scores of these tests determined each school's rating for the given year. If the school got a good score, it would hang up a gaudy banner as if it had won the state football championship. Students first sat for the test in sophomore year, presumably so that they would have two chances to retake it if given an initial low score.

I sat in the school auditorium holding a flat plywood graffiti-covered board on my lap. The moment I finished my test I would have to return to regular classes, which I mostly despised. So I chose to stay with my test all day long, taking naps and pretending to be hard at work whenever the test monitors walked by.

Most students, especially the smart ones, finished before lunch. After lunch, the stragglers, including me, were moved into the library. A handful of us were, like me, there by choice, even in a spirit of mischief. The rest were struggling; a few had special needs. A test monitor hissed into my ear, "You know it doesn't take this long for you to finish this, Rocha." I smiled and replied that I was just trying to do my best and that this was really hard stuff. We had to be finished by 3:30 p.m., so I turned in my booklet and bubble sheet with enough time left to gather my things and head to the gym for an offseason football workout.

I never could have predicted that Bush would make the TAAS test into a nationwide ritual, which he did in the first days of his presidency, by signing into law the Elementary and Secondary Education Act, better known as No Child Left Behind. By now, Obama's Race to the Top and Common Core initiatives have extended the reach of standardized testing even further. Over that decade we saw the birth of a testing-industrial complex made up of giant corporations like Pearson, contracted in multimillion-dollar business agreements with state governments and funded by taxpayers.

The logic of testing is justified by moralistic tautologies and statistical psychobabble—slogans like Bush's "standards without accountability are not standards"—and mostly bogus "science-based research" cooked up in quantitative studies. As No Child Left Behind indicates, the titles of these laws pander both to a desperate public and their elected representatives.

With tests administered by businessmen and graders sometimes hired over Craigslist, the process is immune to almost any serious or continuous public oversight. To speak of accountability is to make a joke in very poor taste. The standards are so low, they might as well be non-existent, as we can infer from the fact that students at elite prep schools like Andover and Exeter—and the Sidwell Friends School, which Obama's and Joe Biden's children attend—are spared having to meet them.

Most of all, the curricula that support and prepare students for these miserable tests manage a trick I would once have thought impossible: they make compulsory schooling even stupider and more soul-killing than before. This judgement may sound harsh and sweeping, but it also happens to be shared by teachers, parents, and students nationwide. Even Diane Ravitch, one of the earliest supporters of No Child Left Behind and an engineer of the testing movement, has thoroughly denounced nationwide standardized tests and preparatory curricula in *The Death and Life of the Great American School System: How Testing and Choice Undermine Education*.

These tests prey on the conscience of those teachers and parents least prepared to critique and question them, the naïve ones who trust schools implicitly. These unwitting accomplices sometimes go so far as to place students in testing pep rallies. This is not a metaphor; just before tests are administered, some schools corral students in the gym and pump them full of fighting spirit. These affairs resemble the events staged by the D.A.R.E. campaign against drugs and are every bit as risible.

Testing is not in and of itself a harmful thing, much less an intrinsic evil. Certain tests are unavoidable. When one's courage is tested, there is nothing one can do to opt out. The test of love is one we all hope to pass. However, each test, like each law, must be accountable to a truer and more rigorous standard. When laws are unjust, they become unlawful. When tests are stupid, they become absurd. When laws and tests harm entire downwardly-mobile populations while enriching multibillion-dollar private industries, they become oppressive. Some students, frightened over the possible consequences to their future of a low score, place that future at even greater risk by cheating.

The only bad test is a bad test, and the only bad school is a bad school. There is nothing magical about testing that requires it be regulated from above like the manufacture of pharmaceuticals. Indeed, one of testing's worst failures is the support it lends to the toxic ideology that deputizes a class of know-nothing experts and professionals to determine who shows intelligence and what makes sense. In the face of such technocratic clout, teachers, parents, and students are at a constant disadvantage. Compulsory testing reinforces all that is bad and harmful about compulsory schooling.

In every possible way, testing has failed. Or rather, it has succeeded only in promoting a set of private interests, backed by capital, that has sufficient resources to stifle its critics.

Even if you are able to help your students opt out of one test or another, hundreds of thousands of others will not be so lucky. This unhappy majority will be chewed up and ground down into a premature intellectual death. Educators and parents must join forces across ideological and partisan lines to announce that the tests have failed, at a scale beyond individual choice and protest.

It may be some time before we can agree on *deschooling*, but at least all people of good will can *detest* the schools.

May 6, 2015
Ethika Politika

Education: The Craft of Desire

There is a universal and inextricable relationship between desire and belief.

This relationship contains and reveals the natural, religious, and erotic order of things. It is no surprise, then, that New Atheists are among today's fiercest defenders of religious belief. In their evangelical zeal, their strawman debates, their group therapy sessions and echo chambers, they reveal and revel in desire.

Here are two well-known facts about desire: (1) We do not know what we want; (2) We do not want what we want. We want to want more than what we want.

The most fundamental objects of desire are, in this sense, the disclosure of desire and the desire for Desire.

*

A child cries.

"What's wrong?"

"I don't know!"

The child is tired and needs some food, a warm bath, and a soft bed, but she isn't conscious of wanting exactly these things. She only knows that she wants *something*.

Not knowing what she wants, but wanting to know, backs her into a tense place. That tension accounts for a big part of her misery.

She wants what she wants, she wants to want it, but she also doesn't want to be told to eat, to bathe, to lay down and go to sleep.

She doesn't want what she wants. Inwardly she does, outwardly she doesn't.

The external masks the internal.

This is part of what desire is: a vexing mystery close enough to make demands on our hearts, minds, and bodies, but distant enough to elude our grasp. Thus, desire remains within the realm of the desired, rather than the realm of the attainable.

The desire for Desire.

Education is all about desire.

Education is the craft of desire.

You don't need to read Plato to understand that.

*

A Dr. Pepper commercial begins with a young man dressed in standard corporate attire. After drinking a can of Dr. Pepper, he tears off his oxford shirt and tie, revealing a maroon undershirt that reads "I'm One of a Kind." At once, the young man is joined by a flash mob of lookalikes who have all drunk from the same liberating elixir. Dressed identically in logo T-shirts, they perform a song and dance routine with military precision. Except for one dancer, whose shirt reads "Rebel," they make up a Pepper-drinking phalanx.

*

Drinking Dr. Pepper awakens our innermost desire for individuality, which is only satisfied by a reversion to total uniformity. (Minor, calculated variations and a single exception only serve to prove the rule).

This is the revolving door of the great myth of freedom that libertinism has bred deep into the modern imagination. This is the one ideological commitment we all share to some degree. Ignore, for the moment, the myth itself and the ideology it has produced. Look instead at the educational structure, and the way it crafts our desire.

Desire comes before and extends beyond freedom. Even freedom must obey desire. We are not free when we get what we desire; either we desire more of the same or we start desiring something new for a change. We desire Desire and revolve back into the place we never left. When we realize our desire for individuality, we clothe ourselves in a different suit, a different uniform, but a costume nonetheless.

The external masks the internal.

Surely that young man once thought (as I once did) that wearing a suit and tie every day would fulfill his desire for status and purpose; now he feels a new desire for the freedom of his youth. But fulfilling that desire returns him, viciously, to his corporate uniformity. Again and again. No escape. No freedom from desire.

Now we turn to the myth of freedom itself and its libertine ideologies: classical liberalism, early modern conservatism, communism, socialism, American progressivism, Rawlsian liberalism, neoconservatism, neoliberalism, globalism, and more. Democrats and Republicans. Ron Paul.

The myth of freedom assumes that freedom will consummate desire, that we desire freedom in the first and last place, that freedom is the proper object of desire. Henceforth, the craft of modernity has been one of freedom, a craft of building freedom. Freedom-fighting. Braveheart.

For Catholics this should ring hollow. Dr. Pepper is sugary and tasty and freedom has its own seductions, but we should know better and ask a qualifying question: Do I know what I want? Do I even want what I want?

The craft of God is love, the heartfelt master craft of desire by Desire. As products of this divine, erotic craft, the education that crafts our desire is Desire itself: Christ is our teacher, rabbi, and master. This is the beauty of the Sacred Heart of Jesus: the desire for Desire.

We long for the one who Desires us.

The craft of desire, then, is rooted in fidelity. Not freedom. Fidelity to Desire. The restless pursuit of holiness, that thing we always desire but never want, because we spend too much time throwing tantrums and drinking Dr. Pepper, the syrupy substitutes.

We do not know the desires of our heart and we do not want what we desire—we don't want what we think we want. There is always more. This is why education is nothing more and nothing less than the craft of desire.

December 31, 2012
Patheos

Real School Choice

Thursday night was my first chance to watch the Republican National Convention. I won't add to the glut of tired commentaries except to reflect on Jeb Bush's speech about schooling and school choice.

By definition, authentic choice cannot exist within a compulsory system. They are antithetical concepts. Any choice worthy of the name cannot be constrained by an institutional system of compulsion. Real "school choice" then, will become possible only after the disestablishment of compulsory schooling.

Sadly, both of today's mirror-image political parties accept compulsory schooling as more than a descriptive state of affairs: they seem to endorse it as a normative value in and of itself. There is a disturbing messianism to the credentialist creed of schooling today.

Nobody on either side is willing to lay real "school choice" on the table. We kid ourselves that we are being generous when we allow parents to choose between home, private, public, and charter schools. But we believe our own lie only because we've forgotten that schooling does not and must not have a monopoly over true education.

For true education, any school smaller than the world is too small.

I may seem to be overemphasizing the need for rejection and denial, while forgetting about the good news in the Gospel. But I tend to proclaim the good news in a minor chord, deeply influenced by the apophatic, the *via negativa* and the *via dolorosa:* ways toward God that lead through the dark night of absence and suffering. Love hurts. This creates a tragic vision of the world that is more than a truth. It is a dark aesthetic revelation of reality. Tell me not what is true, show me what is real. Show us your face and we shall be saved.

Here is the practical challenge: How will this vision of a time where schooling is no longer compulsory, but where the world itself is a school, serve to educate people in an authentic way? What is the purpose behind tilting at today's credentialism? Suggest that compulsory schooling be abolished, and people ask nervously what will replace it. "If I stop taking these sugar pills," they wonder, "what will happen to me?" The placebo of ideology is as precious as Frodo's ring.

Here is a constructive response, inspired by children's play: My two boys have been playing make-believe with their cousins all morning. Earlier, while the grown-ups took their coffee, they performed a rather disjointed play in three acts. Don't get too excited: it wasn't very good—at least I didn't think so—and I didn't particularly enjoy watching it. But that was not the point. I didn't need to patronize them by fluffing up their self-esteem in order to truly esteem what they were doing and how importantly real it was. It was not entertainment or amusement.

I could see that their play was serious; signs of gravity were everywhere. For one thing, the players behaved in a high-handed way toward the audience. "Sit here and watch the play." "No! Don't clap yet. It's not over.

NO! Not yet!" They constantly fought over who was to do what, who should stand where, who was going next, and what they were supposed to be doing in the first place. "And where did Gabe go? Gabe! GAABE! Where are you?!" "I think he went inside." It was clear to me that they were not taking their make-believe lightly.

Afterwards, I sat trying to revive yet another manuscript I wrote during grad school into a proposal for the Philosophy of Education Society, my field's top conference. I could hear my boys running around, busying themselves with still more imaginative nonsense. How annoying it was to me! (Reality can be very annoying sometimes.) I did not find their tireless play precious, at least not then; but I did consider it to be the most important thing going on at the moment. It seemed so crucial, in fact, that I decided to write about it instead of working on my still-unfinished conference paper.

While adults work, children play; and their play is usually more serious and earnest than our work. If we worked as seriously as they played, the world might not be any better or worse, but life would surely be far richer, more enchanting, and less mediocre.

I never joined them; I didn't pass out ribbons or stickers or other cheap external rewards. For one thing, I wasn't in the mood. More importantly, any such meddling would have been deeply disrespectful to the sacredness of their play. I wasn't good enough then to play at their level of rigor. I was working.

People often argue that children need to play and go to recess to have "fun." I don't see it that way. Fun, to me, is only coincidental. These valiant defenders of fun, I suspect, have never really played. Or they forget that real play, the play I am describing here, usually ends in tears, disappointment, fighting, or all three.

Play is not important because it is fun. I doubt that children are nearly as interested in amusing themselves as we are in seeing them amused. The fun is for us, not them. Children play in deadly earnest. How strange that nowadays we celebrate children who work and adults who play! (Just contrast elementary school science fairs with collegiate and professional sports.)

My sons and nieces understood and practiced the art of play with all its dead serious nonsense. The fact that I found it childish and tedious is not important; to focus on that aspect would be to lose myself in translation. The more important, educative reality is that this was sacred time devoted to the most ambitious, important undertaking anyone around here attempted all day.

This is what the school in and of the world allows us to do and be that the smaller, compulsory schools do not. This is school choice at its finest. It goes beyond the consumerist fancy of selection, venturing into authentic freedom, where the only "choice" that really matters is the choice to elect what is unavoidable. To whom shall we go? You have the words of everlasting life.

If someone saw these children playing and asked why they were not in school, I wouldn't have bothered pointing out that my nieces actually are enrolled in school but were not required to attend that Friday, that my youngest is too young to attend, or that the older one is a different story for a different time. Instead, I would have laughed and said, "Of course they are in school! Why aren't YOU in school today?"

The abolition of compulsory schooling will entail more than disestablishment of schooling institutions; it will also mean a return to a school of the world, a curriculum of life. When the school is destroyed, everyone goes back to school. No exceptions. No choice other than the only one that really matters: the choice to imagine the real. No more work. Only play. No more fun or amusement, only what is most serious.

September 12, 2012
First Things

Against Excellence

Americans, especially those involved in the public school system, love to talk about excellence. Rare is the mission statement that omits it. In such a context, "excellence" connotes academic proficiency, ideal psychological adjustment, and all other factors that equip human beings to thrive in modern developed society.

What does it mean to excel? Everyone knows: To excel is to win, to outperform someone else. "Excellence" bears out the true purpose of all models of wide-scale social testing because excellence is really about a contest of pure relativity, the calculus of which determines who gets to survive and thrive.

So much attention has been devoted to the biases allegedly built into standardized testing that few pause to reflect on how unique that testing really is. How many American institutions employ a single test as a measure of membership or qualification? Aside from the bar associations and Motor Vehicle Departments of the various states, practically none. Participants in all other spheres are graded more subtly. We don't test the population of the United States to find its most suitable presidential candidates. The Church doesn't test baptismal candidates to decide who merits the sacrament. Find a single test that has proven entirely salutary. Find one that is not linked to a gulag system.

When weighing the merits of various applicants, corporations know better than to rely on their test scores or even on their school grades. Even the testing corporations themselves do not use tests in this way; surely they must be aware that their own watery standards of excellence are ones they cannot meet. I sometimes dream of giving testing executives and policy makers their own easy tests, for ritual absurdity.

*

Long before *The Hunger Games*, Shirley Jackson's 1948 short story "The Lottery," published in *The New Yorker*, imagined a dystopia where a rural community chooses its annual sacrificial victim through a raffle. The final line is chilling: "'It isn't fair, it isn't right,' Mrs. Hutchinson screamed, and then they were upon her."[2]

The community of Jackson's story isn't cavalier about its cruel ritual, nor do its members seem especially bloodthirsty. They dread the lottery and feel bad for the winners. Some even voice displeasure—"Seems like we got through with the last one only last week"—but nonetheless they see the business through to the bitter end, with fear their only consolation.

Some dare dream of change: "They do say . . . that over in the north village they're talking of giving up the lottery." Others are more cautious: "Pack of crazy fools . . . Next thing you know, they'll be wanting to go back to living in caves, nobody work anymore."[3]

*

Some tests are worthwhile. Standards exist that are worth being held accountable to. Paul, of course, refers to winning a race, and Christ frequently speaks of the Kingdom in ways suggesting disciples prepare themselves rigorously. Here, surely, is a contest to compete in.

But scripture speaks of a contest without singular tests; indeed, it is a paradoxical contest in which the last finishes first and the first last. This is not a contest that demands mere excellence. This is a test that demands even more. Life is only achieved through death. This is not a contest of might or will; it is an exercise that glorifies what is most hidden and wholly other. The

---

2. Shirley Jackson, "The Lottery," in the June 26, 1948 issue of *The New Yorker*. Retrieved from http://www.newyorker.com/magazine/1948/06/26/the-lottery on February 11, 2017.

3. Ibid.

prize is holiness, not success, union, not separation. The commitment must be total and absolute, and its object transcends any faddish standard.

Anyone who has excelled at something knows the dark truth of its high costs and fleeting rewards. Even the school that excels must meet the mark again and again. How many excellent students have suffered, in the long run, through their apparent, immediate success? Surely there is something more excellent than today's excellence. Surely there is something more to education than schooling. Surely there is enough courage left to detest arbitrary contests that abound within and beyond the school. Surely we must reject at least a few conventions that draw and quarter life into oblivion, excellence be damned.

May 26, 2015
Ethika Politika

What Can Go Wrong with Classical, Great Books, and Montessori?

Education requires, as Pope Francis recently observed, *pinzas*, or tweezers. This is very frustrating for most people, especially those most concerned about education, and it is this very frustration that often prevents us from coming to any real understanding.

Cheap opinions and prescriptive programs and quick fixes abound, but even when these options are "effective" and produce "results" or "success," the more fundamental problems remain and, too often, embed themselves deeper.

This is why education needs to be spoken about with words chosen carefully, but also in a philosophical spirit willing to lose and dirty itself. There is no serious discussion of education that is not, beyond the literal topic or theme, already *educational* in itself.

But who really wants to attend to the tedium of love? Who wants to guess and clean the messy excrement and simply hold the beloved for no other reason than love itself (and the hope for a sound sleep)? This is a disposition, a mood, a feel for things shown in work that avoids the seductive selling of snake oil.

*

If you are still reading, then we might be getting somewhere. This is important foreplay. Touch matters.

*

As with most serious crafts, education has a number of important preliminaries that cannot be conflated or rushed through.

Without being too hasty, let me name four things that must be considered with a certain amount of respect for the conceptual distance separating them: education, teaching, curriculum, and schooling.

As mere terms with *definitions*, they can represent whatever you want them to; but as things with *descriptions*, none should be equated with any of the others, even when they overlap.

This is why pedagogy—and, more radically, mystagogy—is an art.

The most common entry into nonsense and miscommunication occurs when education is mistaken for schooling and not sufficiently distinguished from the work of teaching and the questions pertaining to curricula. Confusing generic schooling with *compulsory* schooling creates even greater problems.

But the worst offense is branding education with an -ism or a name. That almost always slimes the surface, placing it at risk of slipping into the abyss of ideology.

When education becomes ideological, it is time to burn it down and start over. After all, there is literally (and metaphysically) nothing to lose. This was at the very heart of Ivan Illich's little-understood notion of *deschooling*.

*

Classical, Great Books, and Montessori are curricula. Each one is grounded in its own ideas about education, which also holds implications for styles of teaching. None of them requires a school, but many schools rely on them. This basic fact, that these three curricula do not rely on schooling much less compulsory schooling, is a major point in their favor.

Therefore, to talk about Classical, Great Books, or Montessori curricula is not the same thing as talking about the schools that employ their material or methods.

I'm trying so hard to tread slowly and softly because my opinion of Classical, Great Books, and Montessori curricula begins with admiration. All three were created through the best of intentions. By critiquing them, I am by no means calling for their abolition. In fact, the most sensible people I know who make use of or endorse these curricula do so for good reason. They appreciate some particular feature because experience has taught them that it works. Their famous names and the prestige attached to them matter nothing by comparison.

Each of these curricula arose from a movement motivated by a spirit of critique. All of them, in their various ways, attempted a critique of modernity. As starting points go, there is none better. I object only to certain particulars and their potential for imbalance or abuse.

*

The so-called Classical approach is a misnomer. So little about the curriculum owes anything to classical antiquity. Its real origins can be found in the Trivium of the Middle Ages. Mired in nostalgia, its apologists hate to consider whether their program could stand an update—or even a turn further back toward the ancients.

The Classical model is much more closely related to the many neoclassical restorationist revivals that rose and broke throughout early and middle modernity. Its underlying assumptions are the assumptions of classical liberalism, and it seems a natural fit in countries born of or reformed by it. But ultimately, the medieval Trivium and eighteenth-century liberalism make for a goofy combination. Imagine Thomas Aquinas addressing the Continental Congress and you'll get the idea.

This brings us to the Great Books curriculum, which shares a great deal of territory with the Classical curriculum. When applied holistically, the Classical approach has more bandwidth than Great Books, but in practice the reverse is often true. In any case, the two share certain weaknesses.

Beyond the canonical issue—i.e., the dispute over which books deserve the title "great"—the major shortcoming of Great Books is the fact that books mark its horizons. Not many will recognize the danger in filling one's head with quality reading, since today's consensus holds up literacy as an unqualified good. But focusing too narrowly on reading is short-sighted to the point of being dangerous. The greatness of "great" books is to be found beyond their pages. They must refer to an incarnational reality; in order for a book to be great, the word must become flesh. In addition, Great Books suffers from a certain scriptural emphasis a bit too Protestant for my taste.

Montessori is more hazardous to critique, since so much of it bears the stamp of a single innovator, namely, Maria Montessori. Even more than apologists for the other two, Montessori boosters tend to treat their curriculum as an ideology. That temptation can only be resisted by a thorough and critical study of her sources.

A fascinating combination of romanticism and Catholicism can be found in a Montessori curriculum, but it easily becomes prescriptive and programmatic in a way foreign to, for instance, Rousseau, who insisted that the ideas expressed in *Emile* were not to be implemented or imitated literally.

*

What are the alternatives? Anything and everything except another "alternative." Even a good alternative. Even Classical, Great Books, or Montessori.

The most radical and revolutionary change is the one that ignores the façade and goes straight for the guts. To change everything, we must be willing to change nothing and simply recover what we have lost, holding tight to hope, that nostalgia for the future.

Pedagogy without mystagogy is bankrupt, and not only for theological reasons. This bankruptcy has caused our collective imagination to fail.

These critiques are not especially practical. They won't lend themselves to instruction manuals or winning political policies—that's the point.

We need move beyond finding this or that to replace that or this. It is time to begin, again and again.

January 17, 2014
Patheos

Dead White Guys

At the time of my high school graduation, I embodied minority educational empowerment. I was a poor Mexican-American boy, a first-generation college student, itinerant but bright, raised in the Catholic Church, full of pious ideas and wet dreams. Thanks to the philanthropy of Bill and Melinda Gates, I was enrolled at an orthodox Catholic college to study the great books, philosophy, and all that jazz. I was even invited to pray at a LULAC banquet, as an exemplar to the Latino community. An invitation I declined.

I sometimes understate how hard I worked during the undergrad years, but I really did read and study and learn far more than I should have, given all my extracurriculars, wholesome and unwholesome. Let the record reflect that I left Franciscan University of Steubenville with a solid foundation in the Western canon, Franciscan thought, and personalist phenomenology.

Next, newly married, I matriculated at the University of St. Thomas in St. Paul, Minnesota to study education. (My education in education also had its practical side—I taught K-8 Spanish.) On my first day at St. Thomas, I learned how awful St. Augustine (a North *African*) was, and what a waste of time it was to read books by white, European men. So we read books by other white, European men, beginning with Marx and Weber.

Then we got to critical race theory—Cornel West's *Democracy Matters* had just been published—and all that "Can the subaltern speak?" kind of stuff. I learned—again, primarily from white men—what a wretched thing the Western canon was and how disempowered I had been at the hands of Homer, Augustine, and Dante. Learning the very thing I once took for the path to socio-political empowerment had been a total waste of time, they explained. I'd sinned and was in need of redemption. I was a miserable Mexican wretch who needed to wallow in the mud of historic injustice to be cleansed from too many bubble baths with Don Quixote.

I was meant to abandon it all and start anew with fresh, *critical* ideas. But the freshness wore off quickly and the ideas became more and more predictable. Vocabulary was key. The lexicon of "hegemony," "privilege," "problematizing," and so on. I learned it all and was quite open to it, but when it came time to select a PhD program, I went to study with this crazy old Deweyan progressive—a "bourgeois liberal," as Richard Rorty would have called him—because he called me out at a conference (which I attended in a *guayabera*), for referring to myself as "underprivileged." He told me to feel privileged for being intelligent. I went to Ohio State and found Nietzsche, Foucault, Jean-Luc Marion, and most of all William James. More white men.

These men left me more suited than ever to mount an argument against the patriarchy of Western metaphysics within its institution *par excellence*, the modern university. And for much bigger and more serious reasons than demographics. We cannot experience folklore, real life, the flux of the commons, by importing the folkloric into this institutional space, nor by fleeing the institution. The only way to find it is to imitate the mad priest in *The Count of Monte Cristo*, digging and scratching our way through with passionate fidelity. This noble doggedness informs the spirit of Ralph Ellison's classic *Invisible Man*.

Some time ago, R.R. Reno published a review titled "Theology After the Revolution," which influenced me deeply. The gist was that today's critical theologians, unlike practitioners of the *nouvelle theologie*, had lost touch with the objects of their own critique. In class I often draw a comparison between serious, intentional disobedience and accidental disobeying: an "I reject you" versus an "Oops!" If one is serious about being critical then one cannot dissent clumsily or by accident. One must *understand* the object of one's departure as much as possible. You've got to do your homework. Period.

This is why I have become so fed up with popular academic trade books. You know what I mean: *Mexicans CAN!: A Critical Approach to*

Teaching Brown People How to Find Their Inner Aztec Gila Monster in the Margins of the Diaspora: A (Post)Critical Approach. If you don't know what kind of book I mean, go to an academic conference book display, where examples abound.

Unlike theology, educational theory may never have been subjected to a sure-footed critique to begin with. Regarding the educational theory of his own day, William James, in a letter to G. Stanley Hall, wrote, "Pedagogic literature seems to contain such vast quantities of chaff that one hardly knows where to seek for the grain." Chaff may have been abundant then for different reasons than in today's academy, but the results are the same: emptiness, a void of the type late-modern horror writers personify in the figure of the zombie. This ghastly pop-cultural projection captures the predicament of the West: we are so afraid of our inevitable demise that we must commit suicide to prevent it. Thus we have the ultimate Dead White Guy we see portrayed in the evangelical film *God's Not Dead*—the undead god.

October 25. 2012
First Things

A Curriculum of Life

What if your child died at the age of eight? What biographical details would make it into her eulogy? Her perfect school attendance? Her wonderful grades? How well-behaved she was in school? No. It would be about her smile, her love, the way she laughed. Sadly, many children who are simply prepared for adulthood, just as adults who merely prepare for retirement, find the time and space of their lives monopolized by what is not most important.

Tomas, our eldest son, turned six on August 8. By state law he is exempt from compulsory school attendance this year. Kindergarten is optional, but next year he will be expected to enter some form of schooling. Last year we decided to milk the freedom afforded us by law by not enrolling him in school, and this year will pass like the last. What we'll do with him next year remains an open question.

My wife and I felt an almost magnetic pull to justify our decision to keep Tomas out of school. Prevailing ideologies can have that effect. Complicating our fight through that force field, well-intentioned family, friends, colleagues, and strangers assaulted us with questions, demands for explanations.

We are still undecided on exactly what kind of education we want for Tomas, or for any of our children. What we are certain is that what we decide to do and not do will constitute their education, for better or for worse. For us, the most important thing is to live by preparing well for death, with or without schools and their institutional counterparts. As Catholics, we cannot settle for a pedagogy that lacks mystagogy.

The problem I've found in "homeschooling," "classical education," and even "unschooling" is metaphysical: all three approaches maintain the trappings of schooling. They may not take place in brick-and-mortar institutions, but they operate within an institutional psychology. One example is their approach to curricula. A curriculum for school is just what it purports to be: a curriculum for school. It is self-serving; preparing people for degrees and employment, for raises and retirement and so on. But when do we prepare for life and death? For theosis?

Having weighed the alternatives, my wife and I have recently begun our own experiment, our own search for an education that has the potential to prepare Tomas for life by letting him live today, rather than fixing his gaze permanently on the next stage. We have built our homemade curriculum around the "Three L's": Logic, Literature, and Love. We chose these three subjects partly because all three are founded in the Catholic liturgy. If all goes according to plan, they will work in a complementary and comprehensive way to guide us in educating Tomas without concerning ourselves today with his future schooling.

Logic

The first of our "L's" is based on our need for a rational sense of order. We need logic if we ever hope to understand subjects like grammar, mathematics, and science, or master practical skills like cooking, cabinet-making, and taking out the trash. Logic unifies all these experiences. Whenever Tomas and I talk, we make simple visual and conceptual comparisons, and we've just begun studying some elementary analogies: What are they? Where can they be found in everyday life? I also purchased a very good workbook, *Analogies for Beginners*, for him to play in as he wants or as I direct him.

We will eventually move to if/then statements. For the moment, though, we're restricting him from doing much more than very intuitive visual work in the form of simple addition and subtraction, as well as reading and writing. In this way, we hope to introduce him to the logic of mathematical operations, along with the painfully illogical grammatical rules and usages governing the English language. In terms of complexity and academic sophistication, Tomas can take it as far as he likes, but the point is not academic. The point is to provide a foundation for the general use of his intellect.

Literature

The second "L" builds on the belief that story and myth (*mythopoesis*) are vital for reasons much more serious than literary fancy, training in reading comprehension, or the development of memory. Logic often pervades stories, but we also want to emphasize literature's aesthetic, non-instrumental side through reading, writing, storytelling, and story-making. I've banned "fact books" for precisely this reason. We already have two sets of encyclopedias and yearbooks and a few other reference materials—these should suffice for now. The rest of his books are to be based in story, myth, fable, and poetry. Tomas has been reading for some time already, but we still have some fine points left to iron out. We want to help him improve his penmanship, for one. Beyond that, we want to equip him with whatever mental constructs will enable him to begin writing down his own stories. He already makes them up. Play is usually very rigorous story work. This notion of story extends to coloring, drawing, visual art, listening to and making music. Like logic, it should permeate everything in the right proportion and to the proper degree.

Love

The third "L" is based on the absolute and unchanging beauty of love that reveals itself in a life lived fully and richly. It is not purely sentimental, but it's not abstruse or theoretical, either. The love side of our curriculum requires that Tomas spend his time with people who love what they are doing, or who at least do not hate it. We will help him avoid people who loathe themselves, the places where they work, and the routines they follow. At home, I invite Tomas to see what I do in my study, to show him my love for the craft of study and writing. I will one day bring him into my classroom, not to learn anything particular, but simply to dwell and be present while I do something else I love. We'll go fishing too. We will also send Tomas away from home to spend time with other people who lovingly practice crafts or ministries. I think that he will witness the incredible tedium and immense rigor that go into doing something with love. Perhaps he will find a craft of his own, but, as wonderful as that would be, it is not the goal. The goal is to teach him how best to invest his time and his heart.

This curriculum of life requires of Tomas only that he learn to live well and dwell in the presence of those seeking to do the same. First and last, God willing, will be the daily example of his mother and father. As his primary educators, we must offer the full use of our hearts and our time.

My wife and I may be the primary educators of Tomas (as well as our younger children), but we do not kid ourselves that we are their exclusive educators. My professorial skills are of limited use here. We may one day decide to send Tomas and his brother to be schooled at a church or a public building, or school him from a textbook at our kitchen table. But we must never allow a curriculum for school to replace a curriculum of life; schooling mustn't take over the education that comes through living. Whenever it does, the inversion risks miseducation. It robs our children of the present gift of life they have been given by God.

If, heaven forbid, they die young, I hope they will have lived beautiful lives, perhaps lives even more beautiful than those who survive them. Our goals for their education, then, are not prescriptive or pedagogical; they are aesthetic and mystagogical. They will require more than a curriculum for schooling or for anything else; they will require a curriculum of life.

September 26, 2012
First Things

Deschooling Religious Education, in Six Claims

1. Compulsory schooling came to the United States in the nineteenth century, through the Whig common school movement. The Whigs modeled their program on the Prussian school system, founded after the advent of the Prussian research university. The first compulsory schooling laws were passed in the late 1850s, in New Hampshire and New York. The laws' backers were convinced that poor Irish Catholic parents could not be trusted to raise their children alone. Thus, the legal concept of *in loco parentis* was born.

2. *Compulsory* schooling is what we today refer to when we use the term "schooling." Like the prison, the hospital, and other facilities meant to house and *reform* humans, the compulsory school is an institution unique to modernity. In many instances, these secular institutions see themselves as assuming the functions once filled by the Church and the family. Suffice it to say that when most people today speak of schools, they are not referring to a generic school. Instead, they are referring to a modern state-run institution and object of compulsory attendance.

3. Initially, compulsory schooling and its philosophical premises encountered resistance, most of which died by the dawn of the twentieth century. In the early 1970s, it faced a new wave of opposition, among whose spokespeople was the Catholic priest Ivan Illich, author of a short book titled *Deschooling Society*. Unlike contemporaries devoted to the *un*schooling movement, Illich saw *de*schooling as something greater than a program for reforming state schools, or even an alternative in the form of homeschooling. Ilich aimed to deschool all of society, which he, like Michel Foucault, believed had institutionalized and objectified the human person. For him, the process included compulsory schooling but extended, ultimately, into every facet of life.

*

From the discussion above, we've seen that (1) compulsory schooling is a recent and characteristically modern invention; (2) the everyday language of "schooling" refers to the modern institution and its counterparts, not some broader, more generic category; and (3) Illich's idea of deschooling is a social critique, first and foremost, not a proposal for shutting down primary schools or starting an anarcho-libertarian homeschooler's fad.

*

4. The Catholic notion of education is classical. It builds on the noetic ideas illustrated by Plato in his *Republic*. It is inspired (Spirit-filled) and ensouled. It builds on an ontological idea we find in Augustine that places knowing under the authority of becoming, and becoming under the primacy of love. The *Ordo Amoris*, the Order of Love, leads toward God and, therefore, toward mystery. This is mystagogy. Unlike pedagogy, mystagogy is not reducible to head or intellect. It cannot be conveyed through a cognitive or behavioral psychology. This is why a truly Catholic education does not require a school and a truly Catholic school cannot submit itself to the norms of the modern day compulsory school.

5. The modern logic of schooling is all about pedagogy, built on a notion of learning that operates from the head down. It was designed to produce docile learners. This emphasis flavors modern schooling jargon, including phrases like "learning outcomes," and "mastery goals." It is also the engine driving Common Core, as it drove many of its predecessors, including No Child Left Behind and Race to the Top. All of these mechanisms were tailored to fit and justify the compulsory school. According to the theories of knowledge and mind that support these ideas, the process of knowing is

purely cognitive and behavioral and good for an industrial economy. This modern logic of schooling is, from a Catholic point of view, false.

6. You can find thriving Catholic communities, past and present, where there are no classes or classrooms. No schools. Most of these communities are poor in socioeconomic terms. I've seen them in Mexico and other parts of Latin America. In these communities, the parish church itself, sometimes bare and even unsightly, is the only common classroom. Children undergo catechesis through the liturgy, through prayers, homily, music, community life and tradition and story—and in the domestic churches in the homes of the faithful.

In such communities, families, though not perfect, take seriously their calling to educate. Literacy is not required, only dwelling and being, living together in faith and often suffering and joy. To say that these communities lack facilities for proper religious education would be libelous. It may even be that these communities offer a much deeper religious education than many schools, secular or Catholic. As Pope Francis teaches us, we have much to learn from the poor—the Church must become a poor Church, for the poor and of the poor.

*

There is a fundamental gap between the secular idea of pedagogy, delivered through modern compulsory schooling, and the Catholic idea of mystagogy, delivered through a religious education that can begin wherever two or more are gathered, whether a church, a van, or a bar. Even a compulsory school, in spite of itself, can provide the setting for mystagogy. Grace can never be excluded. There must be no despair, just as there must be no presumption.

Deschooling religious education, then, is a fundamental reordering of *education* according to its essential *religious* principles, which oppose both the modern institution of compulsory schooling and its logic of pedagogy. The alternative, mystagogy, can take place in a classroom, but classrooms are not uniquely suited to it and deserve no monopoly over it. Religious education is simply a matter of educating religiously, and the poor can show us the way forward better than I or certainly Matthew Kelly can.

February 11, 2014
Patheos

Deschooling Religious Education:
Beyond the Fear of Failure

In 1840, Horace Mann, the first Secretary of Education for the State of New Hampshire and later the first in the United States, wrote an article for the third volume of the newly-founded *Common School Journal*. His subject was the Whig party's beloved and controversial common school movement, and his treatment contained these words:

> Let the common school be expanded to its capabilities, let it
> be worked to the efficiency of which it is susceptible, and nine-
> tenths of the crimes in the penal code would become obsolete;
> the long catalogue of human ills would be abridged; men would
> walk more safely by day; every pillow would be more inviolable
> by night; property, life, and character held by a stronger tenure;
> all rational hopes respecting the future brightened.[4]

Mann was referring, of course, to what would become today's compulsory schooling system. His appeal was rooted in fear. Mann conveyed Whig anxiety over the combined effects of Irish-Catholic immigration, British-style industrialization, and the young republic's inevitable urbanization. Other factors contributed to the uncertain mood that prevailed during this period. Both the election of Andrew Jackson, that implacable populist Democrat, and the Western expansion option, opened the door to all manner of chaos.

In turbulent times, then, compulsory schooling was imposed as a preventive measure, a means of consoling by controlling. It has retained its original defensive posture. To this day, in secular circles, discussions of schooling drip with the language of business, including risk management, the looming economic apocalypse, the survival of the fittest.

Through compulsory schooling, the state asserts a now unquestioned right to act *in loco parentis*. The school is meant to immunize children from the effects of any mistakes their parents might make. In that sense, compulsory schooling equips parents and children with a safety net, but the real beneficiary is the *state*, which guarantees its own security by homogenizing its future citizens.

The history of catechesis is not my academic specialty, but I find the précis at *New Advent* both thorough and accessible. According to the Church, parents are meant to be the primary educators of their children, and Catholic catechesis forms a big part of education.

4. Mann, *Life of Horace Mann*, 142.

One common misinterpretation of this teaching demands to be addressed at the outset. In the Church's view, parents are the *primary* educators of their children but not the *sole* educators. The Church has been blessed with great teachers, none greater than the Rabbi himself, who had no biological children of his own. It was Ambrose, not his mother Monica, whose teaching helped Augustine over the intellectual hurdles to conversion. Libertarian homeschoolers who claim the Church's backing are stretching their case, to say the least.

In the fullest form of Catholic teaching, the parish, the neighbors, and the rest of the community assist parents without usurping their primacy. The habit, common to Catholics occupying all points on the political spectrum, of pitting the principle of subsidiarity against the principle of solidarity, distorts the Church's intention and helps nobody.

When we talk about deschooling, then, we should avoid rushing to prescribe drastic solutions. We should not, for example, think in terms of sending children home to lead a cloistered existence with their parents, who probably feel overwhelmed as it is. We parents don't deserve the suspicion under which some professional educators habitually place us, but nobody does us any favors by romanticizing our calling or exaggerating our gifts. Many of us are hard pressed to pull off a barely adequate job.

But here is the beautiful truth: admitting to shortcomings—our failures and fears and weaknesses, our projections and scars—does nothing to compromise our dignity as mothers and fathers. When the Church awards us the primary role in our children's education, its confidence extends to so-so and bad parents as well as brilliant ones. Even the orphan and the bastard are educated firstly by their parents, though in these sad cases, it's the absence itself that imparts the lesson.

We are born of a Divine womb, we call out, "Our Father . . ."

As parents, we share in that divine role, not because we are especially good, but simply because we are. *Being* a parent is, in this educational sense, sufficient in the first place.

Freud's sexualized psychoanalysis was surely wrong about a great many things, but it was right that the earliest and most primitive familial bonds form the foundation of a child's character. An education so foundational and radical, rooted in an ancient rabbinic tradition of teaching and the mystagogy of religious faith, cannot be replaced or replicated by anything so impersonal and self-interested as the neutral state.

*

Deschooling religious education cannot be an overreaction. We must keep both the baby and the bathwater. In this sense, deschooling is ontological: it is first about being, not knowing, and certainly not learning. It is not an answer or a solution because both would be beside the point. Mann and his Whiggish reformers were motivated by fear. Reform or progress of this sort is metaphysically corrupt. In this sense I am an unabashed conservative.

In our parishes and churches, the sacraments have been thoroughly schooled. We treat them as we would a high school diploma. A religious credential. A passing grade. Catechesis has become the required schooling for the credentialing of the sacraments. Religious education must be deschooled. We cannot catechize out of fear. The Gospel is not a strategy or a plan. The Church is not an institution and is most certainly not a modern compulsory school. The sacraments are not credentials and the religious education required for them cannot afford to be reducible to pedagogy and lacking any sense of mystagogy. Any analogy where the Church imitates the compulsory school is a scandal to the Gospel.

*

Augustine, perhaps the greatest catechist of the early Church and certainly the most prolific, ended his earthly vocation just as Vandal armies were laying siege to Hippo. Within a decade, they would blot out North African Christendom.

When Fr. Conrad Harkins, OFM, my sophomore honors professor and a medieval historian, told me that, I was shocked to process it.

"The Gospel failed?" I asked.

"I don't know, Sam," he replied, "We do not measure the Good News— it measures us and we live by it, in grace and love."

February 13, 2014
Patheos

Liturgy as Mystagogy

Introduction

"Are the three Kings here yet?"

—Tomas Rocha (age 5)

On this day, the Feast of St. John the Evangelist, I would like to embark on a project that is very near and dear to me, one that connects many of my interests and passions, namely, the promotion of liturgy as a means of mystagogy.

In RCIA (short for "Rite of Christian Initiation for Adults"), the word "mystagogy" refers to the period of catechesis that takes place after baptism or other sacraments of initiation. Rather than depart from this usage, I will extend it to its logical conclusion, that is, to include the catechesis that continues for years and even decades after the introduction to the sacraments.

But what does this term "catechesis" refer to? In Catholic circles, its everyday meaning refers to formal programs, including Sunday school, CCD, RCIA, and RCIC. Whenever I hear the term "catechesis" I usually think of something *religious*. This is too limiting for my purposes. While retaining the word's religious connotations, and without excluding formal classroom instruction, I want to broaden its meaning to include education that is not schooling.

This brings us to liturgy. In fact, this is our first lesson: that the liturgy shows us what catechesis is and, in that process, catechizes us. Most people think of liturgy exclusively in terms of what takes place in a church during a formal ritual, especially at Mass. This definition is accurate enough, but liturgy has other meanings besides. There is more to Mass than "the Mass." The Mass doesn't end; nor does liturgy end. (Recall the liturgy of the hours.)

Liturgy is the heart of the Body, the pulse of the Church.

This is how the liturgy has already begun to teach us; this is how liturgy is rabbinic. Just as education can take place anywhere and continues forever, so does catechesis. There is no place or space or time in our earthly lives where we are not immersed in liturgy. It is the water we swim in. This liturgical reality shows us the ubiquity of catechesis, or to be more exact about it, of mystagogy.

By definition, all post-baptismal catechesis is mystagogy. We never graduate from mystagogy; no school can monopolize or contain it. We only participate in mystagogy—in the mysteries of our faith—more fully or less so.

During these Advent and Christmas seasons, I have been blessed to see the liturgy perform its mystagogy on my two sons and me. Here I will not attempt to outline a strictly theoretical or theological system; my purpose in this series will be practical, to show how we can convert orthodoxy into orthopraxy. It should also become clear that our sense of what is orthodox is largely constituted by the orthopraxies of the Church, the practices of daily life.

For this reason, I offer this series with a strong sense of urgency.

We live in a culture—if we can call it that—where the liturgical pulse has been lost and, even worse, prostituted. I am not primarily speaking of secular culture. I am talking about the daily lives of many good and practicing Catholics. We do not live our daily lives in step with the pulse of the liturgy. We do not dance to the beat that is being played by the band. We just flail around, clapping off the beat, singing out of tune. Lacking this aesthetic sensibility, our lives are often indistinguishable from those who know nothing of liturgy. We settle for pedagogy when we ought to seek mystagogy.

In the entries to follow, I will outline some very ordinary and everyday aspects of the liturgy that might reawaken, invigorate, and satiate our need for mystical re-enchantment. Our need for God. These aspects come from my daily life and the lives of my children.

I'll end this introduction with a story:

At about two in the morning, my son Tomas came into the dining-room where I was writing. As he rubbed the sleep from his eyes, I asked him how he was doing. He said he was fine. In a matter of seconds, as he became more alert, he asked me, "Are the Three Kings here yet?"

What struck me in that moment was how much anticipation he had for Epiphany. As I will discuss in a later post, we open almost all our presents on the Feast of the Magi, so Tomas had some material incentive to ask this question. But there was more than this in his voice. He was asking after the Kings as you or I would ask after a loved one who was coming to visit.

A key to the art of teaching is the ability to convert an acquired interest into a native interest. This is no mean feat; attention is always fleeting. That Tomas had Epiphany on the front end of his sleepy mind at two o'clock in the morning showed me that the liturgy is not only a spiritual treasure but also a vast and effective curriculum.

A curriculum for mystagogy.

Next I will describe this sense of liturgy as mystagogy in fuller depth and detail.

December 27, 2011
Vox Nova

Saved by Beauty, a Testimony

As this series begins, I want to be especially attentive to the stories and experiences that anchor and propel it. One of the greatest mistakes made when we talk about educational and curricular things is to pretend that we are giving lessons from a distance. A teacher must always make an effort to de-distance themselves from students.

The teacher who believes that she is teaching something to her students strictly *for them* is deluding herself and failing to attend to the complex dynamic in progress. I always teach in two directions at once: inward and outward, *ad extra* and *ad intra*, for them and, secretly, for myself. Sometimes the internal and external lessons collide, undoing us all.

As much as the births of my children have amplified the mystagogical beauty and power of the liturgical year, I cannot pretend my experiences of fatherhood are the sole source of this series. That story began some time ago.

Here is my testimony:

One of the greatest compliments I've received came to me secondhand courtesy of Fr. Plagens. Father called himself a liturgist. You probably know the type, most parishes have at least one on staff. One day he told my father, "Sam really knows how to *move* on the altar; he's a natural liturgist." When my dad relayed the message to me I was only twelve or thirteen, but I understood what he was saying all the way down to my meat and bones.

Movement on the altar was already very important to me. I worked hard as an altar server, always trying to stay in sync with the celebrant and the overall rhythms of the Mass. I preferred to serve alone because most servers I knew were too clumsy and too inattentive. An awareness of time and space is essential for altar service: if you do things right, moving and making the unavoidable noises at exactly the right moments in just the right way, you can all but melt into the Mass, erasing your own presence. For me, it was about this disappearing. It was art. Reverence followed naturally.

As a very young child, perhaps seven or eight, I swelled with pride and joy when I was asked to serve as the cross bearer at our family friend's first Mass, which he celebrated the day after his ordination. The cross was magnificent and deserved to be held just so. The responsibility of bearing it well and walking it down the aisle with perfect dignity and at the perfect pace bore down on me as heavily as the object itself. If I was to lead this mystical dance, no performance short of a perfect performance would do. The cross was big—tall, thick, golden—and I was a small, skinny kid. But, gritting my teeth, I held it at the right height and angle.

I tell these stories by way of illustrating my intuitive sense about the aesthetics of liturgy. Call it a gift or a blessing, but when I was still drawing stick figures, I recognized that liturgy required elusive qualities: balance, proportion, dynamics, harmony, rhythm, contrast, and dimension.

Nobody taught me to judge these things. Most of my early religious education classes only threatened to blunt these sensibilities. But I cannot say I was born with them. I acquired them from growing up in churches and spending countless hours on altars and in pews, both during formal liturgy and in the informal solitude of the empty sacristy, the office, the chapel. These spaces, too, are deeply liturgical. To this day, I love to explore a church.

In a very literal way, I dwelled in church. Also, for most of my childhood and adolescence, our daily lives at home were built around the liturgy in a very strict, intentional way. As my early years coincided with the tail end of the charismatic renewal, my native liturgical setting would not have passed muster with Archbishop Lefebvre. For making liturgical music, my instrument of choice was, of all instruments, the guitar.

I began playing at the age of five. I learned in order to play praise and worship music at home and church, so I addressed the task with a strong sense of duty and purpose. By "learned" I mean I was taught at home by my dad at first, and later in church by other guitarists. I eventually had the ambition to write praise and worship music. Along the way, I learned some hymns; but now I know the canons of Jim Cowan and George Misulia better than I do Mozart's *Requiem.*

I was soon moved from altar boy to worship leader. My sense of liturgy was somewhat rare among charismatics, but the charismatic movement did have its standards of propriety, its sense of what was "worshipful." I became director of liturgical music at every parish we belonged to from junior high until I graduated from high school. I led music ministry teams at Franciscan University of Steubenville and directed a full choir in Austria during my semester abroad. In discharging the duties of these offices, I learned how to blend a guitar and non-classical vocal style and contemporary music with a more traditional liturgy. I also led a small touring praise and worship band and played at conferences and retreats.

Lest you be misled, this was not always an intentional journey; its destination and purpose were often unclear to me. Liturgy was not my only or main activity. But I now realize just how deeply infectious it was and is. Liturgy infected the way I saw and played on the football field and later on the rugby pitch. Liturgical sensibilities came very much in handy when I acted in high school plays. They kindled my love for public oratory, then debate, and later academic philosophy. They made me, first and foremost, a teacher. These days, they prevent my writing from falling apart at the seams. Composition is liturgical.

Despite the profound impression that liturgy made, and continues to make, on my life, I did not see its origins as particularly spiritual. Liturgy was not primarily a sign of devotion or piety. It was so ingrained that I rarely, if ever, thought about it, much less unpacked it as I'm doing now, despite the nagging fear that I'm failing to do it perfect justice.

Since this liturgical impression and disposition was more existential than spiritual or religious, it failed to anchor my faith. One day, as a grad student, I made the bitter discovery that my devout childhood had run its course without leaving behind any comfort or consolation fit for an adult. Nostalgia for the liturgy did nothing to prevent my walking away, angry, defiant, and without regret.

My spiritual foundation eroded quickly. At the time, philosophy did little to reinforce it, so I abandoned it altogether. Gradually, I came to the realization that in place of what I had always trusted as *The Church* stood a tiny, fake replica of "the Church." Like Zoolander's school for ants, my Church was exposed as a cheap and abusive fraud. It had held my loyalty for so long only by manipulating my emotions. Though I knew in my heart there was a bigger God somewhere, I could not connect with him, only with a scaled-down, counterfeit version, which failed to impress me.

This crisis of faith overtook me when I was in Columbus, Ohio, beginning my doctoral studies. I had reached the age where my family no longer expected me to be a good Catholic. At the time, I was still attending Mass, but at churches that reminded me of country clubs. With both carrot and stick gone, I began sleeping in on Sundays. It felt great! To this day I do not regret this hiatus. For the sake of contrast, I needed to experience the absence of liturgy.

Then I attended St. Joseph's Cathedral, a surprisingly small and cozy structure, where I experienced my first high Mass. The splendor was like nothing I had ever experienced. The preaching sucked, but the music, the pageantry, the worship aids, the architecture, the decorations—these were perfect. Even if God did not exist, or was too remote and incomprehensible to matter, beauty abounded. As the organ played dark, rich fugues, I closed my eyes and drank deeply. My eyes filled with tears.

The sopranos did start to grind at my ear a bit, but the beauty of the Cathedral itself was enough to make me a regular at 5:15 p.m. Mass, which was simpler but just as beautiful. And the preaching! The homilist and celebrant was Fr. Joseph Goetz, a retired priest from the Diocese of Cincinnati. An emeritus professor of theology, he held a doctorate in philosophical theology from Cambridge University where he was a classmate of John Milbank. His homilies were as rich as the organ music. Together, they drew me back to where I had never been before.

I was literally saved by beauty, not from death or damnation or petty things like that—this is not the kind of salvation I am talking about here— but from the disenchantment that comes from abandoning religion. I was saved from the secular desert. I was saved from the abolition of the sacred, of the holy. Beauty saved me and showed me, again, the invisible face of God.

I felt as though I had crawled out of Zoolander's model church and walked face-first into something dense, solid, and real, like the marble pillars at St. Joseph's. Experiencing baroque liturgy made me swear off playing praise and worship music. I vowed never again to play my guitar at Mass, or even attend a Mass where guitars would be played. All of my musical talents I poured into gospel, jazz, soul, reggae, and Latin folk music.

If you want to make God laugh, the old saying goes, tell him your plans. At a time when my family and I were strapped for cash, a suburban Lutheran parish offered me a job playing guitar. Unhappy at breaking my promise, I took it, planning to quit as soon as I found some other source of income. But during Lent, the lead pastor and music director—both dear friends of mine now—asked me to help them beautify a service held in the ugliest space imaginable, a gymnasium. I gave in, and the experience softened the edges of my new reactionary dogmatism.

Moving to Crawfordsville, Indiana, I found the Mexican Catholic community, which attended Mass in a small and ugly church. The liturgy included no music, and the ambience was barren and doleful. I knew I had no choice: I had to play guitar at Mass again, I had to direct liturgy. I've been doing that for a year and a half at this writing.

What this testimony shows is that, for me, liturgy is not simply a prescriptive curriculum that offers a cold "mystagogy" to students in the pews. No, liturgy is intimately double-directed: outwardly towards our times—to a disenchanted generation, mine and yours—and also inwardly to my ongoing, internal, aesthetic conversion.

Beauty may not save the world, since the world is not in need of salvation, but it sure saved me. This is an important part of what liturgy as mystagogy is.

December 27, 2011
Vox Nova

Towards a Pagan Religious Education, Above and Beyond Learning

He said to me "Son of man, feed your stomach and fill your body
with this scroll which I am giving to you." Then I ate it, and it
was sweet as honey in my mouth. (Ezekiel 3:3)

Along with an existential, aesthetic sense of what liturgy is, this series is rooted in an ontological or being-centered sense of what education is. This ontological sense of education forms the basis of what I mean by "religious education" and, by extension, mystagogy.

It has become standard nowadays to think of education as nothing more than the acquisition of knowledge. On this point, most philosophers, theologians, and catechists agree. Modern education is exclusively epistemological and psychological—literally, a heady affair. Welcome to the information age, baby.

This view of education is deficient on many levels, but never more so than when it conceals the fundamentally *religious* nature of education. Again, by "religious education" I am not describing the isolated events that take place in classrooms, schools, or even in churches. Religious education—mystagogy, for the baptized—describes what happens during liturgy. Here, too, liturgy is ubiquitous. It forms a cosmic and oceanic context.

The life of the human person is fundamentally liturgical: it moves and sways and grows to the ebb and flow of the liturgical tides. It is primal, mystical, and mythic. It marks all of our moments, those remembered and forgotten, from birth to death and beyond. In this way, the liturgy is deeply pagan.

If my use of the term "pagan" needs to be explained or justified, this story should serve to do both.

One of the greatest teachers I encountered at Franciscan University of Steubenville was Fr. Conrad Harkins, OFM. He taught in and out of class, and succeeded in shocking me out of many misguided notions. A true Franciscan and scholar of medieval history, he emphasized the *worldliness* of Catholicism.

On the first day of my honors seminar, he told us to read the *New York Times* and secular literature. He said to read everything, be afraid of nothing, check out popular, "pagan" books from the library. He poked fun at the stuck-up, holier-than-thou Catholics at Steubenville. He was magnificent. He railed against the puritanical, cloistered attitude to worldly things I'd become accustomed to.

I read the *Da Vinci Code* because of him, and laughed at how second-rate fiction could raise such a fuss. He calmed my fears of the world. For a time I may have overcorrected and become a little too world-friendly, but this was healthier in the long run, surely, than holing up for the rest of my life in a cultural bunker.

Fr. Harkins's Franciscan love of the world transformed my vision of Catholicism. One day during my senior year, I stopped to visit him in his office. At some point, our conversation wandered to the forthcoming Mel

Gibson film, *Apocalypto*. I mentioned how conflicted I felt about the film's historical subject matter. I was disgusted equally by the genocidal aspects of the *conquista* and the barbaric pagan practices of the Aztec empire. His response—sharp and quick, as usual—ran along the lines of "Any religion that doesn't engage in human sacrifice is not serious. We are cannibals too, you know?" Christianity, he went on to explain, is radical for replacing the pagan human victim with an incarnate God. Instead of human sacrifice, we practice embodied theocentric sacrifice. This is what scared off the Jews at Capernaum and what offends Protestants today.

The pagan core of Christianity shows how the Church, rather than sterilizing the primal religious spirit, unleashes a deeper, wilder magic where man is no longer the sacrifice offered to the gods: God becomes the sacrifice for man's sake. The liturgical sacrifice, then, is not a sterile, civilized ritual; it is not prim or proper; it does not pull us away from the vulgar flux of the world. No. It draws us deeper into mystery, into the night, into the undomesticated, terrible, enchanted world of mysticism and myth. After all, "for God so loved the world." *Amor mundi* is a part of the *ordo amoris*.

The art of liturgy is communicated in the pagan language of *mythopoesis*: in story, poem, epic verse, fable, parable, song, dance, mystic vision, and myth. Through the mythopoetic language of liturgy, we become educated. We imitate, mimic, and emulate what we sense and experience. More importantly, we *become* the things we imitate, mimic, and emulate. This is what education first and foremost is: being and becoming. Knowledge and learning are merely instrumental to the process.

Again, education is not, primarily, a matter of absorbing information or acquiring knowledge. And, insofar as education is ontological, it is religious. As we have seen, any serious religion must be pagan. Religious education, then, is about the constitution of the human person. It is about life and death, gift and sacrifice. It is about who we were, who we are, and who we might become.

Anyone who understands the rich and morbid aesthetic of Catholicism surely recognizes this pagan sensibility. This is why I think that Protestants who call Catholics pagans are exactly right. Spot on. We should be proud of our paganism. It makes us serious in ways that fugitives from paganism are not.

For the same reason, those who attempt to close the gap between the mythopoetic and scientific worldviews are deeply misguided, and why the tortured, *evolving* apologetics of creationism are so badly mistaken. The problem is not bad science; it is bad religion. We cannot reject myth. To reject myth and poetry, or to attempt to domesticate them with modern science, would be to secularize and disenchant religion.

The old pagan rituals, myths, and symbols may have been false in one sense. But the enchanting pagan sensibilities that made the person fundamentally *religious*, a part of nature and the image of nature's God, succeed in imparting an even deeper truth. They connect us to God's Incarnation, the sacrifice of flesh, and the consumption of that flesh.

We all know the saying "You are what you eat." It is absolutely true: the act of eating is fundamentally constitutive, directed towards becoming. This is true in everyday dining and even more so in the Eucharist. Religious education is also a culinary process. We consume through *mimesis*, we become what—indeed *Whom*—we consume.

December 31, 2011
Vox Nova

The Educational Significance of Advent

A home is a domestic church. As such, it can look, sound, and feel like a church. Even the home that houses no creed, especially if there are children present, has a pedagogical effect. Why? Because liturgy is mystagogical. One of its purposes is to teach and form the faithful, to catechize us both during and away from formal liturgical events. Churches are decorated and arranged for more than ornamental purposes. The pictures, colors, structure, style, and order of a church are all deeply catechetical. The images teach and show. The forms of the rituals are the curricula for unspoken lessons. The homily is but a supplement to the vestments worn, the songs sung, and the intentional, repetitive order of it all. Liturgy is educational in the deepest sense.

In today's post-Christian society, Advent may be the most educationally significant liturgical period, if for no other reason than because it goes against the grain. Since no one seems to observe Advent—including many Catholics—the domestic church that celebrates this season stands out, teaching an additional lesson about the radical exception of the Gospel. We are not of this world. We *prepare* for Incarnation. We do not skip over the need to wait.

*

When I was a young boy, my *abuelito* Rocha took me to the traditional Mexican *posadas*. There I saw a rich Advent tradition, rooted in Catholic faith and Mexican folklore. It was alive and fun. Everywhere were reminders of the Nativity story. Mary and Joseph's journey and search for a resting place were converted into lessons about making a place for Christ and hot chocolate. At home growing up, we abstained from Christmas until, well, Christmas. Though the forced delay seemed alternately harsh and hokey, it made sense. Even as a child, I understood the reasons why.

Our Advent season these days is usually spent traveling, so we do not often get to experience the whole season at home, but there are many ways to teach Advent to our children, and to enable Advent to teach them (and us) about the faith.

Here are six tips for your home and family:

1. The unadorned tree. I know about the Jesse Tree, which is lovely and a great idea, but we've come up with a derivative simile. We put up a pine tree and call it an "Advent Tree," leaving it bare until Christmas. Come Christmas morning, the tree is transformed into a beautiful Christmas Tree. The decorating part you can improvise according to family custom or your own imagination.

2. Advent music and winter music, but no Christmas music until Christmas. If you were a parish liturgical director, would you play "Joy to the World" as the recessional hymn on the second Sunday of Advent? No. Never. You'd be run out of the parish on a rail and scourged at the nearest peace pole. So why would you make the same gaffe in your domestic church? There are plenty of Advent hymns and plenty of songs about winter, so there's no need to confuse everyone by playing Christmas music.

3. Advent calendars. All kinds. Expensive. Goofy. Homemade. Portable. They're not hard to find, even now, and they make the wait fun. You can make yours instructive by inserting Bible verses behind each window, but the Rochas have had better luck baiting theirs with candy.

4. Use your Advent wreath. An Advent wreath is a beautiful decoration, but it is also a powerful educational tool. There are all sorts of ways to make one and a variety of ceremonies and private observances that can mark its installation. Try one. Is there anything close to your ethnic heritage? A folk song from the Old World? Check it out. If your children are very young, this might also be a choice opportunity to begin their catechesis in match safety.

5. Gaudete Sunday! Rejoice—in rose, carnation, or whatever shade of pink strikes your fancy. Never mind if the color clashes with the drapes; by standing out, it shakes up routine, foreshadowing the Messiah who brought a sword. Take advantage.

6. The gradual Nativity scene. There is a Mexican tradition of *acostar el Niño*, or "laying the Baby down" on Christmas Night. You can't do that if the Baby has been lying there prior to its scheduled birth. Children are sensible creatures and they understand the progression of history and biology. It's best not to throw them any curveballs. We like to begin the scene with the setting. As the animals and shepherds wait round the manger, Mary and Joseph begin their journey from the furthest side of the house. With every passing day, they creep closer and closer. On Christmas, we lay the Child down to signify his arrival into the world. (Having a detachable manger and Child helps.) Also on Christmas, the Kings begin their approach. They arrive on Epiphany, bearing most of the gifts.

These are tips, not dogmata. None is absolutely required. The only requisite is the intent. Be thoughtful. Be a teacher. Prepare for the infant Rabbi.

*

From observing Advent properly, adults themselves can take a few lessons on the rigor of keeping Christ in Christmas and the practice of radical hope. But most of all, these lessons are essential for our children. We can debate which liturgical knickknacks are best suited to the purpose, but there's no disputing the educational significance of doing something.

If you care about catechizing your children, you already have a powerful tool at your disposal. That tool is the mystagogy of the liturgy. The only necessity is fidelity. How faithful is your domestic church to the imagery, sounds, and themes of your Church? The answer will measure the quality of your curricula.

I wish you all a blessed Advent.

December 1, 2013
Patheos

Discussion on the Mount?

Over at the *First Thoughts* blog, there is a post titled "The Lecture Works and It Always Has." Although the post oversimplifies the issue, it does a good job of stating the obvious fact that there is special value in the art of lecturing that will not diminish anytime soon.

Unfortunately, lectures may soon disappear from many of our colleges and universities. Many experts, especially those who claim an interest in "instructional development" and the like, believe that the lecture is a moral evil for placing a "sage on the stage" to bully pupils into blind submission and boredom. But lectures will survive in everyday human life. They are highly effective ways of communicating, and can be quite beautiful and transformative.

Criticism of the lecture is overbroad to the point of resembling caricature, but it contains some truth. I've always said that the only bad lecture is a bad lecture, and there are few things more mind-numbing and soul-crushing than a really bad, abusive lecture, even when that lecture comes disguised in hybrid form. A discussion seminar can quickly transform into a mini-lecture, for better or worse.

At issue here is something more profound than the comparative merits of various forms of knowledge delivery. Should professors profess? Should teachers teach through the art of profession? Do we have any use at all for sages, priests, parsons, rabbis, oracles, prophets, presidents, elders, preachers, ministers, and the rest?

Make no mistake, those who see nothing but evil in lecturing will not stop at killing the lecture. They won't be satisfied until they've killed the *lecturer*.

Thankfully, these people are usually dimwits who fail to realize that they lecture at great length about not lecturing. So don't be scared and don't take them seriously. They subvert their own ends by professing about not professing.

*

The unique value of lectures is not limited to the classroom. It is made use of by all teachers, in and out of schools, including parents, workers, and friends.

*

Jesus was a rabbi, a teacher. When he taught, scripture tells us, he usually sat down.

Last week at *First Things*, Stephen Webb reminded us that Jesus was sensitive to the acoustics of teaching. He preached from a boat because sound carries better over water. This shows the craft of the lecture, the technical know-how required in oral profession. It also unites the art of homiletics to other performance arts that work in sound, including music, rhetoric, theatre, and teaching.

Even Socrates, Plato tells us, often used the monologue in the midst of his dialogues. There is nothing Socratic about a discussion where there is no teacher.

Today is the anniversary of the Gettysburg Address.

*

If teaching is an art then the teacher must have something to show and offer.

Not all teachers profess through their words. I believe there is room for the silent lecturer, the exemplar. But among us humans there is a longstanding tradition of listening to or reading the words of a professor, one who offers a profession of faith and reason and imagination.

The result may not be learning or even the transfer of knowledge. This is the gravest mistake of the those who attach teaching to learning, as though the professor's vocation were to shovel practical facts and trivia into people's heads. The art of teaching may lead to unlearning or even to confusion and *aporia*—in this manner, even the terrible lecture can teach us something.

In the end, the teacher is not there to facilitate learning, the teacher is there to be there. The homilist takes his place and dwells, reminding us that Christ came not to leave us with instructional updates: he came to dwell amongst us. Jesus wept. Teaching cannot end with pedagogy, it must lead further and deeper into mystagogy. Otherwise it is mere instruction.

*

Timothy Leonard, a mentor of mine who studied in Rome under Bernard Lonergan, told me of the day that Professor Lonergan entered the room, a sage indeed, and proceeded to give what would be his best lecture of the semester.

Lonergan spoke five words. "We are undone by love."

Deeply moved and unable to add to that, the class ended.

November 18, 2013
Patheos

The Excess of Stephen H. Webb

In the fall of 2010, at Wabash College where we were both teaching, Stephen Webb challenged me to a foot race. I accepted, so the two of us lined up on a sidewalk crack. Before the signal came, Webb bolted off. As I ran to pass him, he pushed me into the road. Laughing, with wildfire in his eyes, he tried to grab my shirt to stop me from passing him again.

A couple of years later, Webb wrote to me, saying, "I was, if you recall, going to write about you, beginning with this sentence: 'A screaming came across the sky. . .' (stolen from *Gravity's Rainbow*) but never got the chance." Now, having received the news that he took his own life, I feel the same way. The memory of all those missed chances aches.

Webb wrote in the therapeutic way common to true writers. His emails often made up a single paragraph of several hundred words of pristine prose punctuated effusively with exclamation marks. Sometimes it was hard to keep up, but you wanted to. I now find myself reading through the books and emails that survive him, trying to recreate a sense of communion with my lost friend.

In his 1993 book *Blessed Excess*, Webb asks, "What would be a life without excess, extravagant actions, extreme claims and visions—without, in a word, hyperbole?"[5] This theme on rhetoric and hyperbole consumed his early work on Karl Barth and even William James. In 1999, Webb would publish a theological ethics on the same question in *The Gifting God: A Trinitarian Ethics of Excess*. This work of the 1990s pointed to a Dionysian persona that Webb embodied deeply, even painfully.

Before Jean-Luc Marion's notions of excess and the gift became fashionable in the English-speaking academy, there was Webb. As a scholar, he was neither a trendsetter nor a follower. He wrote on Bob Dylan, dogs, and disability because he loved Dylan, his dachshunds, and was nearly deaf. Webb wrote theology because he loved God, philosophy because he was passionately curious. He adored John Updike and composed several unpublished novels—the one I read, *Stopping the Sun*, is splendid.

Webb's life and thought were seamless in tangled, knotted, but above all supremely honest ways. He was not smooth; he wore his faults with the same humility that transmitted his brilliance. He could not compartmentalize himself. He was explosive, partly because of his poor hearing, and perhaps because of inner turmoil. His laughter thundered, reverberating through the nineteenth-century wood of Center Hall, echoing across his basement ping-pong table, chasing me down the sidewalk. He was the same person at school, home, and the soccer and rugby pitches where he watched his children play.

Webb was much more than a professor at Wabash. He was a son of the college, taught there by his late mentor Bill Placher. To his students, Webb was larger than life, the vanguard of intellectual conservatism, a fully

5. Webb, *Blessed Excess*, xi.

human genius. To his colleagues, Webb was either befriended and beloved or deeply misunderstood. Those misunderstandings were never neutral, innocent, or casual—nor were they forgettable. His wildness could intimidate, yes, but it also encouraged and inspired. He left his mark wherever he went.

Even in times of trial, Webb was selfless and generous to a fault. He loved in an intense and worldly way. He sang Dylan to his wife Diane at the karaoke bar, treasured his time doing prison ministry, and adored his children by pestering them at home and bragging about them in emails. He gave of himself freely and joyfully, and sought a theological community that would offer him the same. In his final works he reached out to Latter-Day Saints wards with gusto and sincere goodwill. In the end, the fellowship he sought eluded him. He was always moving on to the next project, more often than not one conceived of in brilliant and quirky ways that both thrilled and baffled his friends. His heart was perhaps too restless to see those of us who loved him.

Webb has run ahead of me again. I wish I could have caught him and pulled him back. Everything I know about his death fills me with regret, but I know that his race on earth, however hampered by depression, was driven by an excessive love. With the last words he published in *First Things'* online edition, he strove to unite his struggle with our Savior's: "Jesus himself must have experienced depression. . . . The depressed, like Jesus during his so-called lost years, are hidden from sight, waiting for their lives to begin."[6]

The excess of depression is an alienating excess. It overwhelms the depressed person to the point where they cannot hear the loving voices that call to them, even when the voice belongs to God. In his parting address, Webb said what polite people do not say: that God does not limit himself to a generic concern for generic depressives who live somewhere *out there*; that Christ knows depression in a concrete and intimate way. Webb succumbed to his depression, and I grieve for him. But the man I knew exceeded his maladies. For me, he was and remains the image of love in excess. It is this about him that I see at the center of my sorrow, and it consoles me.

March 16, 2016
First Things

6. Stephen H. Webb, "God of the Depressed" at *First Things* online edition, February 19, 2016. Retrieved from https://www.firstthings.com/web-exclusives/2016/02/god-of-the-depressed on February 11, 2017.

A Beautiful Teacher: A Tribute to Maya Angelou

I had the opportunity to listen to Maya Angelou on February 28, 2010, when she delivered a one-hour talk at Ohio State University. I was nearing the end of my doctoral studies, finishing my dissertation, and I expected to be underwhelmed. I'd grown a thick layer of cynicism where celebrity artists and intellectuals were concerned. I was primed to scoff at this media darling of a poet and her adoring fanatics.

But Maya Angelou's presence alone captured my attention and respect. It changed my whole mood. She was taller than I expected. She wore a finely draped black dress that pulled across her elegant waist, and a string of pearls around her neck. She seemed like a giant, a goddess, with a face and disposition as maternal and warm as they were fierce and spirited. She wore a brace on her right hand.

Her talk was mostly autobiographical. She spoke carefully and with erudition. She filled her observations and memories with verse, in various languages, from the works of classical antiquity to her own compositions. There was no flamboyance in her; her confidence was quiet and well earned.

She spoke of memory and counter-memory, all-too familiar themes, but she did more than speak: she showed her discipline and love of memorization when she recited, which she often closed her eyes to do. I took it as evidence of a full heart. "This," I realized, as I listened to her preach and proclaim, "is a *professor*."

Her talk was steeped in the prophetic Black tradition. It was *baptized*, immersed in religious imagery. There was nothing secular about it. This was church and she spoke more truth about the human condition than all the purportedly social sciences in which I was immersed on campus.

She was there as a teacher, an artist. Soon afterwards I would take great delight and inspiration from reading her humane interview at *Paris Review*. Her example has made me require my students to learn certain things by rote—a reversion to barbarism, according to some of today's experts.

There was suffering to be accounted for—racism and misogyny and more—and she sidestepped none of it. Yet she invoked no clichés nor simplistic ideologies. She simply told her story and convicted us all. But there was also joy. Laughter, her beautiful laughter.

When the hour was up, exactly on time, I sensed I had been transformed. Softened a bit and hardened, too. Less cynical. More resolved than ever to be a professor who was willing to take risks in order to profess and confess.

She was a beautiful witness to me of something all too rare these days: a teacher. I will miss her.

Godspeed, Maya Angelou! May flights of angels sing thee to thy rest.

May 28, 2014
Patheos

Franciscan Theatrics: Papa Francisco's Gangsta Ways

"Show, don't tell." This could be the Franciscan evangelical motto. The Franciscan tradition is rooted in story—stories of St. Francis doing crazy, wild, and beautiful things. The Poor Man of Assisi was, in many respects, a fool. He saw life in its most literal and direct terms. He was a childlike artist, a finger painter. He was not a priest.

When called to rebuild Christ's Church, Francis began with his hands. Only later did he realize that the task was not chiefly architectural. This is the man who placed a manger under the altar and animals in the sanctuary in order to show the truth of the Nativity: *puer natus est*. Francis was a deeply embodied ascetic; even as he died, sick and blind, he took the trouble of apologizing to his broken "Brother Body," for having been so hard on him.

This foolishness was also his genius. The literary tradition is full of fools who, in their simplicity, see the world as it truly is. Francis was a real-life Quixote, a canonized Sancho Panza. Francis was so real—so *excessively* real—that we can best appreciate him by likening him to the great fools of fiction.

There is also another side to this. Perhaps the fool, hearkening back to Socrates, is simply acting. Pretending. Maybe the fool isn't so foolish after all.

I don't care for either reading. Thinking of the fool as a buffoon is too naïve and disrespectful, surely, but thinking of the fool as a manipulator is surely an overcorrection. There must be some randomness to the matter. I prefer a switch-hitting fool, who plays buffoon *and* manipulator, never knowing exactly which role he's playing at any given moment.

The Francis more commonly in the news these days, Pope Francis, has been widely praised for his acts of humility. His riding the bus, his in-person payment of his hotel bill, his cancelling his own newspaper subscription by phone, and his historic upcoming Holy Thursday Mass. Others have noted how papal humility can itself be prideful and even selfish. Both positions have some merit. But they also miss a key point: the theatre of the papacy.

John Paul II understood the pulpit and the theatrics of the stage and Benedict XVI understands the letter and the book, but Francis understands something simpler still: the theatre of the mundane. He demonstrates an almost *Seinfield*-esque grasp of the significance of the ordinary. (Yes, on this reading, *Seinfield* was a Franciscan sitcom.)

When St. Francis presented his Rule to Innocent III, the pope admonished him to use it to preach to pigs. Hastening to the nearest pig sty, Francis plopped himself down in mud and pig shit, and had a good wallow. Having thus proved his obedience, he returned to the curia with his original request. In this way, funky Francis got what he wanted—although Innocent III refused to put his approval in writing.

The extreme humility of Francis was also strategically subversive and theatrical. Francis chose to show, not tell.

In another story, Francis learned his order had moved into a house in violation of his severe rule. By way of reproving the backsliders, he climbed atop the house he believed they'd occupied and began tearing apart the roof, tile by tile. Then someone informed Francis that he had picked the wrong house. Oops!

The latter-day Francis, our pope, has mostly been adorable—refreshing for some, quixotic for others, borderline duplicitous for a few. Perhaps he's using his charm strategically, perhaps not, probably both. All of the above.

If he keeps it up, he will probably embarrass himself. So be it. Like his namesake, Pope Francis understands the theatrics of evangelization. He's a total gangsta, a fool who is unafraid to show more than he says, to embody the Gospel and mix the sacred with the dirt and excrement of the profane. The challenge for us is the same: how do we show more than we say? All I can say is this: Papa Francisco, how I love your gangsta ways!

March 23, 2013
Patheos

A Tale of Three Cubicles

ONE

When they assigned me to the beam-cutting station, I asked to be reassigned. I wanted to weld. It seemed honorable and I wanted to be somebody. But I guess no one asks to be a welder once they get to the cutting stations.

I was given the materials: gloves, sleeves, apron, and mask. I needed boots. No tennis shoes. I don't recall the details or the exact time, but I passed an initial inspection of some kind. I had to start out as a gofer, which sucked. I took naps and wasted a lot of time. I was then assigned to weld with a rowdy crew who only began to accept me once they heard I liked to drink lots of Keystone Light.

We had a good time and they taught me a lot about shop politics. They were a tribe. Their best welder, the leader of the pack, knew the bosses needed him bad, worse than he needed them, so he'd work until he decided he had enough overtime pay and wouldn't show up again till the next pay cycle. Unless there was a rush order or a major backup: then he'd make them pay him time and a half. He was shrewd, but not an asshole. He knew he could make more money elsewhere, but he had things under control here. He ruled his tribe as well as anyone I'd ever seen.

There was also a talented up-and-comer who had just bought a brand new Dodge pickup and had a knack for getting his girlfriends pregnant. There were inside jokes and initiation pranks. I didn't fall for them and they respected me for that. But I saw this poor, stupid soul almost crack his skull taking part in the broom-kicking competition. They admired intelligence, no matter where it came from, books or whatever, and they hated an idiot. They asked me what philosophy was and I was in no position at the time to tell them, but I think I managed to bluff my way through.

I got a strong sense that they didn't want to be patronized, these were independent men of an alternative cut. They carried themselves with a fierce dignity. Not insecure like academics and writers and office workers. Scared me sometimes. They horsed around all the time, but they were also serious. Life and death kind of stuff. There's no room for joking around when a ton of steel could fall on someone's leg.

The shop floor was segregated between whites and Mexicans. In between were younger Mexicans, who only spoke English and hated the older, Spanish-speaking Mexicans, mainly for hating them. I roomed with one of the young ones. He was browner than me but only knew how to cuss in Spanish, and his accent was awful. I was different. Yes, I was a college boy, but I also liked to carry on with the rednecks and could speak fluent Spanish with the wetbacks.

I had been terrible in high school shop class; I never tried hard enough. But here, on the floor, I was learning to weld, day by day. Working with the big beams was easy because you didn't have to worry about burning through the metal. You could go slowly and deliberately and run a beautiful, glowing scar down those seams. After a few weeks, I was allowed to move up to aluminum, a more delicate medium.

The work station next to mine belonged to an older Mexican man who sold tacos during break and functioned as something between a court jester and a sage. He was the *fool* of the shop, in Cervantes's and Shakespeare's sense. Chema. That was his name, or at least what everyone called him. I was sent to help him one day, because he was running behind on his quota of twenty-five frames per day. Not too strict, but not too lax. Each frame had to be approved. The inspector, a nice good ol' boy who'd been doing this for-ever—he'd probably started off as a welder—would measure the angles and lengths and check the welds, circling the bad ones with chalk for do-overs.

We made stadium bleachers. Summer outside temperatures ran at about one hundred degrees Fahrenheit; inside the shop, it was hotter. When you started welding, you had to turn off the fan, to prevent the blowing air from ruining your weld. The bead was supposed to be a thousand degrees hot, and you felt every degree of it. "Keep your chin down, son" they warned me. After the first week, I understood why. From raising my chin and expos-ing my skin to the white-hot welding bead, I had burned a tender triangle onto my neck, with its peak all the way down on my upper chest.

Chema didn't seem to sweat much; he was conditioned for this work. But he was terrible at measuring and reading the plans for creating the frames. He wasn't stupid: he was going blind. Everyone knew it, even the foreman, but no one was going to put him out like that. They sent me there to read the charts and let Chema teach me how to tack down the L-joints to create a pattern on the work table for making support frames.

The frames were small, so the station didn't need a big lift, just a small overhead for picking the frames off the work table. You had to move quickly on those thin beams, otherwise you'd blow holes in them. The frames were all but fixed to the table, to ensure proper measuring, so you had to be able to weld in all directions, at all angles, without moving the materials. Right-side up and upside down. Horizontal and vertical.

Chema taught me all that stuff, somehow. He liked me because I was "*un artista*." An artist, a musician. In the back of the station there were things Chema built with leftover steel. A chair he sat in a lot. Three towers of cas-sette tapes, filled with music that blared from his station all day long. He was the deejay for the mostly Mexican cutting-stations of the front of the shop. He didn't just play *norteño* or *conjunto* music—he played *trova*, *cumbia*, all the variations of *salsa* and *merengue*. He played it all. A Latin music ex-pert. He knew the names of all the rhythms and patterns. He liked *corridos*, because they were historical and sad. He was a cultured man. He danced around, foolishly, as I did almost all the work. He was my muse.

I found the Latin clave in that hot welding station and it's infected the way I hear everything. When a 4–4 soul groove is playing, I hear a 2–3 clave and it makes my phrasing stand out and sound interesting. Chema loved to talk to me about music and food and women and how stupid everyone in the shop was, white and Mexican alike. How he woke up at three-thirty every morning to make his tacos and got in by five to ride the clock until six, when he would start making coffee. (He had his coffee at four, at home. *Good* coffee.)

He said that selling tacos was all about profiting from the laziness of others. In his eyes, every taco he sold was a stain on the customer's character. He therefore insisted that I get mine for free. I had a close call where I almost lost my fingertip. He was horrified. How could I risk my hands, my art, my guitar, for this?

My maternal grandfather—Grandpa Montaño—came to visit one day. I don't recall what brought him there, but when he saw me covered in soot and sweat, I could tell he was proud of me. I had proved that I could work hard in a way he could understand. He treated me like a man and told me to get back to work. Never felt sorry for me. That made me feel like I was somebody. I got what I came for so I took Chema's advice and left that dangerous dance floor of a workstation for an easy, stupid job tending kids at the YMCA for the last month and a half before returning to school in Ohio.

TWO

Bilingual Benefits Representative. That seemed pretty good. What was it? Target Corporation, corporate headquarters. Sounded important enough. Fourteen dollars per hour, plus 10 percent off at Target stores and lots of discounts on limousine rentals and WNBA tickets. (I took advantage of both.)

Before landing the job, I was teaching Spanish for $26,000 per year before deductions. With my commute and everything else, I was beginning to feel like Tolstoy's Ivan Ilych: underpaid and underappreciated. Unlike Ilych, I actually was being underpaid—like everyone else at that small parochial school.

I put on my suit and interviewed. A breeze. In training I quickly realized that everything was a joke, but fun. Teaching had come easily, but this was even easier. I expected it to be harder and more serious. I gave a presentation during one of our innovative group learning projects about offering puma rides. Everyone laughed. It boosted morale. My reviews were sky high. One of the trainers pissed me off, so I got him fired through my exit interview and evaluation. No one had liked him anyway.

We all started on the general call floor—English calls only. There was more training required for Spanish calls. The trainer was nervous because

her Spanish wasn't tip-top and asked for my help. I already felt like I was being groomed for a promotion. Great. Shirt and tie every day. Everyone was
counting down till they could transfer out and up. Except the older people,
who were there for life. Programmed. Not us. We were fresh out of college,
looking for a shot at middle management.

We'd dream during lunch hour, in the corporate cafeteria. Our in- and
after-call times were supposed to be short, but we weren't supposed to hustle
anyone off the phone. Sounding natural, reciting the prescribed greetings
and following all the prescribed steps was the key. Everything was recorded.
Surveillance somehow made things feel more official and dignified. This
was Target: *everyone is a team member.* This meant that everyone was
treated like a chimpanzee. Training. Bananas. When I knew the answer, I
was watched to make sure that I looked it up anyway and recited it verbatim
from the manual. That way, everything we said could be held accountable to
the same, standard language. "Even if it's wrong, say it anyway and report it,
then it will get fixed for everyone." (Everyone, that is, except the person who
got the wrong advice about her family's health insurance.)

The cubicles were pretty spacious; you could twirl around in your
chair. When calls were slow I'd read and write and goof off. There was constant morale-boosting going on—team-building activities! I started playing
all the stupid games and even invented a few new ones. I brought a little
rubber ball, the kind that bounces everywhere and forever, and my buddy
and I played a game to see how many times it could bounce without breaking anything. If you could get it trapped under a desk, it would bounce at
least twelve times. Win! Once it got out and flew into our floor supervisor's
cubicle. She was annoyed but not that much and even thought it was funny.
That's when I realized her job was even dumber than mine was.

Every week we'd have a short ceremony when our stat reports arrived
and they'd tell us who rated best that week. If you got over ninety percent
they gave you a little sheet of paper. People kept these pinned on their cubicles. Badges of honor. Corporate helmet stickers. I won a few. But soon I
realized how hard it was to go below eighty percent. I'd leave my phone off
the hook, explore the new building or sit on the toilet reading a book: my
stats didn't drop into the seventies for a long time.

Facebook wasn't really permitted, but it wasn't blocked. Me and another buddy who worked downtown would message each other, writing
backwards—that way, no one could read what we were writing. It was just
another fun way to make the time pass. I started job searching. Nine months
was too long to wait for a promotion; four was just long enough. I regretted
leaving the school. I was shooting too low and holding myself back (from
what?).

All the managers either infantilized their employees or acted like well-behaved children themselves. I needed more money; the pay was nothing here. I saw people's salaries, even the ones of the store workers making seven dollars an hour with no benefits. No one cared about anything. My calls were getting worse because I started hanging up on assholes and people I didn't care to talk to. One person reported me for telling her she was killing my stats when she demanded I send her a screenshot of her benefits page. Didn't the idiot know that wasn't in the manual?

THREE

The opening details are mostly unimportant. The hiring process was convoluted and indirect. But the upshot is that I quit my job at Target for a new job, closer to where we lived. I was a consultant for a middleman company that was working on an IT project for Medtronic Corporation. Both firms had to hire me. I was still an hourly employee, but I was making ten extra dollars per hour. My official title, which I only learned after a week or two on the job, was something along the lines of "Coordinator."

Most of the employees were subcontracted from IBM; many of them came from India. I was in charge of getting them on- and off-board. It was entirely different from Target. There was no job description or training; I was simply to figure out my job and do it as I saw fit and report to my supervisor and manager. Surveillance was very low, too. The person who had held my job previously had been hired as an official Medtronic employee to support the project manager. She was helpful and positive, but she'd left her position a shambles, largely because the person before her was incompetent.

At first it was chaotic but liberating. There was room to make some stuff up, room to live a little. I never entirely understood what I was supposed to be doing and, honestly, I don't think anyone else knew either. My manager was a wonderful man, a Spaniard from Asturias. A slender and tall widower, a cultured man with a thick Spanish accent and also a practicing Catholic. A rosary hung from his computer screen. He played bass at his parish. I was the only other Spanish-speaker in the building, so we soon became friends.

The only part of the job I understood was that I was to eat lunch with my manager and talk to him in Spanish about interesting things: books, feminism, music, guitars and songwriting, religion, and more. My cubicle was just outside his door. Almost every day we would lunch for at least one hour and talk until we got back to his office. This relationship infuriated my supervisor to the point where she began trying to undermine me. My manager wouldn't hear a word spoken against me. He was convinced that my skills were being wasted, and he didn't seem to care what I was doing or not doing. He wanted me to be moved into a more serious, dignified position, where I could write and think about the conceptual side of the project.

I was not working very hard, and a lot of what I did do, I faked. All I did well was correspond with our main contact from IBM—a French woman who never came on-site—and look important. I also liked to eat popcorn every day around three in the afternoon with the Indian IBM-ers. They all thought I was Indian, too, until one day I revealed that I wasn't. They liked me enough anyhow to let me join them for popcorn whenever I pleased.

The project itself was interesting: it was about trying to standardize corporate language and processes across three or four global headquarters. "Centerpoint"—that was the title. It was a centralizing operation, a Tower of Babel problem. The purpose behind the piles of money and workers was to improve communication in carefully planned phases. I understood it quite well, a little to my surprise, and think I could have helped, but not in my current position.

As interesting as it was in theory, my day-to-day work was becoming more and more tedious, and my supervisor was out to get me. For my part, I was cutting lots of corners. I was shirking entire assignments. Like keeping a current map of everyone's cubicle assignments and making sure that the remote-access passwords of the people who quit or were fired got deactivated. I built a huge spreadsheet and color-coded it. It was as absurd as Borges's famous taxonomy in "The Analytic Language of John Wilkins." As Ivan Illich would later put it in *Deschooling Society*, my spreadsheet was irrationally consistent. I could explain it in meetings or in professional conversations because (1) no one listened or cared and (2) the color-codes and the Excel data gave it a sense of order and fake rigor. "Great work, Sam," I'd hear. "Keep it up."

By the end of my time there, I was going on long walks around the building under the pretense of checking up on things (like my much-neglected floor map). Suddenly I'd feel as though I were suffocating, about to explode inside. I later learned I was suffering anxiety attacks. Ohio State was recruiting me into their PhD program at the time and I was also accepted at Syracuse, but in my heart, I was still unsure what to do. I confided in my manager one day and he told me he'd support me no matter what I did. A classmate told me I should take the security and money and stay at Medtronic. "Take the money and run," he said.

But graduation and doctoral studies were still a few months away and I now hated my job. The doctor told me I was clinically depressed, which depressed the shit out of me—*clinically*, I suppose. I couldn't enjoy my lunch or popcorn anymore because my supervisor's supervision was starting to feel oppressive, and I was running out of fake jobs to pretend to do. Doing fake work is very taxing on the nerves. I began looking for other work that I could do as an independent consultant—some music, some translating, some other things here and there—to get us to the time when we'd move to Columbus.

I never said goodbye, I just picked up my things and left. They could fire me on the spot any day, so I didn't see why I should give them two weeks. I still don't. Plus, I wouldn't need the references: I was making a clean break from corporate cubicles. I was going to the academy: back to the craftwork I so dearly missed. Not steel and dancing, this would be books and teaching.

Epilogue

I was destined for the collar. Everyone seemed to see that, and believe it, too. Fr. O'Malley, the priest who converted my father and baptized me, would take me out for a steak dinner sometimes. He'd always say, "When you're a priest, you can eat steak every day."

That stuck. I love to eat. I felt obligated to say that I wanted to be a priest when I grew up. Not sure why, but I knew there was no firefighting in my future. I was a devout and precise altar server until I took over music ministry and liturgy planning from junior high into college. In high school there were vocation retreats and visits from the diocesan vocation director.

I'd lived my entire life in rectories and church offices. I grew up knowing and loving and despising dozens of priests. I understood the vocation as well as any high school student could. Fr. Sam, a wonderful mentor to me, offered to pay my college tuition—the implicit condition being that I'd one day be ordained in the Society of the Precious Blood.

I couldn't accept. It wasn't the fear of becoming a priest someday—that I could deal with, as I'd been dealing with it my entire life. It had more to do with not wanting to let down Fr. Sam, a man I truly loved.

As cocksure and bright as I seemed on the outside, I had no idea what I could do in college. No internal sense of competence or confidence. Always guessing. No one cared to tell me that I was over-preparing through debates. After showing promise as a high-school debater, a state scholarship and some philanthropic money sent me to Baylor University's two-week debate institute. Besides eating in the cafeteria of Hardin Simmons University before a playoff football game, I'd never seen a college campus before and I had no idea, really, what it would be like there.

My roommate was Jewish. We were enrolled in the exclusive "expert" tier. I was certainly no novice, but I probably belonged in the intermediate group. I figured I'd never get to do this again, so I'd better see what the best people were doing. It was the summer before my junior year. The year earlier I'd beaten the best debater in our district, a senior from Ballinger, Texas, for the final spot at regionals. During freshman year, she and I debated in my very first tournament, and she ended up dusting me in the semi-finals. But at regionals, I was in over my head. I needed better content and more polish. Even my proud, paraplegic coach admitted that I needed outside help: debate was new at little Brady High School.

Debate was new for him, too. Before his accident, he had played and coached basketball and won state titles. Now he was my coach and we were going to win trophies and medals and go to state together. So I needed to get better. A Lincoln-Douglas debate is a one-on-one combat over value propositions. The foundation was always philosophy, or some legal derivative. I needed to learn about philosophy and get more training in the rhetorical techniques being used by the big-leaguers, the top kids who competed in the national circuit.

Walking the Baylor University campus was something out a dream or a movie that I'd never had the data to process. It felt free and frightening— better than church. I'd never heard of a coffee shop before, but I did have a taste for coffee. Prayer meetings always served coffee and Dad always let me drink it, with milk and sugar.

Common Grounds was dark and packed with debate nerds. I had received an envelope with $215 spending money but had no idea what to do with that much in so little time. Somehow, I felt obliged to spend it *there*, at Baylor, not to try and save it and take it home with me like I would usually do. Coffee proved expensive. I learned the ritual of ordering and waiting and where the bar was with the napkins and stirring sticks and salt-shaker things to add flavors to the coffee. Cocoa. Then conversation. The dance. Sparring.

I befriended a group of novice-level debaters who thought I was more important than I really was, and I acted the part. The first morning opened with a welcome, followed by a lecture from a professor in the communications department. He was wearing a blue Oxford shirt with huge, sweaty pit stains. He spoke passionately, with words and phrases so animated, they sounded magical. His rhetorical skill was something I'd read of, but never actually witnessed firsthand. I started to wonder if I would ever be able do what he did.

I also recalled the great preachers I'd heard and began to realize that my father was one of them. He had *pathos*.

Then came the other lectures, from among our tutors and guest philosophy and law professors. We learned the basics of ethical theories and political philosophy. The lectures were brilliant and exciting: I took notes in a way I'd never done before and wouldn't find occasion to do again for a long time afterward. Those notes filed up two blue legal pads. I kept and treasured them for many years.

At first I didn't dare to say a word when the lecturer posed a question, but I always rehearsed an answer in my head. Often as not, I was right! The big shots never answered the easy questions, they waited to ask questions of their own. I started thinking of questions to ask. Then objections. It just kept going.

Soon I was tangling with the big shots at the coffee shop. Each of us received a small paperback library of primary philosophical texts, the classics from Plato to Rawls. They came with introductions and tips on how to convert the ideas into debate fuel. I read them every night till I had to start preparing my debate cases for practice rounds and the tournament. I did well. Before leaving I went to the college bookstore and bought four books: *The Penguin Dictionary of Philosophy*, the *Oxford Companion to Mill*, Rousseau's *Social Contract*, and a compendium on political philosophy. My money was all spent and my mom picked me up. We listened to Cat Stevens on the way home. I sensed she understood that I left that place a different man, headed in a new direction.

My doctoral advisor was shocked at my upbringing and my ignorance of academic pedigree and decorum and who's who and where's where and whatnot. My first year, we rode the bus together—he hated to fly—to Chicago for a regional conference. On the second day, we went to the University of Chicago, to see the campus, walk the halls, and witness the Lab School, founded by John Dewey, the misfortunate patron saint of the philosophy of education.

It was a damp, gray day. The gothic architecture dripped gravity and self-importance; walking the halls, I felt an electric buzz from the residue of brainwork. I wept, out of reverence and shame, as I never knew such a school existed. To me, Chicago was just another big city. My advisor didn't help. "You could have gone here, Sam," he said. "Maybe someday you'll teach here." He led us to a used bookstore where for five dollars I bought a rare early edition of William James's *Human Immortality*. I read it on the train ride back to our hotel. The book engrossed me totally, as I read, I did my best to process some of what I'd just experienced. Now I was sure I would become a professor. I would work to make up for lost time and opportunity, to redeem myself retroactively.

About a month ago, I watched Fr. James Schall's most recent lecture, "The Final Gladness." I took note of Schall's delivery, which was expert—erudite, rich and soothing, though a little on the dull side. It was the work of a true professor, a person professing. Had God called me to become a priest like that? Had I, in a sense, become a priest, though a secular kind of priest who enjoyed the right to marry and beget children—a figure more like my father than Father?

At that moment, I realized my honeymoon with the academy was long over. I was becoming cynical and unhappy. Insecure, too. The light in my eyes was dying. I was losing my vocation, or something like that. Doubting it, like I'd always doubted, and ultimately rejected, the idea that I was born to wear a Roman collar.

I don't know what a vocation is. Even after all these years and diocesan posters and pressure, I still don't understand it one bit. I understand its etymology, *vocare*: a calling, but that's about it. This thing we call "vocation" remains, for me, a total mystery. The call is as inscrutable to me as the One who calls. I still don't know what I want to do or who I want to be when I grow up. Maybe a writer? A musician? I am a professor now, today, even though it is out of fashion for professors to profess these days. And when will I be "grown up"? When I'm dead?

These are sentimental and silly questions, juvenile and flighty aspirations, but they are the roots and spirit of the stories I've recalled and shared nonetheless. A cubicle is a just a workplace. Like the one I sit in now. I have a very nice desk, a writing desk. Simple, but simply perfect for the time being.

January 20, 2013
Patheos

PART IV

FUNK PHENOMENOLOGY

¡No le Aflojes!

In loving memory of Andres Rocha (1914–2010)

No le aflojes, mijo. Don't let up, son. These were last words I heard my *Abuelito* Rocha say to me. He died a peaceful death in his home yesterday at two o'clock.

He was born in 1914 on a horse ranch in south Texas. He was one of the last *vaqueros* of the mythic American West. But his life was not a rosy myth. He worked hard for very low wages. He picked cotton in the South and vegetables in the North. He packed produce in the local packing shed. He lost his fingertips to a workplace accident.

My *Abuelito* was wise and generous. He possessed the best aspects of both pride and humility. Even into his eighties, he would go to visit the *ancianos* (the *really* old people) at the nursing home. Materially poor from birth to death, he always gave what he had to those he loved and those who asked for it. Often, when *el cheque* (the Social Security check) arrived, he would have us grandchildren line up, then he'd give us two dollars apiece. He saved one hundred dollars to give me and my wife as a wedding gift and apologized for not being able to give more.

Like Abraham Lincoln's, my *Abuelito* Rocha's schooling lasted only through the third grade, but he was deeply educated. He taught me my multiplication tables and showed me what true love looked like in his love for my *Abuelita*, my Dad, and me—all of us really. He wrote in an ornate cursive script that curled and looped. He knew who he was and judged no one with his words. I never heard him slander anyone.

He was not a perfect man. But in comparison to most other people I know—myself included—he lived the life of a saint. He was very particular and refused to bother with things that didn't interest him. He loved to tell stories and he told them in vivid colors and landscapes.

This past Christmas, while I was in the heat of writing my dissertation, he spoke to me over the telephone from his bed. After asking about my wife and the boys, he told me *"No le aflojes, mijo."* He was referring to my ongoing dissertation, of course, but I also take him to have been speaking for the ages. Never, *ever* let up, he meant. Never become complacent. Stay restless. Be in love, always.

The legacy my *Abuelito* left behind for me was a call to constant action: to continual renewal and conversion. He remained active until the day he died. He prayed and studied scripture for hours daily. He never intended that his life of self-discipline should serve as a lecture to others. It simply spoke for itself, and its testimony was even more convincing for being implicit.

He lived much of his life in a world very different from ours. The modern world of the city never fit him like the *rancho* did. He cried at his father's grave when we visited it, and tears always came to his eyes when he spoke of how the man died after being bucked off a horse he was trying to break. He never complained or made any excuses for himself. He never gave in to nostalgia.

Whenever anyone asked after him and my *Abuelita*, he would say that they were both good, aches and all, and that they were blessed. The blessed life he led was one where he lived his restless words and never let up on being alive and in love.

February 9, 2010
Vox Nova

What is a Border?

In debates over immigration, platitudes rule the day on all sides. Confusion is the result. A kind of magical thinking immunizes certain nostrums from critical analysis. One of these is this thing called "border." It may seem too simple, but until "border" is demystified and made accountable to simple intuitions, we will have no idea what we're really talking about.

To begin with, a border is something like a shape in relation to color. It demarcates where one thing ends and another begins. In this sense, borders are everywhere. A border exists as a simple, ordinary fact of perception.

In cartography, borders begin in the same way. Water and land create what we might call *natural borders*. It is no surprise, then, that geopolitics uses these normal ways of thinking about borders to make more ambitious distinctions, lines that demarcate the beginnings and the ends of nations and peoples.

Here we begin to encounter problems. Basic perception and even the evolving demarcations between water and land or mountain ranges and forests, are not arbitrary in the geographic sense. They literally map onto the physical world.

The borders of geopolitics, however, are usually the results of wars, or treaties written to avoid or end wars. Unlike natural borders, *geopolitical borders* are not only exceptional to the physical world, they also serve as the means to ends that should, I believe, be subject to vigorous debate.

Nations draw borders in order to protect themselves from whatever and whoever exists just beyond those borders. In *The Butter Battle Book,* Dr. Seuss does a nice job of depicting this dynamic in the absurd war between the "butter-side-uppers" and the "butter-side-downers." A geopolitical border, then, is a way of demarcating the land and people of a nation. Such a demarcation declares one side *this* and the other side *that*.

In many cases, these demarcations seem as natural as perception or geography. After all, even an ocean declares one land mass *this* and the one across from it *that*. Naturally, those who find themselves on one side of the ocean have a sense of belonging to their side but not to the other side.

There's nothing wrong *per se* with these feelings or with the natural borders that nurture them. But when geopolitics imposes itself on natural geography, we find ourselves in very dangerous territory. Here are two dangers of geopolitical borders (GPB):

(1a) A GPB is the product of history. Depending on that history, it could be either a blessing to human relations or an ugly scar of power and domination.

(1b) Since a GPB is attached to a particular history, it follows that there were times in the past when the GPB did not exist. In other words, a GPB is not a natural part of things like shape is in relation to color. Even our continents were once undivided, geologists tell us.

(2a) A GPB has been, is *already*, and likely will continue to be the cause of tremendous violence and suffering.

(2b) Insofar as the violence and suffering caused by a GPB is unjustified, a GPB can be a form of injustice.

All of this should bring us to consider the following suggestions: *In any debate over immigration* or citizenship, *the simple presence of a border is not an authority worth appealing to.* In the end, I think that if we adopted a less magical and superstitious view of borders, we would see the actual people that are demarcated and ask ourselves whether these demarcations are just or not. Insofar as they are just, they are useful and, perhaps, legitimate. Insofar as they are unjust, they are not useful and, perhaps, illegitimate.

My grandparents were born on neighboring ranches in South Texas. Over the course of the nineteenth century, their families lived under the rule of, in this order, the Kingdom of Spain, the Republic of Mexico, the Republic of Texas, the United States of America, the Confederate States of America, and finally, the US of A once more. During their earlier lives, they never thought about nationality. They spoke Spanish and worked with horses and cattle. It wasn't until the WWII draft that my *Abuelito* and his brothers realized that they were US citizens.

For the rest of their lives they lived in South Texas and traveled as migrant workers. They never learned English well; my *Abuelito* never spoke English at all. But if you told him to go back to "where he came from," he would have gone further north, not south. They welcomed everyone into their home and family. This included many undocumented people from Mexico.

For them, the issue of the border was a practical one, not a magical one. The grand issues of geopolitics never drew any lines between the neighbors they were called by the Gospel to love—certainly not the widow, the alien, or the orphan. These were not platitudes for them. They visited the San Juan Nursing Home until they were homebound; they fed and housed immigrants in their own house and their small one-room *casita* (little house); and they adopted my Dad and his brother, my Tio Juan, as their sons.

They would have shaken their heads at the question "What is a 'border'?" They knew what it was and acted accordingly. My grandparents are wiser than most of us. For us—myself first and foremost—we need to remember what a "border" really is before we can act justly.

Final questions: What is a "border"? What demands does it make on our lives? And what demands does it *not* make?

April 27, 2010
Vox Nova

The Politics of Guadalupe

In loving memory of Fr. Sam Homsey C.PP.S. (1910—2004)

As a teenager, I played basketball on a small cement slab behind the parish rectory where we lived. At the time, my dad was pastoral coordinator at St. Patrick's Catholic Church, in Brady, Texas. I was told that the place where I played was also the entryway for a small chapel dedicated to Our Lady of Guadalupe. In that small chapel, there would be Spanish-language Masses offered for the Mexican faithful.

I didn't think too much of it until I met Fr. Sam. Fr. Sam was a Lebanese priest, though he preferred to call himself an Arab. He belonged to the Society of the Precious Blood and continued serving until the day he died as a passenger in a car accident. At that time, he was well into his nineties and showed no sign of slowing down.

Cement slabs like the one I played on were common in the Diocese of San Angelo back in 1980, when Fr. Sam first arrived in Ballinger, Texas, to serve as pastor of Mary, Star of the Sea. By then he was well into his life and priesthood and had just finished missionary work in Chile. Long before that, during the Second World War, he taught high school and served as the pastor of two Black Catholic congregations in Nashville, Tennessee. He was never bitter about racial tension, but he never pretended it didn't exist.

As a seminarian, he was proud to be the only Arab, even when it disadvantaged him. He sang tenor in the choir and, though weighing in at a mere 165 pounds, played center for his college football team. He spoke or read English, Arabic, Hebrew, Latin, Spanish, French, and German. His Spanish oratory far exceeded the skills of many second- and third-generation Hispanic priests. Rather than spend money, he preferred to give it away to fund the education of bright young men who felt called to the priesthood. Indeed, he offered me a scholarship, which, uncertain of my vocation, I turned down.

When he arrived in Ballinger and encountered the "Mexican church," *La Capilla de Nuestra Señora de Guadalupe*, he didn't make a fuss or write letters to the newspaper or the bishop. He simply informed the Mexican faithful that next week's Mass would be celebrated at the parish sanctuary with the entire Catholic community. To the English-speaking faithful, he made the same announcement. I don't know all the details, but Fr. Sam did tell me, his eyes twinkling with mischief, that the bishop, irritated over not being informed in advance of such a monumental change, hit the roof.

In Fr. Sam's account, many Anglo-American Catholics were furious over the inclusion of Spanish Masses, along with the Mexican faithful, in the life of the main church, or as some of them openly called it, "the white church." Among the Mexicans, there was also a good deal of discomfort at the erasure of their *iglesia Mexicana*. But the protests were not equal in vigor—clearly the greater share of outrage came from the "white church," and much of that from parishioners who wielded influence in the community.

In this manner, resistance notwithstanding, Fr. Sam Homsey began the racial integration of West Texas Catholic parishes. That was in 1980. By now, it's become the new normal.

That's not to say that racial divisions have altogether disappeared. Most West Texas parishes have an early-morning or Saturday-evening Spanish Mass and a later-morning English Mass. There are also plenty of bilingual services, especially at Christmas and Easter. During some of those liturgies, mutual suspicion and resentment hangs in the air.

In these mixed gatherings, you will always hear a few people reciting the Our Father in their own language, even when that happens not to be the language prescribed by the missal, as a calculated gesture of defiance. Planning a bilingual liturgy can involve a delicate balancing act; deciding what will be said, sung, or read in each language means juggling heavy political freight. Though no one wants to make the other side feel slighted, everyone wants to see their own well represented.

In the life of the typical West Texas parish, an organic fusion of cultures is evident in many people—including some of my dearest friends from Brady, who have shown me only love and brought me only joy. But there are still those places where unspoken law divides people along racial lines. To cite an example from the Mexican side, you hardly find a *Guadalupana* (a member of a traditionally Mexican women's society) of other than Mexican descent.

How does this story relate to Our Lady of Guadalupe? Well, in a roundabout way, it helps explain why her story appeals so powerfully to so many Mexicans who adore her and St. Juan Diego. In a culture where even some Latinos and African Americans prefer light skin for its social cachet, the title *Virgen Morena* ("dark-skinned Virgin") runs against the grain in a way impossible to ignore.

In the classic Mexican song of the holy day, *La Guadalupana*, there is a verse that sounds nationalistic:

> *Suplicante juntaba sus manos, Suplicante juntaba sus manos. ¡Y eran Mexicanos! ¡Y eran Mexicanos! Y eran Mexicanos su cuerpo y su faz.*

> *Supplicating she held her hands, Supplicating she held her hands. And they were Mexican! And they were Mexican! And her body and face were Mexican.*

"And they were Mexican!" is a very explicit way of saying, "Mary was Mexican-looking!" Even today, the lyrics retain their power to shock. Mary came and visited this indigenous peasant, Juan Diego—big news in itself—and he recognized her as his countrywoman! What a surprise! Who would have thought? Mexican-looking people getting preferential treatment from heaven itself!

These are the politics of Guadalupe: It is a holy day for Mexican-looking people. And there are so many Mexican-looking people who are not Mexican. Anyone who is oppressed by the look of their hands, face, and body, can look with devotion to that dark-skinned Virgin and find hope. And this hope is not simply for the soul; it is for the body, mind, and politics of the day.

For the rest, to be Catholic and still look down on an immigrant, a migrant worker, or withhold fair wages for such a person's services, is to be blind to the political challenge of Our Lady of Guadalupe. This may be why

I have been told by non-Mexican-looking friends that this day makes them feel uncomfortable. Small wonder that it took Fr. Sam, a rather Mexican-looking Arab, to recognize the plight of others and act on it decisively.

We cannot all be Mexican-looking, but we can all become Mexican at heart. Some of the most Mexican-at-heart people I know have been of European, Asian, and African descent. There are too many Mexicans who merely *look* Mexican but have forgotten the politics of Guadalupe in their own treatment of others, and even, perhaps, in the way they treat themselves.

The politics of Guadalupe are still needed today, not only in the world at large, but also in *our* parishes and *our* homes. Far too many Catholics, in their private lives, harbor preference for those whom they see as their own kind, even as they play at togetherness during Sunday Mass. Far too many Catholics will accept the sign of peace from a dark-skinned hand but would never offer their daughter's hand in marriage to its owner. It is a familiar queasiness that comes from attending Mass as an "equal in the Lord" to a Eucharistic minister or lector who wouldn't not allow you to date their daughter because you are Mexican-looking. Far too many Catholics pervert their faith with racial or national pride. Mexicans should never claim Our Lady as a founding mother of *La Raza* ("The Race"). And the list goes on and on for so many of us.

On this day of Our Lady of Guadalupe, rather than become superstitiously enamored with ourselves and our own kind, we should try to find the most overlooked and ignored people we live among and appear to them as Mary did to Juan Diego—and as Gabriel did to Mary, and as Jesus does to us. For Catholics of all colors, the Dark-Skinned Virgin should be a deep symbol of the preference for the poor, the weak, the oppressed, and the suffering in the heart of our Mother and her Son. We must appear in a flesh not unlike their own.

In an appropriate way for this season of Advent, the politics of Guadalupe prepare us for the politics of the Incarnation.

December 12, 2009
Vox Nova

A Canon of Everything

While much has been made about the politics of canonicity, there is nothing particularly exceptional about them. Anyone who has taken a photograph has surely engaged in some form of canonizing. Whenever we focus on this over that, include or exclude, emphasize or deemphasize, we engage in a thumbnail version of the sort of thing the academic canon wars are about. This is not to deny that selectivity in academia can have repercussions graver than those that follow from the creation of a family slide show. My only point is to establish the simple, descriptive fact that such decisions are neither exceptional nor extraordinary. They are as commonplace as cleaning one's office, deciding if this obscure article, or that random and only marginally interesting-looking unread book, or this nostalgic piece of correspondence should be kept or thrown away—or put into the growing undecided pile. To ignore what is descriptively obvious about canons and disputes of canonicity would be to ignore the thing itself.

Canons are not only ordinary in this way: they also possess a perennial, reflexive, and relational dynamic. As sands in an hourglass shift from one side to the other, so does the canon show what is present and what is absent. In fact, many have begun to read canons through the lens of absence, through what is not there, looking for evidence of the shifting sands of canonicity. As the emphasis changes, a new canon emerges. There are several anti-canon canons we can think of: the canons of critical race theory, critical pedagogy, and more. While there are no immortal canons, there is surely an immortal aspect to the shifting sands of canonicity.

One objection to the description I have offered thus far could be that I have ignored the relationship between orthodoxy and canonicity. After all, a canon is not only the decision of what to include or exclude, it also implicitly marks the point where orthodoxy ends and heterodoxy begins. The canon of New Atheism is more than a generic choice between this and that text; it also articulates a creed, with strong normative implications that create a powerful sense of orthodoxy. The same could be said of the previous examples in critical race theory and critical pedagogy. The very fact that I need not even mention the essential authors is evidence of how well we know them: the gospel of bell hooks, the epistles of Peter McLaren, the apologetics of Richard Dawkins.

It does not take a Foucaultian analysis to see the power dynamics of canonicity. Ironically, the canon of Foucault—from 1963 to his final lectures—is itself a *powerful* example of these dynamics. I do not think we can afford to ignore the question of power and the politics of recognition, presence, and absence that are embedded in any canon. But it is *how* we think about them that is important. Because of the cyclical, elastic reflexivity of canons, we cannot afford to think of canons in a non-reflexive way.

We need to be open to a canon of everything.

November 30, 2011
Vox Nova

White History Month

No tengo madre ni padre,
Ni mando a la escuela hijos,
Hombre no soy, pero tengo . . .
¡Tengo nombre y apellido!

I have no mother or father,
Nor do I send children to school,
Man I am not, but I have . . .
I have a first and last name.
— Juan Antonio Corretjer, *Yerba Bruja*

Reclamo el derecho simple de ser lo que somos.
I reclaim the simple right to be who we are.
— Manuel Zapata Olivella, *Chambacú, Corral de Negros*

I reject the popular and self-righteous paranoia that requires our speech to be politically correct; and I am equally dismissive of the reckless, self-indulgent, and often dangerous attitude that revels in being politically incorrect. My distaste for this unimaginative binary begins with the fact that I have no idea, no clue at all, what "political" adds to "correctness" or "incorrectness." What do politics add to being "correct" or "incorrect"? Is there a difference between being "correct" and being *politically* correct"? And why would anyone want to be incorrect in the first place?

I don't care for correctness much, either. I want more than that. I don't desire to *merely* be "correct." I don't want to settle for the sanity of correctness, nor the insanity of its converse. Give me truth instead: the elusive, excessive, overwhelming truth. Correctness abounds in this age of constant information and innovation, but truth seems awfully scarce. I've even heard it said, "Never has there been so much knowledge and so little truth." There is noise, but no music.

In other words, I don't give a damn about the narrow assumption that our speech has to be either politically correct or politically incorrect. And I am offended by the idea that, even beyond my words, I am required to exist as one thing or the other. If you want to understand me today, you will have to disabuse yourself of these destructive mirror images and begin to imagine something bigger and better—something true. To be painfully clear: this is not a conservative or a liberal chapel talk, just as I am not a conservative or a liberal; those terms do not begin to define or contain me. I am more than that. Like Walt Whitman, I contain multitudes and so do you. We all do, really.

In a way, this opening clarification gets right to my point, and my point is this: we discuss race and ethnicity—and identity in general—in such timid, anemic terms not because we lack intelligence, insight, or experience, but because we lack imagination. Without imagination, things become small and simplistic and demand ideological positions that are just as small. With an impoverished imagination we settle for junk food instead of real food and malnutrition becomes the norm, not the exception. We settle for getting as rich as possible and, in the process, live our lives poorly. As Tolstoy warns us in *The Death of Ivan Ilych,* we settle within the ordinary and terrible fate of the living dead, and the person who *refuses* to settle often feels like "a loner in a world of clones" as The Roots' recent album *How I Got Over* laments.

Just think about it: eating healthy today is considered to be exceptional; plain, organic food is a specialty item at the grocery store; Wendy's is running a special ad to tell us that it makes "natural-cut fries" (as though there were "unnatural-cut fries" somewhere) with ordinary potatoes; the pixilated *image* of Beyoncé has replaced her sensuous *body* and VIZIO is bragging about it in their television commercials. No wonder things so often feel counterfeit: the inauthentic is what we have come accustomed to. We are all too familiar with eating fake food and watching disembodied mirror images of ourselves. Without a robust, curious, and inventive imagination, this absurd way of living appears normal and becomes acceptable. But this is an illusion and we are in need of *dis*illusionment, which is impossible without a healthy imagination. As our bodies need real food and vigorous exercise, so too with our imaginations. How can we nurse our personal and social imaginations into better health? This is what my talk is about.

Fostering a healthy imagination is not only about making things up for the future; it is also about remembering old things, things from the past. We can find new images and novel ways of thinking by recovering the archives of memory that live in the stories of history. In this way, the study of history is a rigorous exercise of the imagination. It is precisely this sense of history that motivated Carter G. Woodson to initiate Negro History Week in 1926 during the second week of February, so as to coincide with the birthdays of Abraham Lincoln and Frederick Douglass. This initiative would lead to the institution of Black History Month in 1976, during the United States sesquicentennial.

Carter G. Woodson knew very well that oppression was not primarily a matter of physical intimidation or legal compulsion—oppression, for Woodson, was most violent when it became psychological, when it got into your head. We all know that control over someone's body is one thing, but control over their mind is something quite different. In *The Mis-Education of the Negro,* Woodson notes that the lynching of the mind, mind-lynching, is more effective, dangerous, and destructive than the lynching of the body. For Woodson, the study of history, the recovery of collective memory, was a way towards freedom of the mind. History was a call—as Bob Marley would later put it in his final composition, *Redemption Song*—to "emancipate yourself from mental slavery."

The institution of Black History Month, then, was not a matter of celebrating a holiday. It was a serious, sober, and urgent call to study history as a way to imagine oneself anew and to free one's mind, again and again, from the bondage of mental slavery, from the shackles of a hidden, forgotten identity. History, for Woodson, was not something to be celebrated. It was something to be studied, pondered, struggled with, and ultimately empowered by, through a sense of one's place in the world. Black History Month was more about existence than equality. It was a response to Malcolm X when he said, "Who are you? You don't know. Don't tell me 'Negro,' that's nothing. What were you before the white man named you 'Negro?' And where were you?" History, for Woodson and Malcolm X, was a lethal weapon in the fight for justice, not a cheap noisemaker in the party of politics.

The fact that many people who claim to celebrate Black History Month have little to no idea of its history and are unfamiliar with the thought of Woodson, Malcolm X, and others is itself proof of why *celebrating* history is a bad idea. Too many people celebrating it don't know what they are doing, they have no reply to the interrogations of Malcolm X. Everybody knows that too much celebration makes you complacent, lazy, and unmotivated.

After Saturday's basketball game I saw a fine example of this: Coach Petty gracefully refused to participate in his team's celebration of his long career out of true love for his family, his team, and the game of basketball. He was grateful, but he reminded Wabash that we still have "unfinished business." (The playoffs.) He surely knows that too much celebration is as toxic for life as it is for sports. This example shows what G. K. Chesterton meant when he wrote, "The two sins against hope are presumption and despair." Since there are no eternal victories, then there should be no eternal celebrations, just as, since there are no eternal defeats, there shouldn't be eternal mourning. By celebrating history we *de*-historicize it; celebrating history is at cross-purposes with what history is.

Because of this view I hold, I am glad that we didn't take Martin Luther King Day off from school. You see, I have no interest whatsoever in celebrating Martin Luther King Day. I do, however, have a great deal of interest in the life and legacy of Dr. King. But by celebrating Martin Luther King Day as a "holiday," we actually disfigure the truth of that life and legacy. For example, the "I Have a Dream" speech isn't really about a dream. It's about trying to cash a bad check—anyone who has heard or read the speech knows this (and those who haven't shouldn't pretend to be so enamored with it).

In order to celebrate Martin Luther King *Day*, the Reverend Doctor Martin Luther King Jr.—the *man*—has to be distorted into a Black Santa Claus: an idolatrous personality we no longer take seriously, much like Santa Claus allows people to celebrate Christmas regardless of what they think about the Christian mystery of the Incarnation. Make no mistake: Dr. Martin Luther King Jr. is neither Santa Claus nor the Easter Bunny; he is not a soft, fuzzy, generic caricature who makes it easy for people to pretend they care about his life and legacy or about the disenfranchised and the poor. As Ralph Ellison puts it, King is "not a spook like those who haunted Edgar Allen Poe." Yet, by making him into a national celebrity, we have made King invisible in all the ways celebrities are invisible: we no longer see him as anything other than "one of your Hollywood movie ectoplasms."

Celebrations are numbing ointments that dull the truth of history. In the case of Dr. King, celebrating Martin Luther King Day desensitizes people to the fact that King's check still goes unpaid and the bank of justice is still compromised by racial supremacy, hatred, transnational capitalism, and more. Slavery in the United States may be over in the generic legal sense, but it has not gone extinct in many other places; slavery is alive and well, especially in the mind, the heart, and the soul.

And, to those who confuse the election of Barack Obama with a partial repayment of Dr. King's bad check: Dr. King would have been more impressed had we elected a poor president than a Black one. Since we didn't elect Cynthia McKinney or Alan Keyes, we have yet to see a Black president from the genealogical line of Carter G. Woodson, Malcolm X, and Dr. King—that is, a Black woman or man with ancestral ties to slavery and the civil rights movement has *never* been elected president in this country. And surely Dr. King would have rejected the idea that Obama's election marks the beginning of a "post-racial" era.

How do we save Martin Luther King Jr., "the man of flesh and bone, fiber and liquids?" How do we preserve him from this frightful fate of invisibility? Moreover, how do we emancipate our minds from the soft, popular impressions of him that our generation has been weaned on? How do we remain faithful to the truth of his biography, his life story? Here is my recommendation: We need to stop celebrating him as some kind of symbol or hero or celebrity and begin to study him as a real person. We need to read his writings and listen to his speeches. We must struggle to understand the context that shaped his worldview, and more.

The larger point is this: if we take history seriously, then we shouldn't celebrate it; we should study it instead. Otherwise, our celebrations become empty, dangerous, and often dogmatic rituals that distort real lives and bodies into comforting delusions that weaken our sense of the truth, invert reality, and enfeeble our minds and imaginations.

For all these reasons and more, we should stop celebrating history. If you really care about Black history, then stop celebrating and start studying. If you find that task too demanding, then, frankly, I doubt whether you cared about Black history in the first place.

Now, don't get me wrong: I like to celebrate. Anyone who knows me at all knows that I love to party. And precisely because I love to party I also know that no one really wants to celebrate history. I've never been to a raging "History Party"—have you? In many ways, just as celebrations de-historicize history, history ruins a good celebration. I am not discouraging playing, partying, or having fun; but we do need to know when to play and when to study.

At this point you might be wondering: What happened to White History Month?

"White History Month" is not just a provocative title. It is also a pro-posal. I don't simply want to talk today; I also want to suggest things we might actually *do*. White History Month is a way to apply and put into prac-tice the implications of the view I have begun to set forth. If we abandon the *celebration* of Black history—and any history for that matter, includ-ing Wabash history—and begin to *study* it in earnest, to take it more (not less) seriously, then we will soon find that Black history takes white history for granted. In other words, like the relationship between shape and color, there is a necessary connection between the center and the margin. Eating a donut takes the donut hole for granted, but without a donut hole a donut is not a donut.

In the past, when all history was primarily European, it took this so-called whiteness for granted and treated it as normative and natural. Higher education nowadays spends a lot of effort promoting the racial and ethnic histories of people considered non-whites, but in similar fashion, it rarely asks questions about where so-called "white people" and white history came from—it leaves whiteness unquestioned and, in doing so, makes it just as normal and natural as before. In other words, leaving whiteness uninter-rogated inverts the reality of what it is and leaves so-called white people exempt from self-reflexivity, from asking themselves the questions of Mal-colm X.

One reason for this is because whiteness is often considered an absence of identity. I often hear so-called white people say that they have no culture or that they are not ethnic or diverse. This is strange for many reasons. First of all, unlike the study of masculinity, where we cannot ignore the temporal flesh of the body, there is no such thing as a white body. Let me put it physiologically. The physical site where we find "color" is on the largest organ of the human body, the skin. The surface of the skin is called the *epidermis*, and the *epidermis* is "colored" by *melanin*. When we refer to someone by color, we often think we are speaking descriptively about what we observe, what we are actually looking at, when we see another person's *epidermis*.

But if we were actually doing this we would never use the color "white" to describe anyone because that color never exists in the *epidermis* at all, there is no *melanin* pigmentation that remotely resembles the color "white," even in albinos who lack pigmentation altogether. To put it another way, a painter would never reach for the color "white" to paint anyone's body. Look around at these chapel paintings. None of the bodies of these so-called white men surrounding us today were painted with white paint; while their bodies suggest masculinity they say nothing about literal, pictorial whiteness. As a descriptive, empirical matter: white people do not exist. The exact same thing can be said about Black people, by the way. That's why Black people—and many other peoples—make a big deal about being light- or dark-skinned and often refer to themselves as "chocolate" or "brown"—just visit "Chocolate City."

Since I've never seen a white- or black-colored person in my entire life, and since this experience reflects a physiological fact, then the history of how people came to be named "black" or "white" will offer some reply to the question raised by Malcolm X. This time, the question becomes a bigger issue for all people who identify themselves using language that they don't understand and didn't come up with—all of us, in other words. For the so-called white person, just as the so-called Negro before, the question would go as follows: "Who are you? You don't know. Don't tell me white, that's nothing. What were you before the rich man, or the man you cannot even imagine, named you 'white'? And where were you?"

How many of you are of some kind of Irish ancestry? How many of you have Italian, Scottish, Greek, Polish, or German heritage? How many of you so-called white people are Catholic, Jewish, Mormon, or Atheist?

For those with Irish ancestry, the historical record is clear: you were not always considered white in this country; you somehow became white. In fact, you were once Black in America. The same goes for Italians, Scots, Greeks, Poles, Germans, and many other people of European descent. Albeit in a different and more complicated way, there are also important historical overlaps here for Catholics, Jews, Mormons, and Atheists.

Consider the questions again: Who are you? You don't know. Don't tell me white, that's nothing. What were you before the rich man, the Whig, the Protestant, the Theist, named you "white"? And who were *they* before whoever named them that named them that? Who invented you in this way? How did you move from the margin into the center? And when did you decide to have more in common with this rather than that person? When did you lose your culture, your ethnicity? Are you invisible?

As a Mexican and a Texican—and I don't call myself a "Mexican-American" because that would be redundant; after all, on the last map I checked, Mexico and Texas were both in North America—as a *Tejano* and a Latino, I am quite familiar with the historical transformation from margin to center in this country, the move from this or that to white. After all, Latinos in the United States have tried to become white at different times and were legally classified—albeit not socially treated—that way until the *Hernandez vs. Texas* Supreme Court decision in 1954. Plus, Latinos make the light- and dark-skinned distinction too, you know; it is the basis for the difference between a *criollo* and a *mestizo*. I also know that becoming "white" is for strategic and political purposes, not existential ones.

Anyone with darker tones of *melanin* in their *epidermis* who spends time with people of lighter tones of *melanin* in their *epidermis* knows how to "act white"—I sure do. As a punishment for mastering this trick, I am also used to getting called a "coconut" —brown on the outside and white on the inside. I admit it: I *can* be a coconut at times, when it suits me—after all, Latinos come in all stripes, European, African, indigenous, and more, so "acting white" shouldn't be a threat to being a genuine Latino, whatever *that* is—but I can also be a chocolate cake with light brown frosting when I play and sing the blues, and I am unquestionably *Mexicano* when I sing a *corrido*, play a *requinto*, or let loose a *grito*. I am all these things and more. Their plurality does not threaten or enrich my identity; it simply is. To be more transparent about this, I never knew about many of these possible selves until I studied history—literally—and realized that my narrow assumptions about Latino identity, about my own identity, needed to be expanded to account for the vast geography of Latin America and the vast variety of Latinos. As the prophetic Black tradition and the Rastafarian movement saw and read themselves into the plight of the Hebrew slaves in Egypt and Babylon, I read my own self into the lives of others and realized that no one—not so-called Black or white people, not Latinos—*no one has a monopoly over suffering and the desire to intimately know who one is.*

I often mourn for those who have been fooled into thinking of themselves as white, and therefore flavorless, culturally irrelevant, and on the margin of questions about alienation and existential pain. I even feel bad, from time to time, for those who react to this in the opposite way: by becoming white supremacists, neo-Nazis, and Ku Klux Klan members. They are mind-lynched, too, you know; they are slaves to their own self-hatred, to their own racial and existential insecurity, impotence, and ignorance. Malcolm X's questions apply to them too.

Now, some people who are frustrated with (or afraid of) the conflicts embedded in this thorny subject of race propose that, in the United States, people refer to themselves as "Americans" and be done with it. This seemingly easy suggestion reminds me of a scene in *The Great Debaters* where the character, Henry Lowe, recalls Tacitus: "Once, a Roman General brought peace to a rebellious province—by killing all its citizens. Even his fellow Romans were shocked. One of them wrote, '[*Ubi*] *solitudinem faciunt pacem appellant*'—which means, 'They create desolation and call it peace.'" Those who would erase race and ethnicity in the name of national unity threaten to bring racial and ethnic peace by means of cultural genocide. Furthermore, unlike Australia and Australians—where the nomenclature of the continent and the nation coincide—calling oneself an "American" makes about as much sense as the French claiming the term "European" for their own specific use, the Chinese monopolizing the term "Asian," or the Egyptians taking total control over the word "African."

There are other ways to appeal to larger categories and leave the smaller ones behind, and they are not all genocidal or poorly named. Humanists who reject any race but the "human race" are not spouting dangerous nonsense like the previous suggestion, but they are wrong nonetheless. The truth is that whiteness and blackness are historical inventions, socially constructed labels that are empirically non-essential. In short, they are myths. Race is a myth. But the myth of race is itself a powerful, productive, and intimate reality. Racial myths don't go away overnight, nor should they. The *mythos* of whiteness and blackness contains all kinds of things: the good, the bad, and the ugly. We cannot confuse these myths with natural reality, but we can, and often must, operate within their real legacy, shadow, and structure. Race is a myth and, as such a thing, a powerful reality.

To understand this point better, consider the following example. We all know that our house, the physical structure, has no essential or natural reason for being what we call "home." Someone made our house at some point and time; it is not eternal or fixed; we can move, it can burn, and the world will continue to exist. A house is not the same thing as a home. Calling it "home" instead of a "house" is based on a domestic myth: the myth of home. At the same time, the feeling of being at home or not at home when you are either close to or far from your house reveals the power of this myth and the way it operates in your real life. Last year, my grandfather wanted to die at home, in his house, instead of at the hospital, and he did. I could never fail to understand, much less respect, his desire to be at home just because it was attached to an arbitrary, constructed house. There is a real difference between the magic and mystery of his house and a sterile, cold hospital room. Correctness might dictate that we have to have it one way or the other, but the truth of the matter is both: *we need myth without superstition; we need magic without incantations; we need mystery without deception; we need race without racism.*

In order to answer Malcolm X's existential challenge we must see things in both ways. We need to recognize that there are no white or black people in one sense, and, in another sense, we need to find out where these names came from and how they operate and become powerful. I know that being Latino, Mexican, *Tejano*, Hispanic, Chicano, and the rest is a myth, the myth of race. But, at the very same time, many things about that mythology make me who I am—it is a house that helps me feel at home. And while I hold many of these racial and ethnic myths dear, I must never forget that they come with real, serious, and even dangerous, limitations. Let me be clear: We should not abolish race for being a myth, nor should we essentialize race in order to preserve its mythos. We should treat it like Cordelia's love for her father: "according to my bond, no more and no less."

This is why we need to have White History Month at Wabash: not to celebrate it, but to use it to thicken up our thin, cracking discussions on race, culture, and the rest. White History can deepen our imaginative abilities in order to avoid the impoverished options offered by the two-headed monster we call the Democrats and the Republicans, the conservatives and the liberals.

If all the food at a buffet looks and tastes like shit, then don't eat it; make your own food instead or, perhaps, starve with dignity. If someone asks you, "What do you want to be when you grow up?" say, "Yes" or "Beautiful," or reply, "*Being* is sufficient for me at the moment," or "I think I'll be a human person;" or give Bartleby's reply, "*I would prefer not to* [answer your (stupid) question]." Don't fall prey to the limited options that have put a straightjacket on our imagination and impede us from dwelling in authentic communion with each other. To do this, we will need the capacity to know that we have this option to begin with, and then we will need the additional mental and spiritual resources to create something different, even if that different "something" is very old. If there ever were a place where we might, just might, be able to do this, it would be Wabash. I truly and wholeheartedly believe this. As I said before (at the MXI Sunday dinner), this is an enchanting place. It is why I am so honored and excited to accept the college's generous invitation to extend my time here into next year.

So here it is, this is my official, twofold proposition: I propose first that Wabash stop *celebrating* history—Black history, white history, and even Wabash history—and that, in its place, we promote the serious *study* of history, in and out of class. This is not to suggest that we abolish the months dedicated to these histories. Instead it is a call to take these months seriously and add to their number, which leads to the next part. Secondly, I propose that Wabash add White History Month to the official college calendar, and investigate questions of whiteness and white identity throughout the entire year, alongside other questions, across the college and the curriculum.

As with Woodson's 1926 proposal of Negro History Week, my own proposal today is not about equality, it is about existence—it is about seeking authenticity in a world of the living dead where artificiality has become normal. A disenchanted, secular world of inversions and posers, where the News is old, the rich are bankrupt, and the schooled are miseducated. Without White History Month, without the careful study of the invention of white identity, we will only imagine parts at the expense of the whole, which means we would fail to imagine anything at all. In perilous times such as these, we cannot afford to willfully commit another failure of the imagination. We cannot sin against hope by presuming or despairing.

In that hopeful, imaginary spirit, I end as I began—with translation and poetry:

> I have no mother or father,
> Nor do I send children to school,
> Man I am not, but I have . . .
> I have a first and last name.
> I reclaim the simple right to be who we are.
> —*A mixed translation of the epigraph*

February 24, 2011
Wabash College "Chapel Talk"

Art Perfects Nothing: Review of *The Thorny Grace of It*

Joseph Bottum puts it plainly at *Patheos*: "Forget the culture-wars crap."

He's right, and his urgent, huffy tone is appropriate. I wrote something similar, almost a year ago, and since then I've had countless conversations with like-minded Catholics who are doing the creative work it takes to move beyond the culture wars.

One such Catholic is Brian Doyle.

It is always refreshing to read the words of someone who cares about the craft involved in using them, and Doyle is just such a craftsman. It may seem obvious and dull to praise a book because it reads smoothly, but anyone familiar with today's Catholic letters, including blogs, knows that really good wordsmiths are rare almost to the point of being mythical.

Not to put too fine a point on it, but Brian Doyle sure ain't Matthew Kelly.

No, Doyle isn't marketing Catholicism 2.0, nor is he posing as an apologist, scrubbing, dusting, sweeping, and mopping the Church's image with clichés and pep talks. Doyle is not a consultant, either, nor a self-help guru, nor a how-to-get-it-right-most-of-the-time motivator.

Doyle is an essayist—a writer who can stand toe-to-toe with anyone, anywhere, with all the requisite musculature, rigor, and verve—who also happens to be Catholic and is devoted to his faith.

This is Flannery O'Connor kind of stuff.

*

There was a time when Catholic aesthetics oozed from the pores of just about everything, even by negation. Even "Piss Christ."

I don't think that time has entirely passed.

*

I recently played some lounge music for the opening of a new display at the North Dakota Museum of Art. The main feature is a recreation of the apartment of the late New York artist, Barton Benes. The space's dominant theme is described as African, but I saw something very different. The collection was thick and smoking with Catholicism: morbidity everywhere, relics, Mexican notes of thanksgiving to Our Lady of San Juan, a money-mâché mosaic of Our Lady. A monstrance. This heavy sacramental sprinkling of holiness was doused all over the dead hummingbirds, a giraffe bust, Voodoo masks, ruins from disaster sites, all nesting in a tiny New York-sized apartment, with "Law and Order" playing on repeat.

It was in that flux of art that I understood Doyle's book in light of Bottum's lament.

*

The title-track of the book is a litany, a prayer. It reminds me of William James's essay "What Makes Life Significant," where he describes his visit to Chatauqua Lake, a "middle-class paradise." James is initially seduced by this perfectly artificial place, where soda fountains run incessantly, but when he returns to the wild and crazy world he is surprised to find himself relieved to be back in the mess and sin of human existence.

Doyle's wind-up is playful and light: "The house is mortgaged until the Jesus Blessed Christ returns in His Radiant Glory to resolve all mortgage payments and carry us home to his House."[1] The middle quickens and gets more personal, recalling lost siblings and unborn children. The ending shows the joy that can dwell in pain, and the glory that still has wounds. Doyle testifies, "I don't know Who set all this pain and glory in motion, but I bow in thanks for the sweet puzzle of it all."[2]

There is a confidence in this book that is willing to leave itself alone. Let art be sufficient. The writer's voice knows its range and defects and where the good notes are. The musicality of the long, often bare, sentences, filled with description and comparison, shows an author who knows what *not* to do.

*

The Church entered the culture wars for fear of nihilism, but fighting nothingness head on is a recipe for metaphysical disaster. It breeds fear of nothing, as if it were something. It makes the anti-real more potent than the real. It also presumes to have discovered this anti-reality recently, ignoring its history and anthropology.

Today many of our Catholic brothers and sisters live in fear of the world. Scared of all the bad things that are happening. And the people. Bad intentions, everywhere. Conspiracies. Gripping rosary beads in fear while clutching the remote. They want to know what to fear and how to guard against it and how to get the word out by sharing it online and praying for Jesus and the other good guys to make it right.

We want better arguments and stories—anything and everything—and lots and lots of gotchas and wisecracks. Books, television, and the internet are tools for anxiety, dread, and scams. The art of it all gets lost. In the midst of this grim condition, there are exceptions: periodicals like Doyle's *Portland Magazine*, reviews, collections, and other things not quite so quick to induce paranoid thinking.

1. Doyle, *The Thorny Grace of It*, 115.
2. Ibid., 117.

The Thorny Grace of It is one of these exceptions. It pierces the bullshit of cultural battlefields, unafraid to share the insight that "Catholicism and golf are ultimately about crazy hope."[3]

November 25, 2013
Patheos

Solidarity in Vulgarity: The Funk in Racial Jokes

"I don't want your stupid ethnic dances, I want dirty jokes!"

—SLAVOJ ŽIŽEK

"Gonna have a funky good time, gonna have a funky good time!"

—JAMES BROWN

Like several of my colleagues, I don't own a television.

On those occasions when I do watch movies, sports, or television programs, I rely on the internet. One of the shows I like to watch is *American Pickers*, the series about two guys who drive around buying junk. Being a lover of flea markets, thrift stores, and garage sales, I can relate to these guys. I especially like the fact that they cherish very particular kinds of places: run-down, dirty, rust-filled, verging-on-dangerous sorts of places. If a place is too clean, organized, or well kept, they are usually skeptical and unhappy. When the place is a dump, off the beaten path, teeming with dirt and rust, they are hopeful and excited.

These guys don't want to spend their time in domesticated or sterilized places. They want to be in the wild, untamed, mess of people's ordinary lives. Many times, they literally have to get lost to find their way. That attitude is the subject of this essay.

Watching YouTube videos of the public intellectual Slavoj Žižek is another nerdy pastime of mine. I don't always agree with him, but that's not the point. One of the many reasons I enjoy him is that, from time to time, he puts into speech a thought that I have struggled to fully understand and express.

3. Ibid., 54.

I recently had this experience while watching a clip excerpted from a talk he gave at Princeton titled "Why Only an Atheist Can Be a True Christian." (You can find it by searching "Žižek on Racism" on YouTube.) During the Q & A session, Žižek discusses racism. He responds to the question "How should we fight racism?" with this quixotic answer: "With progressive racism." He argues that there are forms of racist discourse—especially racist jokes—that are not racist at all, but are actually a powerful form of shared solidarity.

Hold that thought.

I also love to listen to and perform music. But I'm extremely picky about my music. I'm not looking for virtuosos. I'm after a pocket, a thick-groove, the perfect feel—I'm looking for music that is rootsy, earthy, that makes me wrinkle my nose, crunch my brow, and rock my head from side to side. I'm looking for real, funky music. The funk.

For music to be soulful to me, for it to be an experience that really hits me, it must be anchored in funk. (And funk must be anchored in the blues.) Whenever I play guitar, whether at a church or a club, I'm looking for the part that dwells in the funkiest depths of the song. Sometimes that means not playing at all, just pick-scratching at muted strings, turning my melodic guitar into a percussion instrument. Funky playing requires precision; no one can get in the other guy's way. It's all about space. Any band that is funky is in perfect balance, a community if a fragile one. To be funky is to dwell with others in a radical moment of solidarity.

What people don't often realize or pay attention to is that the funk literally refers to something vulgar: body odor. Funk is dirty. It is born from the bloody womb of the blues, Negro spirituals, the African "one" beat. It is baptized in suffering and hard work. You can't play good, funky music just because you play the right notes or follow all the rules. You can't really teach funkiness. You have to acquire the ability to dwell in the music in a way that has grit, sensuality, sexuality, and even vulgarity.

The funk isn't just about the bandstand; it's also about how the music affects the listener. The funk is physical, somatic music: it makes you dance and sweat, it makes you shout, it makes you feel—and more. The funk makes you swear beautifully. When you hear something funky you know it. Like Erykah Badu, you might ask the person next to you, "Damn, you feel that?"

There is something about funk that is absolutely authentic. As a genre, funk was born from jazz and gave birth to hip-hop. (Hip-hop drum samples are usually taken from funk bands, especially the work of Clyde Stubblefield, the original "funky drummer" for James Brown.) It is the crucial link between these two improvisational art forms. This is why I make a sharp distinction between hip-hop and rap—and especially gangsta rap. Hip-hop is *always* funky. There is something beautifully real about funky music, funky people, and the funk as more than just music.

Back to Žižek.

I doubt that Žižek knows much about the musical genre called funk, but he is absolutely funky. His lecturing style is endearingly sloppy: he is usually sweating and/or unbathed, his hair is greasy and unkempt, he cannot keep the saliva in his mouth, and he is constantly wiping or picking at his nose. But he is more than just funky in this literal way. Žižek understands the danger of trying to combat social injustice through sterilization or domestication. He challenges us to be more honest. To be funky.

We all know that there are real, intimate spaces in our lives where racial jokes and vulgar language are not only acceptable, but offer signs of the deepest trust and affection. My true friends, many of them on this campus, are not verified by their outward kindness or politeness to me, but instead by their earned freedom to insult me; to tell racist, vulgar jokes and speak in racist, vulgar ways when we spend time together.

There are trendy, pious forms of white guilt where fear of funky relationships is so strong that people try to organize, clean up, and deodorize these authentic ways of living, speaking, and being together. But make no mistake: you can't kill the funk. It is stronger than the soap of white guilt (itself a deodorized form of white supremacy) that is so often carried by so-called white people and, even more ironically, by gentrified people of color.

There is a powerful, funky form of solidarity in vulgarities exchanged between true friends.

The funk is not an excuse to be dirty for no good reason or to skip a shower, but it is real evidence of the inescapable fact that we all sweat, lust, swear, and more. We all love and hate. We are alive. In the same spirit, this absolutely does not mean we should just tell racist jokes willy-nilly or be expected to suffer racist heckling with a good grace, but it does mean that we should be slower to assume that racist jokes are always racist. They may in fact betoken a deep form of affection and solidarity.

These R-rated forms of social life are harder to pursue and attain than more comfortable, civil forms of solidarity. The funk is tremendously difficult, both in music and in friendship.

If you want to play the funk, you must be properly initiated and learn to dwell authentically with others. If you want to gain my personal trust and respect to be able to affectionately call me a "dirty Mexican," you will have to dwell with me. And to dwell with me, you must love me. When that day comes, we will be funky friends.

I'd rather have a real, rude, funky-ass friend than a deodorized, thoroughly gentrified so-called "friend." The former is a friend I might die for. So, Wabash, shall we be vulgar friends—or polite enemies?

December 13, 2011
Patheos

No-Exit Catholicism

It is understandable that some people cringe at seeing Catholicism reduced to an existential condition or a religious disposition, a cultural or folkloric aesthetic. There is something too soft and sentimental, too theologically unchecked, about these forms of "cultural Catholicism." In *Evangelical Catholicism,* George Weigel offers arguments against them. Bishop Robert Barron, in his popular *Catholicism* series, makes some of the same points, although often in a more measured, even implicit, way.

It would seem, then, that it is all or nothing. Full-force *kerygmatic* Gospel proclamation, rooted in the sacraments and liturgy, or a wholly secular none-ism.

But is that really accurate?

Some have argued that this is patently false. Urs Von Balthasar, Maritain, and Gilson all come to mind. Though they seem to be mostly forgotten, misunderstood, or ignored nowadays, a more concrete case can be made through simple observation. For instance, consider the vast canon of art in the West. There is a very real cultural anthropology present, especially in the art of Europe, that cannot be described as generically religious. It is distinctly Catholic. Small wonder, since much of that art was commissioned by and for the Church. In various ways, many oblique and hard to detect, these works of art created an aesthetic consciousness that became embedded in the culture itself.

To live amid Catholic art is to be affected and educated by it. This is public pedagogy in its most refined and effective state. Religious architecture, for instance, consists of geographical and ecological effects, creating a spatio-temporal effect in the human person who dwells within the aesthetic beauty of the church (which, of course, is not to be confused with the spiritual, but every bit as real, beauty of the Church).

Public religious art is, perhaps, too weak a case study to measure against the weight pulled by the confessional and dogmatic creeds often touted as the *sine qua non* of Catholicism. However, it is precisely the weakness of this aesthetic and affective environment, this fragile ecology of sorts, that makes the Catholic presence hard to ignore completely.

A soft breeze.

Another, more personal, example:

My story begins as the son of a lay Catholic evangelist, raised in a missionary family, steeped in evangelical Catholicism in all its rigor and mendicancy. This evangelical background eventually led me to enroll as an undergraduate at Franciscan University of Steubenville. I swallowed it whole: the "essential content" of the core Gospel message, the basic proclamation of the Good News, in the power of the Holy Spirit, rooted in the tradition and teachings of the Catholic Church. It is hard to imagine a more *evangelical* Catholicism than this.

But in another sense, my Catholic story has deeper roots than mere autobiography can trace. I am a cradle Catholic whose ancestry in present-day Texas and the American Southwest saw the blending of blood and cultures, the fall and rise of empires. I came into the world with thick Catholic roots, watered by Mexican folklore. *Posadas* and *Guadalupe*. I *learned* about my faith from my father, the evangelist, but I *lived* my faith with, and in many ways through, his father—my *abuelito*, a simple Catholic man. Both men played vital roles, to be sure, but one was prior and indispensable to the other.

Cradle Catholics can be arrogant and self-important, especially when relating to converts; of this there is little doubt, and I am no exception. But this fault seems to be a rare instance of nativism—albeit a shameful, nasty, and off-putting one—and even the binary assumption of the cradle Catholic versus the convert admits some exceptions.

Nonetheless, cradle Catholics are sometimes misunderstood, I think, when judged pitilessly according to doctrinal orthodoxy and the evangelical tenets of Catholicism. What looks like apathy may, in fact, be the natural consequence of being Catholic from womb to inevitable tomb. Ancestry and culture. In other words, where an aesthetic ecology of religious practice is especially strong, we shouldn't wonder that doctrine sometimes takes a backseat.

In my own experience, the Catholic Church resembles the Hotel California: "You can check out anytime you like, but you can never leave." This is a no-exit Catholicism. Its cultural affectations are useful in describing its external details, but they fail to capture its powerful grip over the imagination, a life, and the soul.

In many cases the expression of this no-exit Catholicism is through the arts and culture. No wonder, then, Catholicism so abounds there, even through negation—even an atheist who has felt the Catholic *imprimatur* will show it sometimes. Contemporary artists, for instance, cannot seem to help themselves, despite the growth of secularist hegemony.

Recently, in the mostly secular academy where I do my work, I have noticed a remarkable number of people who have this no-exit sense of Catholicism. These people were cradled, raised, and/or educated by the Church. Even after leaving (either intentionally or through the unconscious acquisition of habit known as "falling away"), they never ceased to think and even express themselves through a Catholic lens of some kind, in serious ways. Sometimes this expression took the form of serious jokes.

Even the rather anti-Catholic cliché of being a "recovering Catholic" pays homage to the truism that you never stop being an addict; the addiction stays with you forever. You can only hope to recover by degrees and proportions. Odd as it may seem, this notion of "recovery" is, perhaps, a more faithful, albeit inverted, expression of the Catholic universal call to holiness through continual and constant conversion.

None of this is to suggest that a no-exit Catholicism is sufficient on its own terms. There's no sense in replacing one zero-sum game with another. Nowadays, both the public, cultural dimension and the personal, lived experience are often torn and fragmented as religious influence disappears from our culture. Even when things are mostly intact, as I found them when I was growing up, the radical reality of the Gospel remains open to reduction in ways that minimize its power to transform and heal.

But a no-exit sense of Catholicism does at least recognize the importance of the Church's cultural and aesthetic anthropology. It also pays proper tribute to the genealogy and lived experience of the cradle Catholic—and, indeed, of the convert; I've heard many converts swear that they felt Catholic long before their formal conversions. No-exit Catholicism is not necessarily a threat to, or even a critique of, evangelical Catholicism. On the contrary, no-exit Catholicism affirms the desires for beauty and rootedness that complement the evangelical Catholic's desires for orthodoxy and magisterial fidelity.

April 9, 2014
Ethika Politika

How (Not) to Destroy Catholic Art

Catholic art is destroyed at the exact moment when it becomes necessary to have "Catholic" art.

*

The liturgical movement surging through the Roman Catholic Church over the past decade, often called "traditional," attests less to the popular appeal of Catholic liturgy than to its loss of popularity. We would not see self-styled "traditionalists" emerge unless (a) an innovation required re-branding as tradition, or (b) a real tradition were in danger. In the normal run of things, traditions are just ways of being and living.

If you want to diminish a tradition from its organic and natural state, start calling it a "tradition."

Wherever tradition is defended passionately you will find a thick layer of fear and insecurity. In the case of the Jewish people, for example, these feelings are sometimes justified by recent (and not-so-recent) historical events. The same goes for indigenous peoples. As the old joke reminds us, just because you're paranoid doesn't mean that they're not out to get you.

The general point is a simple one: every need hints at a lack. This goes just as well for categories as anything else. Whenever a special category becomes necessary, some class of thing is in danger. Depending on the cir-cumstances, inventing categories and launching movements on behalf of endangered things can produce either good or bad fruits, or a mixture of the two. But the constitutive conditions remain, by and large, the same.

*

Catholic art is destroyed at the exact point when it becomes necessary to have something, just one thing, just one reliable thing, with the Catholic *imprimatur.*

I grew up hearing about how badly we need "Catholic" things. Mer-chandise. Music. Stuff to compete with the Protestants who were better at making stuff that looks just as cool as the secular stuff. Really good vegan bacon.

I also kept hearing about how we need "Catholic" things that are *more* Catholic than the current Catholic stuff. Qualitative degrees of Catholicism.

It escaped me at the time that, for me, Catholicism was not optional. I was a cradle Catholic, a Mestizo Mexican Tejano Southwestern boy. Noth-ing could dislodge the deep genealogical, ancestral Catholicism that had seeped into me and shaped my imagination and dispositions. The special-ized community of Catholics who worried about having "Catholic" things must not have been so lucky.

Growing up in church offices and prayer meetings and weekday morn-ing Mass with lots and lots of priests certainly helped. But there was a time when it seemed as though it didn't. I knew all the stuff, I had all the facts, I went to the right school, I could talk the talk and had walked more of the walk than most. I read the Catechism. But when certain things change and shift, foundations get shaken, all the right answers wear thin, and nothing remains to prevent a fallout.

But I couldn't, and still cannot, seem to fall away entirely. Grace, sure. Of course. But also the fact that being Catholic, for me, is not about a conference I went to or a T-shirt or a socio-cultural brand name—or even, for that matter, a set of doctrines I understand and am willing to check off my belief list.

Mine was, still is, and always will be, a no-exit Catholicism.

*

Catholic art is destroyed at the exact point when and where we become desperate and starving and will take anything, anything at all, so long as it is "Catholic," and create special places for those books and CDs at the store, so that everyone can find it, regardless of how badly composed they are.

Religious art is not what I am after here. But, in another sense, it is what I am after. What makes art *religious*? Its author, theme, use?

I don't know, nor do I particularly care. But I do know that "Catholic" art is the last thing we need. We need art, period. That is rare enough.

Once the art proves worthwhile, worthy of its class and peers and so on, then, perhaps, we will start measuring its Catholic proof by volume.

*

I once assumed that "Catholic" music was all about use value. If you could play or hear it at Mass, or during a praise and worship service, then it was "Catholic." If it was unsuitable for either of these purposes, then it was probably not "Catholic."

What suited "Catholic" music to ministerial use was a built-in opening for *participation*. It had to be sing-along music, so it had to have words. In the context of music ministry, the word "performance" was strictly pejorative. To *perform* was selfish, prideful, and bad.

As I improved on my instrument and my other musical crafts, people started accusing me of performing or showing off. "But I've been playing guitar since I was five and am self-taught and these licks don't come cheap and sound pretty good," I would think. I would also think about how much better it would sound through a decent PA system.

In this way, I began to intuit that making use value the measure of music's Catholicism was deeply wrong. In fact, I began to see that the liturgy itself and the sacraments are too often disenchanted into mere utilities.

Art has no use. Liturgy is useless. Silence. God is not a life-coach.

*

Slowly, I built these experiences into a type of music that already existed, though perhaps not in an intentional way. Soul music, gospel music—the market offers all kinds of religious and spiritual kinds of music. American music is, at its root, religious. The blues.

But—if I do say so myself—few artists have made a project out of composing music faithful both to soul's religious roots *and* unfit for devotional use. I have tried to do that precisely for the sake of fidelity to a deeper and more fundamental Catholicism.

*

To restore Catholic art we need not restore anything but art itself. To restore art, we just have to make it, and be very serious about it.

February 25, 2014
Patheos

Francis's Radical Realism: Performance vs. Ideology

One year into his pontificate, one of the few uncontroversial things to be said about Pope Francis is this: He is our first American pope. Though this claim verges on the obvious, it still paves the way for insight. We are in the midst of something like a shift in current, a reversal of continental polarity. Since the Spanish *conquista* first brought Catholicism to American shores till now, the dawn of the twenty-first century, the Americas have *listened*. Now, through Francis, there is *speech*, a voice.

A Latin American voice.

Even before the pragmatism of William James (and the pragmaticism of C. S. Pierce), American philosophers have worked mainly in concrete—concrete realities, that is. Geopolitical developments in Latin America over the past hundred years have reflected this tendency. Whereas Europe has followed a progression of *ideas* (e.g., rationalism, empiricism, idealism, and so on), postcolonial Latin America has responded to a series of political *situations*.

Francis embodies this situation-based approach in a very direct and pointed way. Sections 231–233 of his apostolic exhortation *Evangelii Gaudium* are summarized by the subtitle "Realities are more important than ideas." Francis manages the distinction between realities and ideas by giving ontological priority to the former. "Realities simply are, whereas ideas are worked out," Francis teaches. The ontological simplicity of reality gives way to a "principle of reality," an incarnational order between word and flesh that favors the *practice* of evangelization.[4]

Francis's notion of practice here is performative. To "put the word into practice," we must "*perform* works of justice and charity which make that word fruitful."[5] This is, perhaps, the key to understanding the significance and underlying logic of his phone calls, kisses, and other acts of kindness that have become a constant spectacle in the public media. (Why should they not? They are spectacular.) They are performances, a series of very real, and often quite ordinary, responses to situations. They are concrete and therefore proximate, giving rise to a unique and unprecedented sense of intimacy. That this intimacy has been perplexing to many only testifies to the radical nature of his approach. In these times, ideological "issues" often take precedence over the human touch, but these iconic papal acts can be, and have been, grasped in pictures, images without language. They are realities and require no further explanation. Francis teaches that realities are greater than ideas without having to say so.

The question of papal continuity, which always appears at some point in this discussion, is interesting in itself. I do not know whether any other pope has been scrutinized as closely as Francis has been for signs of fidelity to, and divergence from, his recent predecessors. What is most obvious in this case is also instructive: the relationship between Benedict XVI and Francis is literal and present. We can see it plainly. The irrationally ideological style of today's popular speculation is, perhaps, most vividly on display as both left and right antagonize a very real friendship between our two popes. Too many would have us believe that Francis and Benedict are nowhere near as friendly as they appear to be.

Of course it does not follow that friends must agree with each other. However, when two popes who, for the first time in 800 years, are both alive *and* in close and frequent contact, we are forced to confront a *prima facie* case for high mutual regard, if not total accord.

4. Apostolic Exhortation *Evangelii Gaudium* of the Holy Father Francis. Retrieved from https://w2.vatican.va/content/francesco/en/apost_exhortations/documents/papa-francesco_esortazione-ap_20131124_evangelii-gaudium.html on February 11, 2017.

5. Ibid.

What I am calling Francis's "radical realism" might be even easier to appreciate by examining the common ground shared by Benedict and his own predecessor, St. John Paul II. As an actor and playwright, John Paul practiced the arts of performance; this, I think, explains his intuitive grasp of the power of phenomenology, an influence deeply embedded in his writings both before and after he became pope. Benedict XVI's Augustinian roots give his writings a sense of the performative, too, most explicitly in *Spe Salvi*, where he maintains that the Christian message must be "not only 'informative' but 'performative.'"[6] Benedict anticipates Francis's radical realism when he elaborates that "the Gospel is not merely a communication of things that can be known—it is one that makes things happen and is life-changing."[7]

From John Paul's love of stagecraft and appreciation for lived experience, to Benedict XVI's understanding of the amorous and performative core of the Gospel, to Francis's distinctively American preference for reality over and above ideas, we see a progression clear as a symphonic movement.

But what are the relevant implications?

One of them is a critique of modern ideology that, in many respects, mirrors that of Alasdair MacIntyre and, more recently, Slavoj Žižek. In fact, it may also point to an interesting (albeit limited) convergence between them.

In *Marxism and Christianity*, MacIntyre credits the prophetic strength of Marx's critique, rooted in the Christian inheritance carried over from Hegel. He also highlights Marx's two-fold weakness: the inability of his theory of ideology to account for itself (How can Marx accuse *others* of false consciousness?), and its constitutive social conditions. (In this case, MacIntyre rehearses the argument he would more famously deploy against social science methods in *After Virtue*). MacIntyre's *strategy* is what stands out here as unique, especially among philosophers, because, as he has continued to show throughout his writings, he takes seriously both the ideological implications of a critique of ideology and all of its social effects, well beyond the narrow boundaries of reason.

This strategy is similar to Žižek's use of Lacanian psychoanalysis to critique the narrativist approach in Freud and other purely linguistic or interpretive approaches. In *The Plague of Fantasies*, Žižek, following Lacan, contends that "narrative as such" is what emerges as the real, not a strategic reorganization of narratives and counter-narratives. Therefore, concludes

6. Encyclical letter *Spe Salvi* of the Supreme Pontiff Benedict XVI. Retrieved from http://w2.vatican.va/content/benedict-xvi/en/encyclicals/documents/hf_ben-xvi_enc_20071130_spe-salvi.html on February 11, 2017.

7. Ibid.

Žižek, unless we take care to account for "narrative as such," and the various ways in which our desire reconstitutes narrative into fantasy, we will end up reproducing ideology.

There has been much debate over the translation, the terms and their exact meanings and intentions, and most of all the economic narrative of Francis's message in *Evangelii Gaudium* and elsewhere. What this parsing of words misses is the *performance*, including the performance of the narrative, but most importantly the performance of the Gospel as a reality instead of an idea. If the Gospel is merely an ideological alternative, a narrativist strategy, then, as MacIntyre notes disagreeably and as Žižek strongly and perversely favors, Marxism may simply be the modern appropriation of Christianity.

Francis's radical realism, then, is to treat the Word as an incarnate thing, as a reality to be shown more than it is said, to let its proclamation live in the performance of its witness, to be captured in pictures of tenderness, embrace, ordinary living. A kiss. Acts such as these are immune to the ideological trap of Western ideas that has turned so much of the reality of the Gospel into intellectual history, moral theology, and dogmatic ideals. A real Gospel cannot be a philosophy or even a philosophical theology. A philosophical Catholicism is what Francis seems to be avoiding, and for good reason.

The result of this realism is radical in both senses. On the one hand, it returns to the root (*radix*) of the matter, to the real itself. On the other, it makes incredible demands that come with very real costs. There is a price to pay when the Americas are given a voice. Francis is direct: "This calls for rejecting the various means of masking reality: angelic forms of purity, dictatorships of relativism, empty rhetoric, objectives more ideal than real, brands of ahistorical fundamentalism, ethical systems bereft of kindness, intellectual discourse bereft of wisdom."[8]

In short, Francis is calling on the Church, and the world, to reject ideology as such, to decolonize and disabuse itself of the deleterious effects of Western intellectualism, to perform an embrace of reality, most of all the reality of Christ and his presence among us in the poor and the suffering.

March 11, 2014
Ethika Politika

---

8. Apostolic Exhortation *Evangelii Gaudium* of the Holy Father Francis. Retrieved from https://w2.vatican.va/content/francesco/en/apost_exhortations/documents/papa-francesco_esortazione-ap_20131124_evangelii-gaudium.html on February 11, 2017.

Moronic Manhood

I grew up in the sort of Catholic circles where "being a man" was, and still is, a really big deal. Since the early days of father-and-son manhood retreats, I've seen no shortage of manhood-focused customs and discourse—and of course the steady stream of popular books on the subject. Most of these were salutary on the whole. Some were not.

Speaking as a former Texas high school football player and collegiate rugby player (and coach), I believe jock culture represents the most nuanced version of manhood. It has earned most of its stereotypical portrayals, but it also admits more exceptions to its rules than most outsiders suppose. Many people would be surprised to see how finely detailed those rules are in themselves.

I especially remember priests who were really big into manhood and "being a man." They seemed to affect the sort of butt-kicking persona that I eventually began to read as a sign of deep personal insecurity. By my college years, I began to suspect that Fr. Badass, giving his talk about being a real man in today's world of wussies, was projecting, not dispensing sound pastoral advice.

Then there is the "masculinity studies" approach, which is basically a gender-feminist critique of a rather unsophisticated caricature of male sexuality as it's been constructed in the West, and sometimes elsewhere. Granted, jocks and priests, along with pop culture, continue to supply these scholars with ample material.

A lot of the manhood stuff, then and now, had less to do with being a man and more to do with *not* being a gay man. During vocations retreat talks, there inevitably came an awkward moment where Fr. Macho, as if to establish his hetero bona fides, would drop in a line about how much he still liked to look at women. Then he'd lead us in a game of touch football.

When it comes to homosexuality, let me be clear: I've read Foucault's *History of Sexuality* (and *First Things'* recent discovery of poststructuralism) and agree with the obvious fact that both hetero- and homo-sexualities are fairly recent and evolving conventions, with disciplinary functions often on display in this sort of manhood talk. Foucault's perspective on sexuality has some surprising consistency with the philosophical work of John Paul II, however frequently that work is exploited for contrary purposes.

I've also read the Greeks and learned about the ancients, whose conceptions and practices of manhood were often deeply homoerotic. Homoeroticism is, I think, one of the significant cultural traits of the West, and perhaps of the human story in general. Add to this the fact that I have many gay friends who are not politic or predictable about their identity, and frequently reject the (often hyper-sexualized) terms of the discussion that would seem to weigh in their favor, and I find myself deeply allergic to the "don't be a gay (or girly) man" implications in certain strands of manhood talk.

If you patronize or practice the fine arts, and even if you don't, you will find it hard not to admire and cherish the remarkable taste, sass, and verve of a gay Southern man. If you like to be treated like a human being, warts and all, there are fewer things more consoling than the humor and embrace of an older lesbian woman. If you don't know these sorts of people, and how wonderful and precious they are, you should. Avoiding them suggests an incuriosity especially unbecoming of Roman Catholics; it also offends charity to imply or project that "being a man" fundamentally excludes the feminine or effeminate. Most of all, it does violence to what it is to be a *person*.

In Catholic circles, needless to say, I've read and heard thousands of jeremiads that run along the lines of: "There is a crisis among men today; men are not men anymore." People make this claim in reaction to almost everything: church attendance, college admissions, social issues, vocations, the decline of the family, and more. Just a few days ago, Michael Voris' show, *The Vortex,* broadcast a stunningly well-executed rehearsal of this position.

I don't doubt that some of the problems are in a sense very real and that some of the available data support these intuitive judgements. But it does not remotely follow that because more men are incarcerated today than women, or church attendance is low among males of all ages, or whatever other figures one might cite regarding fatherhood or anything else, that a sudden and unprecedented decline in a mythic notion of modern manhood is to blame.

It is at least equally plausible that manhood itself, at least of this unrefined sort, has lent special appeal to "Larry the Cable Guy" and "Joe the Plumber" Americana, which has lately become so tiresome, if not positively toxic. There is no denying the family resemblance between these boorish caricatures and the Catholic "real man" as personified by Michael Voris and Fr. Badass.

And when, exactly, was there a golden age of manhood? As I recall from Augustine's *Confessions*, Monica cut a very familiar figure of a lady who went to church while her husband and wayward son did not.

The fact is that "manhood" has become a seductive moniker, and manhood's seductive potential is pregnant with irony. It pastes an intuitive solution onto a range of problems, with interpretive flexibility. Manhood, the ideal of being a *real* man, has become a marketing cure-all: it washes surfaces and can enrich uranium. Write about manhood and people will buy and read. (Why else do you think I am writing about it?)

The problem with the manhood business is not only that it is a business; its biggest problem is a self-defeating lack of self-reflection. Is there really some timeless normative or axiomatic quality about being a man beyond what is descriptively obvious? In fact, this clumsy notion of essential manhood is manly in the sense of being stupid, one stereotype that our sex could afford to lose, no matter how many laughs it gets on *Everybody Loves Raymond*.

Women can be hard to find throughout the canon of the historical record, so reasons why notions of womanhood often fall prey to gross over-simplification and abuse are easily imaginable. But men are literally everywhere in human history and offer countless counter-memories, inversions, exceptions, and digressions. I don't buy the sex/gender binary distinction *in toto*, but neither would I reduce things to a dialectic between two fantasies of masculinity and femininity. Such a reduction wouldn't be manly or womanly; it would be infantile.

God created Adam and Eve, yes, but he didn't program them into ahistorical robots.

The human person is a vast and toothy creature, with enough complexity and contradiction to keep the most advanced supercomputer fully at bay. Compared to other life forms, our species has had a short history, but that history is still quite long when compared to our favorite analog: ourselves. We've invented and reinvented each other across time and place and are likely to have forgotten more than we remember. None of this scares me as a man, a Catholic, or a human person, nor should it scare you—and I am getting sick and tired of hearing why it should.

The manly manhood alternatives out there are sometimes well intended, albeit metaphysically naïve, and can be effective in positive ways, teaching lessons that create and preserve culture. Fashion and style, for instance, have a strikingly aesthetic notion of physical manhood reminiscent of the Greeks. But too often the tail wags the dog and, before you know it, "being a man" starts its loopy, and often comical, parade into self-parody. I relish the irony, sometimes; but irony gets old, too.

Yes, I want to become a better father, son, husband, and friend, to man and woman alike, as the man that I am, but I'm not sure that I need to watch *Braveheart* on repeat to do it or keep up with the latest motivational self-help being sold as an antidote. I sometimes wonder if being a "real man" is simply a matter of reading and retreating a lot about it. I certainly don't need to watch Michael Voris or read Matt Walsh as they preach to head-nodding fans, feeding them as one might feed ducks in a park, showing their strongest and most visible virtues: smug certainty and preachy self-confidence.

Jesus was a man, of this there is no doubt, but I am not so sure that he was all that much more stoic or resilient (or possessed of other "manly" qualities) than his mother. A critic might reply that he was, after all, the *Son* of God. But it is at least a philosophical mistake to equate the manliness of Christ's humanity with his divinity. If Christ "humbled himself to take on our humanity" then it follows to see the masculinity of Jesus of Nazareth as different in quality than the glory of his divine being and personhood. In other words, while the divinity of Christ and his masculine humanity is a whole and irreducible mystery, it seems that any essential burden lies with his divinity.

Truth be told, before holding up Mary, Joseph, or even Jesus as exemplars of manhood or womanhood, we should pause to recognize that all three were pretty weird, both as individuals and as a (holy) family. For instance, a woman today who found herself in the same predicament as Mary did at the time of the Annunciation would be called an unwed pregnant teenager—a social construction if there ever was one. I doubt you could cut a blueprint for masculinity, femininity, or anything else too hard and fast, from the saints. That is in part precisely why they are such inspirations: sanctity is enigmatic. It is also deeply personal.

When imitation is easy and cheap, the original is often found to be lacking. When imitation is hard and elusive and takes a lifetime to master, something substantial must be there. Jesus doesn't need muscles and a six-pack to be our Savior. He can take the form of bread and wine.

I think it's worth our while to do whatever we can to live a real life, to be holy, to run the race with speed and endurance. That manhood has something to do with this I have little doubt, but let's also be humane and rational about it. At the very least, let's try not to sound and act like morons in the process of being and becoming (wo)men. Men and women, I think, should imitate the best qualities of anything that deserves imitation, without condition or pretense, and rejoice that grace perfects nature.

June 2, 2014
Ethika Politika

Michael Jackson: Another Quixote?

First of all, let me be clear: I reject the notion that we should discuss an artist's work without referring to their life. What I have to offer regarding the newly departed Michael Jackson is no mere technical analysis of his music. Michael Jackson's artistic output was so tightly intertwined with his identity that the two were practically fused. It is this fusion that commands my attention here.

Music. Here is a dare for anyone who dismisses Michael Jackson's musical gifts: try to replicate his art. Join a respectable cover band and try to pull off credible versions of his songs from his Jackson Five days to *Invincible*, his last studio album. You'll discover that it's impossible to reproduce the Michael Jackson effect through superior technique alone. To do so, you'll need all the intangibles (and more).

For example, in order to emulate with perfect tone his staccato phrasing and wide range, you cannot simply sing; you must *sang*. In Black musical circles, much is made of this distinction. (People will ask, "I know she can sing, but can she *sang?*") Moreover, getting the beat just right is not simply a matter of being "on the one" every time, like a metronome; you've got to be able to keep a tight groove that breathes just enough to let the body move. (This well-known somatic approach to rhythm is common in dance-based musical genres, especially Latin and Afrocentric music, where the beat is for the body.)

My point is this: Playing the basic forms and beats of a genre or style is one thing, but to really be able to play—and dance, too!—Michael Jackson's music (or Stevie Wonder's music, or Ray Charles's music, or the music of a few others touched by the gods) you need your model to hold you by the hand and teach you. I came into the scene pretty late with little more than a good ear and years of playing at church, but I gave Stevie, Ray, and Michael a long listen. (I did the same for Bob Marley.) From studying the masters, I have gained more in my playing and my ability to communicate myself through my instrument than I've gained by any other means. Even now, after years of discipleship, I never let myself become complacent when the time comes to play Michael's music. Nothing less than my best will do.

By now I've also taken heavy doses of older cats like Wes Montgomery, Muddy Waters, Freddie King, and Django Reinhardt, as well as some current virtuosos like John Scofield, Pat Metheny, Adam Rogers, and John Mayer (yes, he fits in that category to me). But while they inspired me to shed and work on chops, phrasing, and style, Michael Jackson (and the others I previously mentioned) taught me how to let a beat be itself and consume me without sounding loose or sloppy. In a word, Michael Jackson taught me how to groove.

Now, is "pop" a silly throwaway genre? Sure, sometimes. Okay, all too often. But in Michael's case, unless you've achieved a level of expertise that I have yet to come across (which, for all I know, you have), hold your verdict. Michael embodied the most sophisticated approach to Black American music we have heard to date, with Prince as his only possible rival. His global popularity attests to that sophistication as much as it attests to his genius for self-promotion.

At his memorial service, we saw the very best in the field try to do justice to his music. None of the results was better than tolerable, and some were simply poor. (Mariah sounded like a hot mess.) The bar has been set; let them try to clear it, whoever dares. If you want to play in the evolving tradition of the Black American music scene, you must contend musically with Michael Jackson, period.

Identity. Michael Jackson lived a tragic life. Whether he emerges the hero or the villain is not for me to say, after all, and it hardly makes sense to cut it so cleanly. What Jackson did do in his life (including his music) was struggle to become a person in ways that were torturously strange to everyone watching. From his gradual blanching of his skin, to his distortion of his face into a mask both puerile and androgynous, his life was a mystery. Judging by the abuse and unrequited love he suffered as a child and the accusations of pedophilia lodged against him as an adult, it was a dark mystery.

The idea that these bizarre—and possibly worse—aspects of his life should be excluded from our attention is, to me, the strangest thing of all. Why, even as we mourn him, does fascination with his identity excite such controversy?

I see Michael Jackson as a another Quixote: a man trying to live out a fairytale, whose life was a paradox at best, a tangle of contradictions at worst. For Miguel de Unamuno, Don Quixote was an embodiment of the "tragic sense of life," a sense of life fulfilled not in the type of the Quixote, but in Christ.

I am not sure that I am ready to join Michael Jackson to Unamuno's Christological reading of Cervantes, but I would say that Michael Jackson's life is one we should not be ashamed to find fascinating. It is not a lost cause to wonder why his identity was so strange to most of us, even those who wish he would fade into distant memory.

When I am at my most introspective, the identity of this man, who was objectified through abuse from prepubescence and who went on to objectify himself through self-indulgence, body-modification, escapism, and repression, as well as through musical innovation—and who may, God help him, have objectified others, too—is not so strange at all. He is none other than myself. In a way, I am Michael Jackson. We all are.

I realize how cheesy and glib, how bombastic, such a claim must sound. But in my view, any quixotic life that presents us with deep questions of identity is a call to conversion, to re-identification, that forces us to face ourselves, our sister and brother, our enemy, and, in the end, the face of God.

Rest in peace, Michael.

July 12, 2009
Vox Nova

The Perils of Private Consensus:
Or, In Praise of Mommy Blogs

In my essay "Fear of Generosity," I come dangerously close to self-help. It was not widely read when I published it, but it seemed to resonate with the few who did bother to read it. Perhaps certain things need to be said plainly and in terms that verge on the prescriptive. If cheesiness be the result, oh well.

Now I'd like to limn another danger I've observed in public discourse, especially on social media. In fact, it would not be off the mark to see nagging posts like this one as a reaction to the kind of interaction, or lack of interaction, so easily observable on Facebook and Twitter. Call it by any name you like—it's a symptom of a grave cultural illness, one from which we suffer collectively.

*

One of the most salient qualities you will find among people who share their thoughts on the interwebs is woundedness. So-called mommy bloggers—not least among them my own *Patheos* colleagues—show an awareness of these wounds and the pressing need for catharsis and other therapeutic forms of outreach. These women seem to write, on repeat, a refrain that sings, "You are not alone, I am not alone, we are not alone." For all the melancholy, the effect is sometimes comic, and not by accident. These women write to crack themselves and their readers up, very likely in order to prevent themselves and their readers from cracking.

I don't want to caricature these wonderful bloggers as sentimentalists. To the contrary, the sentiment and emotion on display in their writing also reveals its intellectual and literary value. These qualities also strike me as being remarkably *catholic*.

*

The point is that mothers are not the only ones who feel alone and afraid and particularly anxious these days. Lurking in any ideological echo chamber on any issue, from marriage to guns to abortion to taxes to school curricula, you will notice that each side is convinced it is losing badly.

How odd it is that such widespread despair can be found among the truest believers! Conservatives are sure that the Democratic Party, backed by the liberal media, is taking over everything and that they will soon be forced to fight or flee. Liberals are equally sure the GOP, cheered on by Fox News and conservative talk radio, is devastating the environment and further impoverishing the poor and breaking everything beyond repair.

Each side is not-so-secretly infatuated with the other. From here, it looks like a tragic ideological romance, foreplay that seems destined to precede a nuclear, explosive consummation.

Other factors are at play, but dwelling on them too long would add little to the discussion. Some of us like to be routinely outraged, so we join the dance, we copy it through denial, and the exception becomes a part of the norm.

*

If mommy blogs prove anything, it's that we can also, in spite of ourselves, use the new media for good.

On my Facebook page, I see worlds collide. I am still a bit hesitant to let in friends from the academy, but the ones who have taken their places on my list are forced to bump up against members of my family and fellow musicians and church friends and friends of friends and old high school acquaintances.

This sounds like a recipe for a delicious disaster. But so far it hasn't been. Sure, people may often check themselves out of politeness or simple indifference, and sometimes things do get heated, but by and large I've found that all of us are able to do more than get along: we are able to get to know each other.

This leads me to submit a cliché that deserves to be repeated: there is a real danger in the ghetto, the insiders' table, the group that has become comfortable with its own words and lingo and jargon, the small world that has recast everything else in its own image. We all know this, at some level, but I don't think we realize it enough.

*

Long before the liberalism of early modernity, the early Church was *catholic* in a radically Christian way: it was non-sectarian, or at least a non-sectarian sect. It also fostered deep and sometimes lasting disagreements. But it was a "public" in the vaguely democratic spirit of Athens that girds our modern political loins, and it shows all the stretch marks of a public experiment, the suffering of compromise and consensus.

Because, let's be honest, there is no widespread agreement without a great deal of work and, ultimately, calamity. No consensus without disensus, no assent without dissent.

As I watched Pope Francis pay a visit to the Holy Land and try to bring peace to the region, my mind wandered to the early Church—a social and cultural experiment fraught with danger, where the stakes were very high.

*

The wounds between us also show that division can result naturally from real and frank talk. The line dividing dysfunction from sincerity is, perhaps, a fiction. But, I pray, it is also the work of healing that opens up a new space for grace to intervene, again and again.

So, no, this is not self-help. For conflict resolution, no simple, foolproof plan exists.

Instead, this is a warning against private consensus, against the sorts of interactions built on self-referential notions of "common sense," against the fortresses we build to protect ourselves from the love we desire.

We should avoid confusing the tragedy of consensus with the comedy, made from memes, bumper-stickers, and clever bullshit, that has replaced sharing our lives, as well as careful argument, and listening.

We should search for public spaces where we can test and check and imagine what a real consensus might look like, and whether that sort of thing is what we really want after all.

*

I do not think that these prescriptions are necessarily political; I do not mean to draw up blueprints for the reinvention of democracy or an experiment in self-government. Instead, I have in mind a radical religious experiment, one that gets us to that place where mommy blogs venture more than most, namely, the wildly tame and predictable space of the pornographic internet, a place of weakness and vulnerability.

Pope Francis refused extra security precautions and bullet-proof protection when he visited the Holy Land. His refusal is, I think, a cue for all of us. The peril of a private consensus is most deftly avoided when we are willing to be present in such a way that we risk something grave and serious, even when that thing is love itself.

In other words, in order to avoid what is dangerous we must be willing to put ourselves in real danger.

May 26, 2014
Patheos

Art Kills

If we listen to the people who pretend to know, Catholic literature is dead, poetry is dead, pop music is long dead, jazz is dead, classical music is dead, sacred art is dead, and activist art is dead. At this rate, it would not be a surprise to find out someone is running around proclaiming the death of all artistic media and even of art itself.

In response, we can give these claims the lie by pointing to this or that work of contemporary art. Defenses of this type usually conclude with an insinuation that obituaries for art are all ideological. My sense is that these tugs of war reflect differences of opinion on the present state of art less than they reflect different definitions of death.

Life and death, after all, are hardly opposites; they embrace and complement each other. It may be the case that, to the person in mourning, art is dead and, to the person hard at work curating or creating, art is very much alive. This is not willy-nilly relativism. It is simply the good sense inherent in a great deal of clear thinking and, coincidentally, William James's unoriginal conception of pragmatism.

The more fundamental question is neither sociological nor metaphysical. We must ask a different question: What does art do? What happens when art happens? One response is that art kills. Art even kills itself, at every level. Art kills artists; art kills epochs and eras; art kills convention; art kills beauty. Art kills everything. In the wake of art we cling to life and conserve it poorly through fear and through love.

Art kills all through desire.

On this view, art is a killer, a dangerous and violent force like gravity. The alternative view to this fatalistic one is the vitalist position that seems to be generating so much anxiety about the axiomatic death and life of the arts. These disputes of memory and counter-memory, past and present, project equally plastic futures: the apocalypse, nostalgic revival, or business as usual.

The vitalist assumption expects art to conquer all, to change the world, and waxes sentimental about beauty in ways that turn fresh spring water into stale vomit. How many more essays must we read about the enchantment of the arts to be convinced that perhaps art is something altogether different and more radically normal than these mediocre dreams of Eden?

The reduction of all art can be found in its folk expression. There is no form of art that escapes a folkloric foundation. The Gospel demand of death to self treats the selfhood of the human person as a piece of art. The developmental sickness of values in our time, and in times past, often mistakes this personalist firstness of the folk as a trivializing or infantilizing inferiority, on the one hand. On the other, it celebrates it in a naïve and hipster way, without understanding or caring about it.

To understand folk music, for instance, is to know that it does not exist. This is not populist music that "everyone can sing along to easily." These are songs that die as soon as they are born and often become impossible to share because each region and people touts its own expression of the song. What makes folk art universal is its suicidal aversion to notation and memory, its weakness and fragility and willingness to go extinct. This is what Dylan understood so well when he went electric.

The ultimate and rarest climax of folk music is the kind that is achieved through improvisation. By its very nature, improvisation is dead on arrival; it represents the last gasp of a dying soul. The screams and applause for a jazz soloist who moves, confuses, and excites a roomful of people is always tragic, I suppose, but the tragedy is expected and staged. Find a song trapped in a roomful of people who don't expect or know it, and give it no chance for retrieval or YouTube sharing, and you will have an instance of improvisation. What is left behind we can love and should treasure, but the chronological remnant is never the same as the phenomenological origin.

The vitalist mourners and defenders of art have nothing to lose. All we have to lose is the boredom and tedium with which they torment us, their words, and my words about their words. To admit that art kills does not affect this quarrel; it takes nothing from nor adds anything to the studio, the stage, or the daydream. What it asserts is not an alternative. It is a truth that does not need to defend itself; it is sufficient enough to outlast its own demise.

Art kills all. Art kills death.

February 18, 2015
Ethika Politika

When Identity Fails: Insufficiency and Guitar Pedals

There are times in my life as a guitarist when I become deeply dissatisfied with my gear. I look for better models of guitar. I seek out another amplifier. I consider selling old things and buying new ones. I look at vintage catalogs and Craigslist postings. I read reviews of guitar pedals and scroll through message boards frequented by gearheads and fanatics. I long for something to add the missing sound I need in order to become a better musician.

In some cases this research is justified. One summer, I was given a gig with a band in the Twin Cities on the condition that I buy an overdrive pedal that would enable me to cover the range of lead guitar work that I would have to execute. I got the Radial "Tonebone Classic," a boutique piece of equipment that I've kept to this day. In most cases, however, this dissatisfaction signals a deeper existential frustration, one often accompanied by material changes or other events that shake up my equilibrium.

For instance, whenever my finances settle, which happens every few years or so, I tend to acquire any number of desires, new "needs" to account for the spending money with which I suddenly find myself. Some of these needs can be quite genuine, like a new pair of shoes for one of my growing boys. But most of the time these needs are projections of something deeper and sometimes darker.

Guitar manufacturers understand this. Fender and Gibson are not cheap or flimsy guitars—their popularity is evergreen for good reason. The quality and versatility of a Fender Telecaster or a Gibson ES-335 is worth almost every penny. However, beyond their products, these companies pay good money for the endorsement of famous artists. Thanks to these deals, the not-so-famous (or, as we prefer to think of ourselves, the not-yet-famous) can splurge on T-shirts and merchandise that allow us to don the brand as a form of symbolic identity.

In both directions, from the company to the stage and the recording artist, from the ordinary customer to the T-shirt rack, there is a desire expressed for a particular kind of identification with the celebrity artist.

This relationship—between the personal anxiety for belongings and the longing for an associative type of belonging through brand identification—points to concrete instances where identification can't offer the consolation of a complete or satisfying identity after all. Indeed, identity itself seems to be a rather poor candidate for what identity signifies and is, which is nothing less than the desire to be something instead of nothing, the desire for integration instead of alienation—the deepest longing of the human person to love and be loved.

This is but one small way to express my growing sense of alarm at the way questions of identity have come to obsess both left and right. Indeed, the best way to distinguish between the right and the left in the United States is by comparing the individual identities that each claims as its own. That Christians are as complicit as anyone else in playing with the politics of identity is a scandal to the Gospel demand to die to one's self.

In fact we might understand this notion of identity as a false representation of vitality. There is a sense that we live through representation and a corresponding fear that, in the absence of recognition, we will die. Not only are these beliefs ungrounded in reality, they also overlook the importance of "being there." This sense, which lends importance to recognition and representation in the first place, will not stand reduction to identity.

When I choose and craft the tone for my instrument, I select the presence and contour of sound that is required for an altogether different kind of task: a recognition aimed at showing something that is not as clear or plastic as an identity. Indeed, the work of art is often burdened by the task of how and where and exactly when to refer to the thing it tries to show. The mystery of identity is in the difficulty of its presentation and its resistance to easy and cheap representation. This is part of what I mean to suggest when I assert that art kills.

Identity in its present ideological form is about survival. It comes wrapped in a fear that puts everything on life support, the exchange of pulsating plastic lungs for breath. Everyone and everything these days is in mortal peril. The Academy is dying, the Church is in decline, the arts are disappearing, the environment is failing, the right is winning and the left is the new normal. No one except Joel Osteen these days thinks that there is much out there that is not going to pot.

I don't share Joel Osteen's optimism (or his winsome smile). But perhaps his coy act is more honest about the depth of his deceit. I doubt it. All I know, for now, is that when I ache for a new guitar, the answer to the riddle is to practice more and improve my skills and scales and put down the internet catalog.

April 20, 2015
Ethika Politika

Why Serious Catholics Should Hate Catholic Stuff

I love Mexican food.

Bordertown street cuisine, Tex-Mex comfort food, Southwestern red and green chiles and *sopapillas* . . .

Tacos al pastor, tortas, elote (en vaso), carne guisada, frijoles a la charra, CABRITO AL PASTOR.

I love the drinks, the *tamarindo*, the key lime, cilantro, the salt. Heat that actually isn't too hot.

Mariscos, fresh.

Una coca bien fria—a Coca-Cola in an ice-cold glass bottle.

The soups: from a clear, crisp fish soup to a beefy *sopa de res.* Or the spicy balance of *menudo* and *pozole.*

I live in North Dakota. *North* Dakota, an hour north of Fargo. A long, longing way from *Mexico lindo y querido*, Texas, and the beautiful Southwest, where my grandfather, uncle, and first-cousin have owned Southwestern Mexican restaurants for three generations.

I've lived in the Midwest for over a decade now, but my taste for Mexican food has not waned.

I've tried all kinds of restaurants: lunch counters tucked away in Mexican food stores; high-dollar downtown Mexican gourmet restaurants; popular "big menu" spots; better and worse and worse and worse, mostly.

I've grown to hate Mexican food. Because I love it.

I won't settle. Even when I fly south, I am usually disappointed. (Same goes for Texas-style brisket.)

My love keeps me trying to find the food I know I love, and that same love leaves me, mostly, disappointed.

There is no such thing as a chicken fajita. Literally, there is no cut of meat on the body of a butchered bird called a *fajita*. I can smell preservatives in a flour tortilla through the plastic wrapper.

My heart is restless for tacos. Real ones.

*

A year or so ago, *The Atlantic* ran an interesting essay about Jonathan Blow, a video game designer and delightfully unlikable fellow who is passionate about gaming. So passionate, in fact, that he hates most (if not all) video games.

> Blow makes a habit of lobbing rhetorical hand grenades at the industry. He has famously pronounced so-called social games like FarmVille "evil" because their whole *raison d'être*

is to maximize corporate profits by getting players to check in obsessively and buy useless in-game items. (In one talk alone, Blow, outdoing himself, managed to compare FarmVille's developers to muggers, alcoholic-enablers, Bernie Madoff, *and* brain-colonizing ant parasites.) Once, during an online discussion about the virtues of short game-playing experiences, Blow wrote, "Gamers seem to praise games for being addicting, but doesn't that feel a bit like Stockholm syndrome?" His entire public demeanor offers a rebuke to the genre's intellectual laziness. Blow is the only developer on the planet who gives lectures with titles like "Video Games and the Human Condition," the only one who speaks of Italo Calvino's influence on his work, and the only one to so rile up the gamer community with his perceived pretentiousness that the popular gamer blog *Kotaku* used him as the centerpiece of a post titled "When You Love the Game But Not Its Creator."[9]

On a related note, in a super interesting YouTube lecture, Jaron Lanier, one of the first innovators in virtual technology, gives a fascinating look at the future of learning aided by the human use and creation of digital technology. Far from naïve about technology, Lanier, the author of *You Are Not a Gadget* (2010), warns we risk forgetting that "everything about computers is denatured."[10] He generalizes to say, in reference to his disdain for Facebook, Web 2.0, mass media consumption, and even popular music: "You have to go through hating [any form of technology] first . . . be forceful in your skepticism."[11]

In other words, he is telling us to be good, passionate lovers of technology.

Both Blow and Lanier seem to echo Nietzsche's aphorism, "The man of knowledge must be able not only to love his enemies but also to hate his friends."

*

One of the more obvious—and, I suspect, ultimately self-defeating—missteps in the so-called New Evangelization has been the coinage and

9. Taylor Clarke, "The Most Dangerous Gamer," from May 2012 issue of *The Atlantic*. Retrieved from https://www.theatlantic.com/magazine/archive/2012/05/the-most-dangerous-gamer/308928/ on February 11, 2017.

10. Jaron Lanier, "Learning by Experience & Play" YouTube lecture. Retrieved from https://www.youtube.com/watch?v=F9eFZpdSeRU on February 11, 2017.

11. Ibid.

promiscuous use of the phrase "New Evangelization." Looking right at you, Fr. Robert Barron—a.k.a. Fr. Unobjectionable.

More disturbingly, many lay Catholics today seem to think that being Catholic requires an all-or-nothing sort of fanaticism.

If something, anything, is the right sort of "Catholic"—if it comes from the right side of the Church or bears an imprimatur—then it must be liked. Not only do we have to like it, we have to *want to want* to like it.

In certain niches, any (or at least most) movies, art, plays, books, websites, music, radio channels, ministries, bookstores, or whatever, will score an instant hit, given the credible label "Catholic."

"Of course I like it; it's Catholic"—this logic misunderstands what it is to love something or someone.

The fact that I love Mexican food, for deeply personal (and ancestral and autobiographical and sheer physical/aesthetic) reasons, is the very reason I hate most of the Mexican food that I actually eat.

Because I love Mexican food, I am a snobby consumer of it. My love forces me to be choosy.

*

I attended Franciscan University of Steubenville for my undergraduate studies and know firsthand that FUS is the capital of kitsch Catholicism, at least in America. But I learned to love the Church in a unique and enduring way at FUS: I learned how to be selective about things. I met fierce critics of the Church, of the University, and of me, in my classmates and professors—one of them an OFM Franciscan.

I ran with a group of people who lived on the margin of the FUS community—I was (and proudly still am) a "Delt." At bars and parties, I met people who, unlike me, were forced to go to FUS, who resented being bribed or controlled, but who also, for the most part, loved the Church in their own, very real and rich, ways.

*

Sometimes when I say what is obvious to me, others are scandalized. I'm an idiot, sometimes.

On one such occasion, I was graciously invited to talk about Catholic social teaching at a parish, and the three priests of the rectory hosted me for dinner beforehand. It was a lovely time, as these dinners tend to be. Conversation was intense, quick-paced, and fun. There was no shortage of ideas or book talk or wine.

At one point, when mulling over the huge question of how to create Catholic culture in America, I added, as an obvious aside, "EWTN is just awful. It's terrible, totally embarrassing." Conversation skipped a beat. One of the priests was clearly shocked. Thoughtfully and charitably, he asked me to clarify. The pastor cut in with something conciliatory, which knocked our discussion back on track. I started feeling guilty about offending my hosts with such a polemical remark. The night went on and I soon forgot about it.

As I prepared to leave, the pastor excused himself for a few minutes and returned with an envelope in hand. He handed it to me and blessed me. Money was tight and I knew what was in the envelope. I opened it to see how much. Inside, I found a generous check, folded in a plain card, with a note. Below the cursive signature was a postscript: "And you are right, Sam: EWTN TOTALLY SUCKS!"

*

There is a not-so-fine line between the sort of "hate" that comes from love and the other kind, the kind that comes from hatred. Any conflation of the two would be a serious category mistake. Catholics are under no obligation to lose their sense of sight, taste, and smell, and the ability to love something with all the madness of true love, simply because true mad love is other than nice.

An infectious, "nice person" altruism has seeped into our veins, candied our palates, and rotted our minds. I disagree with Pope Francis in letter when he says that grumpy people cannot be Christian witnesses. He should read the Book of Job or the Passion or St. Paul—or talk to the money changers who got their tables flipped over by a furious Galilean. Or, perhaps, in spirit, he is talking about something far more profound than being nice and fun and not hurting anyone's feelings. Who knows?

Truth be told, I sometimes hate writing at a "Catholic" blog. I don't expect to quit anytime soon, and I don't mean to sound ungrateful for the platform, but it sucks sometimes nonetheless. I don't want to write in or to a Catholic ghetto, as comfortable as it is for me to do that.

*

For Greater Glory may have been well intended, but it was a terrible movie. So was *The Hobbit* and all of the *Narnia* films produced to date. Watch *Once Upon a Time in the West* or *The Good, the Bad and the Ugly* or *3 Godfathers*, if you want to see a good western. Anderson, Malick, and Tarantino have done more for Catholics than whoever keeps producing these atrocious films about saints for Ignatius Press.

I didn't see the movie on Augustine's *Confessions* because I love and adore the *Confessions* too much. I knew I wouldn't be able to survive the experience.

If Matt Maher is the best pop music you've heard in a few years, you should really check out Atoms for Peace, or Brian Blade and the Fellowship, or much of the Black music of the 1960s and 1970s. Live, preferably.

At this point I've lost myself in my own pretentious rant, a rant that is itself problematic for the very reasons it means to describe and enumerate. Surely *I* should become a better writer and thinker, worthy of the discriminating critics I am trying to awaken.

But I'm not.

And taste is not static nor is it stable. I'm working on it. That's why I write. Maybe someday I won't have to, or I will choose to for the reasons I cannot presently.

The point remains: the flux of sensory and conceptual life within our flesh and bones and mind is not something we should take lightly or give away or oversimplify. Not even to God. That violates the very heart of the *Imago Dei*.

*

Beauty, truth, amazing, the heavens, food that makes you sit back in your chair and sigh, music that drains you of every feeling you thought you had and more, liturgy that does nothing to move you, but changes you quietly, in the dark, slowly, in silence and stillness, the space and time that produces that tiny primordial shudder from nowhere. Call it whatever you want—*this* is what is out there, in here, together, apart, whole, universal, and plural, all the same and totally different. Longing, yearning, dying for *theosis*. A God beyond all gods.

If that is what we seek, if that is what we believe (even when we cannot believe our own belief in it), then we cannot be so saccharine, so cheap, so easy.

Maybe we need to unlearn and relearn how to desire, how to think and feel and be.

To be a serious Catholic, I think we must especially learn to hate, lovingly. Even Catholic things. Even the Pope. Even ourselves.

July 13, 2013
Patheos

An Aesthetic Critique of Youth Ministry:
Miley Cyrus vs. Bonnie Raitt

Marc Barnes's critique of youth ministry has, predictably, gone viral. Today there is a measured and intelligent response posted at Fr. Robert Barron's site, *Word on Fire*, written by Fr. Damian J. Ference.

The parties in this back-and-forth make use of many scholarly and abstruse sources: church documents and properly understood Catholic teachings and traditions. The important stuff.

I will add only this: there is no reason to assume that, if parents are the *primary* educators of their children, that they must also be the *sole* educators of their children. So there is, as Fr. Damian points out at greater length, room for other people in the process than parents and clergy.

There is room for ministry.

This is slightly beside the point or perhaps redundant to what Barnes and Ference already wrote. The content.

But both of them ignore questions of style and form. For me, these are the most problematic aspects of present-day youth ministry and a great many other things besides.

The problem with youth ministry is not principally a question of orthodoxy—it is a question of aesthetic practice, *orthopraxy*.

I know countless full-time youth ministers. The good ones agree with me on this point. But this basic problem and challenge of aesthetic practice is spread far wider than Catholic youth ministries or even the Catholic Church. It turns up wherever education and pedagogy take place.

The art of teaching has been replaced by a desperate and dangerous substitute that can only be called fuckery passing as entertainment both cheap and expensive. This lame imitation is cheap in the sense of having a brief shelf life but expensive in the sense that you will find very few youth ministers working in poor parishes, urban or rural.

Youth ministry is remarkably suburban in its aesthetic and demographics.

Unlikely as it may sound, Miley Cyrus and Robin Thicke's performance on MTV last night is representative. Their onstage antics were not sexual in any way that merits serious attention. They were anything but sexual. No, what happened on that stage was a cheap, unskilled, and depraved insult to all truly vulgar and sexual performances. The effect was sterile, lifeless, and void.

The twerking was deeply racist, a label I use in its pejorative sense only on rare and grave occasions. Cyrus and Thicke highlighted the ways in which Black art—especially music—is routinely exploited, especially by those who seem to pine for the edge and credibility woven into the blues and hip-hop along with the history of suffering they express. The suburban appetite for faux thuggery and ghettoized counter-identity has a quality of longing, as though responding to a void in the plastic paradise and its meta-physics of endless pathetic pleasure.

There is also an immature maturity to this. The sort of inversion that turns children into adults and adults into children. Youth ministry is brimming with these adult-like fourteen-year-olds and childlike forty-three-year-olds. The studious and devout and serious teenager and the fun, balding, and *crazy*—and above all *cool*, in a weird endearing way—father of seven who wears hip jeans. Just look at Cyrus and Thicke: a girl in lingerie and a man in a zebra suit.

Elvis took a great deal from Black music, but he did it with the fidelity of a true master. Same goes for Sinatra and Richie Valens. While the greats imitate, the not-so-greats exploit. This need not be intentional; it might simply be a natural consequence of mediocrity.

My own music is deeply indebted to soul, jazz, and funk music. I do not take these inspirations lightly. I also have discovered that they find fertile ground in a core folkloric place: my own Latin and Mexican roots. Ray Charles took a great deal from country music. Stories. These lines are so clear to the person immersed. The blues extend from the Mississippi Delta to the Appalachian ridges—and beyond.

Nonetheless, it is irresponsible not to have a very intentional sense of one's influences. My respect for Bill Withers, and my awareness that I will never do justice to his work, forbids me to play "Grandma's Hands." Every responsible artist should cultivate that kind of humility.

This small caveat is relevant to the way youth ministry (and other forms of ministry, too) try to make themselves relevant, especially in suburban America.

Wittingly or not, contemporary youth ministry borrows heavily from the aesthetic and routine of the charismatic renewal movement. Arguably, youth ministry is the last gasp of that movement. It might be supposed that if charismatic spirituality were growing with young people, it would also be thriving among their parents. The obvious fact that it isn't shows more than I can say.

I grew up during and within the charismatic renewal and became familiar with its worship style through lengthy and intimate encounter. In fact, having begun playing at prayer meetings and Lord's Day's celebrations since the age of five, I fairly stumbled upon the charismatic style—and *into* it.

Much later, I found my upbringing came in handy for playing gospel music, contemporary and old: hymns, country gospel songs like "Just a Closer Walk With Thee," virtuosic compositions by Israel Houghton. Thousands of young artists, like Cory Henry, who bring the unmistakably "churchy" sound to everything they do, demonstrate the value of such an apprenticeship. A soul singer who cannot sing church music is not a soul singer. Period.

Watching Bill Gaither's cheesy showcases on the Trinity Broadcasting Network and listening to 1990s R&B ballads, I detected something genuinely religious. That something, whatever it was, had been missing from the incessant 4/4 praise and worship strumming that had been my speciality when I served as a music minister. Suddenly, this absence seemed grave, even fatal.

After graduating Franciscan University of Steubenville, I studied Bob Marley's *Legend*, the iconic album released after the artist's untimely death. An FUS friend, Dallas Carter, was deeply indebted to Marley and, citing his late conversion to the Ethiopian Orthodox Church, referred to him as "Blessed Robert of Jamaica." Marley's work seemed like the perfect starting point for my quest after true spiritual mojo. Indeed, I was soon shocked to discover how many tracks sounded like praise and worship music played properly: "Give thanks and praise to the Lord, and I will feel alright." Biblical references were everywhere. I began to read about Rastafarianism, whose music, I came to understand, was both explicitly secular and explicitly religious.

I went to see Burning Spear perform at First Avenue, in Minneapolis, on the same stage where Prince played "Purple Rain." The music stirred me to my charismatic roots. I recognized that I was attending what the folks at Steubenville called a "FOP," a festival of praise. This was a band playing Rastafarian praise and worship music, lifting its hands, acclaiming Jah with a banner of the Lion of Judah while a bunch of hipsters, hippies, and stoners shook their asses.

The disconnect between the band and the spectators turned the whole thing into a spectacle of sorts. The audience loved the music, but their appreciation looked uninformed.

This, putting aside the more general problems of education and pedagogy, is the fatal flaw in Catholic youth ministry: there is almost no cultural purchase on the aesthetics of the present-day youth minister's "coolness factor." His coolness is all exploitation, insincerity, and posing. He probably doesn't have the slightest idea it's all an act (and a bad one at that). As a suburbanite leading other suburbanites, he has nobody to tell him.

This has nothing to do with magisterial infidelity, or even bad liturgy. It's a crisis of aesthetics and authenticity. The problem is embedded in its signature form and style, and recognizing the problem requires immersion in that style followed by a period of deprogramming.

Small wonder Lifeteen parishes are found so rarely among the poor: poor kids would surely recognize that a cool guy with cool facial hair who dresses like them and pours his heart out (and stages balloon fights over chastity), is not the real thing, whatever official title he might wear.

Finally, there is something distinctly masculine about the model youth minister personality. That form and style are so lacking here might result from the absence of feminine genius.

Where are Bonnie Raitt and Aretha Franklin when you need them?

August 26, 2013
Patheos

I'd Rather Be Whole

Since the release of my Augustinian soul album, *Late to Love*, I've faced a number of questions about the identity of this music I've made and, more intimately, my own identity as its maker.

Many have wondered how my work as a musician can be reconciled to my work as an academic and a father. Others have wondered about the religious identity of my work, across its various media and have been generous in allowing me to offer a series of difficult answers.

Some reviewers, like Pia di Solenni, have argued the case made by Jacques Maritain: that Christian or Catholic artists needn't go out of their way to make their art Christian or Catholic. Artists need simply to be artists, which is to say good ones. *Image Journal*, which is hosting me for a concert on October 22, has neatly packaged this idea into the claim "Christian" should not function as an adjective.

For the last ten years of my life, I took claims like these to be wholesale endorsements of my work and, out of sheer convenience, I accepted them in an uncritical way. Of course, for most of that time, I was not producing very much; I still had skills to hone. Over the last few months of my creative process, however, I've developed some distance from this idea that art need not be religious in any devotional or confessional way. More and more, I am finding a great deal of existential comfort in being classified as a Catholic artist, even with all the baggage that such classification attaches.

I think where we all agree is that art cannot be terrible and that too much of the art made by Christians nowadays is exactly that. My greatest fear is that I'm no exception to that rule. To be a serious artist is to know the most severe weaknesses and limitations of one's craft. We artists try to fix whatever can be fixed, to overcome paralysis whenever it threatens to strike, and whenever possible, to dissect our shortcomings for whatever secrets they may conceal. Few people achieve the technical mastery of an instrument that we witness in some of the greats, but even *their* mastery is fleeting, not muscular, and their quest for it is never satisfied.

None of this is helped by sentimental news stories about nuns who sing karaoke or priests who deliver mediocre, not to say awful, renditions of Leonard Cohen during wedding homilies. Consumers pounce in packs on such viral spectacles, to the detriment of serious artists with or without religious inclinations who might have some hope of producing an indie album. But beyond the ceaseless work of self-promotion and the diminishing returns of marketing, existential questions continue to haunt artists as they struggle to write and perform.

Questions of artistic identity may not really be about art. They don't relate very directly to the work of playing a song or sculpting a sculpture. I suspect that the desires of the artist are nothing more or less than the desires of every person: to be what and who one is, or to at least not be otherwise. The labor poured into works of art may sometimes reflect a sharper and more descriptive image of that desire, but intuition tells me there is nothing special about it. The questions of the arts are not unique to the arts, nor are they elevated above the domain of normal human living.

Any artificial separation between a generic and an artistic way of life, between being an artist and being a person, is a red herring. It is dangerous to argue, as some do, that collapsing the work of the artist into the general human condition will obscure the uniqueness of the arts. Of course art is special. Naturally the human person offers her closest *imitatio Dei* when she creates something anew. Without a doubt the traditions and objects of the arts are the most precious treasure any cultural tradition can lay claim to. All of this is true. Yet behind each work of art, there is the worker, the artist: the person who does not have the luxury of ever being finished or complete.

Whenever I feel myself about to make some sweeping platitudinous claim about art, I remind myself to walk away. It is not my business or concern to figure out how art and the artist can reconcile their identities with any satisfaction. But I cannot help thinking that the tensions between these identities are more commonly felt than we might be led to think.

Speaking only for myself, I know that my music is probably never destined for mass popularity, either among religious or non-religious listeners.

Indie musicians, including many very of good calibre, are struggling everywhere, and making great sacrifices in order to survive. Most musicians whom I admire—even those who are now relatively well known—worked day jobs well into early middle age. The overblown glamour of celebrity causes us to underappreciate the unglamorous doggedness that most artists must cultivate simply in order to remain artists in any meaningful sense.

There is no shortage of quality music being made today. That few of the musicians behind it are Catholic or even Christian fails to move me one way or the other. Here I feel no need to root for the home team. But I am a Catholic artist because I am a Catholic person. Beyond family and friends, all I have in the way of roots and connections is this Church of ours. As Paulo Freire once put it, "I am in my faith." Without being able to explain that conceptually, I know deeply what it means for my own life—the life that provides the essential subject matter for my music, writing, and teaching.

Online commentators have recently been speculating about the dangers posed by the postmodern university to professors of faith. Secular academia, one argument goes, is just too hostile an environment for us. But for me, the exact opposite has proven true. Though some of my brothers and sisters inside the Church have questioned my freedom not to be Catholic in my music, most of my sisters and brothers outside the Church have encouraged me to be Catholic in my academic and artistic work. This may confound expectations, but I see it as evidence of grace.

The intuition behind letting the arts speak for themselves, on their own terms, with as few burdens as possible, is salutary on the whole. This is a good basic guideline. But making professions of faith may in fact be necessary for the artist. I suppose classification will always force things into specialized parts, but for my tastes, as an artist and a person, I'd rather be whole.

October 20, 2014
Ethika Politika

Black Messiah, Cracker Christ, and the Beauty of Guadalupe

After a fourteen-year retreat, D'Angelo took the world by surprise with an abrupt midnight launch of his long-awaited studio album, *Black Messiah*. Amir "Questlove" Thompson leaked the album's original title, *James River*, several years ago, so the renaming was as unexpected as its sudden release. The only direct reference in the music to the album's provocative name comes in the introduction to track two, "1000 Deaths," where Black prophetic preaching is set to a hip-hop beat. The preacher's fiery words arrive at a quick and anointed pace.

> When I say *Jesus* I'm not talking about some blonde-haired, blue-eyed, pale-skinned Cracker Christ. I'm talking about the Jesus of the Bible, with hair like *lamb's* wool, I'm talking about that *good* hair, I'm talking about that *nappy* hair . . . Jesus the Lord, the Savior, the Master, the Redeemer, Jesus the Black Revolutionary Messiah.

The distinction between the Black Messiah and the Cracker Christ is clear enough. We may dispute the exact ethnic identity of Jesus of Nazareth as an empirical question, but the anthropological narrative of sacred scripture does exclude certain races by geographic necessity. For instance, none of the peoples of pre-Columbian Mesoamerica appear in the Bible, obviously, and likewise there are no white people in the Bible, especially since the latter are a very recent invention. (For more on the invention of white people, see my talk "White History Month.")

I'll say it again because it is so obvious that it bears repeating: There are no white people in the Bible. An embarrassing counterfactual to this fact is the recent film *Exodus* that, like The Ten Commandments before it, interprets the story of Moses in Ancient Egypt with a cast of Caucasians in the lead roles.

Whether Jesus was Black or not is a trivia question for Biblical historians, but there is little doubt that the Mary we encounter in Luke's infancy narrative was definitely not Mexican or Aztec and did not speak Nahuatl. Nonetheless, the *Virgen Morena*, a racial title of endearment for Our Lady of Guadalupe, is beloved by the Mexican people for appearing in brown skin when she appeared to an indigenous peasant, Juan Diego. Here the line between biblical history and personal revelation begins to blur as the holy water turns muddy.

An authentic Christian humanism is rooted in the abolition of castes, sects, and all the other divisions we find in the New Testament from the visitation of the eastern Magi to Paul's dispute with Peter over circumcision. The humanistic development of Christianity from an obscure Jewish sect to a dissident religious universalism opposed by the Roman Empire is too easily mistaken for the atomistic liberalism of today. The latter vision of society, shaped by the derivative secular Enlightenment and sponsored by the overdeveloped nation-state, exalts color-blindness as a humanist virtue. A post-racial era has become a dry-dreamed utopia where a neutered and toothless human identity is the desired norm. No wonder the Bible has lost so much of its color, funk, and flavor. No wonder white people are the best candidates for the role of Moses and Pharaoh. No wonder race is seen as a harm and a deficit, a source of victimization and violence. No wonder we long for a whitewashed "ethnozombie," a species of human neither dead nor alive that relies on multicultural statist affiliations to replace ancestry and magic.

Race is a convention, to be sure. It is pure fiction, always flirting with ideology. It can be dangerous and downright monstrous when used as a calculus to decide the value of a life. It can breed self-hatred and shame. This is the picture many seem to agree on, against which savage egalitarians resist in the pathetic style of know-nothing non-denominational ecumenists.

The realities produced by the fiction of race are more beautiful than most of us realize. No one wants post-ethnic food; indeed the idea of non-ethnic food could only actualize as a healthy, dystopian nutrition pill or something that kills food altogether. A feeding tube will never look delicious. The arts are perhaps the greatest testament to what race can do, how it can shape an era, a social imagination, fill a groove to recall an ancient melody. As with all truly beautiful things, there are no romantic escapes here. Racial pride is always too few steps removed from ethnic cleansing. But to wish away the humanity of Christ's geographic place and physical face for a generic Cracker Christ is to mistake St. Paul's humanism for John Lennon's.

The post-racial pipedream is a form of ethnic cleansing that hides in plain sight, without shame, irony, or self-consciousness. It is bloodless genocide. It does not even give its victims the agency of suicide. This is an accountant's altruism, the sort of banality Hannah Arendt called evil.

D'Angelo's *Black Messiah* conjures and conveys something radical and different. The sentiments behind the Guadalupe cult are echoed in the "Black is beautiful" cultural movement of the 1960s from which D'Angelo's soul music draws deeply. Both celebrate the beauty of the colored body, a body that inherits its marks from the ancient peoples of Mesopotamia, a body that, like Moses and Polycarp, stands in the shadow of Empire. The image of the Black Messiah is revolutionary because, like the brown *Virgen* on the tilma of Juan Diego and the flag of Guadalupe Hidalgo, it contrasts the strategic ideological whiteness of the American Empire, an empire that cannot recognize Jesus as a Middle-Eastern man of Jewish ancestry who was tortured and executed by Roman soldiers. It is an empire too used to its blue-eyed, blond-haired Cracker Christ.

I have sometimes wondered why I am able to write the word "cracker" or "honky" or "gringo" in a way I cannot, in good conscience, type the n-word or "spic." That the latter term is one I am able to subvert with my own

Latino identity is beside the point. What is it about whiteness that willingly takes up the role of an absence, a void that blackness fills? This is not merely a question of melanin. This is present in the Irish imagination of C. S. Lewis, who saw Narnia bewitched under a white spell and liberated by color, in a sacramental struggle where we see the cradle of Christmas and the Cross of Calvary in a single thread.

The fundamental paradox we find in the convention of race is much deeper than sociology. It is present in the paradox of Christian humanism: Jesus is the ultimate everyman, a brother to all, a Jew who reached out to the gentiles, a redeemer whose historical humanity is mingled with the mysterious Divine, a God who is fully human. The paradox of Davidic genealogy and geographic particularity, the fulfillment of the prophets and the Jewish covenant, and the mystical Word that became flesh to illuminate all men, is not solved by subtraction. Indeed, it is not a riddle: he is a Child to be adored by kings. As D'Angelo's preacher proclaims, he is Jesus the Lord.

The universals and particulars, the one and the many, substance and accident will remain to be quarreled over and contradicted. We can hold the periodized Jesus in our hearts and minds and make pilgrimage to the Holy Land. We can see Christ as our brother and see him and his mother as our own kin, of our own color, eating our own food. The clothes that swaddled the babe of Bethlehem are kin to the linen cloths that wrapped him a second time, in a tomb. The lights of his birth and resurrection are not two, but one. The cradle and the Cross, the Black Messiah born of *La Guadalupana*, with a Welsh bass player holding the groove: these are the mysteries of our faith.

January 7, 2015
Ethika Politika

Thanksgiving as Forgiveness

"Thank you."—"I'm sorry." A simple redemption lives in those utterances. There is grace there.

During the heyday of the charismatic renewal, at prayer meetings and Lord Day's, there was always a time of thanksgiving, usually during praise and worship. A guitarist would strum a sustained chord and await prayers of thanksgiving to chime in aloud: "I want to thank you Lord for the gift of life . . ." "Thank you Jesus for healing my sister . . ." "Thank you for gathering us all together here today . . ." A skilled worship leader had a liturgical sense of when to start and when to finish, and how to use dynamics to lead right into the next song, usually on the chorus. An antiphon of sorts—*I'm Forever Grateful* or *Give Thanks* or something along those lines.

The insight to this ritual was beautiful: we should give thanks at all times, for all things. Prayers of thanksgiving ought to measure our prayers of intercession and adoration.

The simplicity of those times and rituals, throughout my childhood and adolescence, often makes them less memorable. There is nothing terribly special about them. Nothing stands out. No pyrotechnics. So I focus my attention elsewhere and, oftentimes, create alternate realities. I re-write my past according to the way I choose to recall and recast it in the present. In this sense, I am often thankful in a selective way. There is something inherently ungrateful about that. It's out of tune, out of step, out of balance.

To be truly thankful, one must be thankful for ALL. Thanksgiving is a time to be thankful for more than what we choose to give thanks for; it is time to be chastened by the gift of total gratitude. In this sense, thanksgiving is forgiveness.

An act of total thanksgiving can become a moment of true forgiveness. Healing. Thanksgiving as forgiveness heals without anesthesia—it remembers everything, dulls nothing. Have no fear! We can thank God for suffering, pain, weakness, and doubt. The Cross. There is nothing we cannot be thankful for. There are no wrong answers. We have nothing to repress or withhold.

Today I am thankful for my life. All of it. Every part of it. Every piece that builds and sustains the whole. Even the pieces I try to hide from others and, especially, from myself. From memory. We can't remember everything, but the choice of what to remember and what to forget is not as innocent as it seems. Today I try to give thanks as an act of surrender to the total, wholesome graciousness of existence, life, and being. I am especially thankful for forgiveness, the chance to try again and again. For conversion.

Giving total thanks is impossible. We are incapable of rendering an account of everything. The finite cannot grasp the infinite. This absolute gap is worthy of our thanks too. For only emptiness requires grace.

"Thank you."—"I'm sorry." A simple redemption lives in those utterances. There is grace there.

November 22, 2012
Patheos

EPILOGUE
Philosophy and the Offering of Death

Dedicated to the memory of Martha Stella Bonilla (October 26, 1982—July 15, 2016).

IN YESTERDAY'S LECTURE, I was unprepared to offer anything in relation to the jarring news of the sudden and tragic passing of our classmate Martha Bonilla. Today, in this week's final lecture on philosophy, I am moved by a sense of debt to her memory and by our common need to process this event as something more serious than mere sad news. For this reason, I will attempt a meditation on the notion of philosophy as a preparation for death, which dates back as far as Plato. In educational parlance, philosophy is an invitation (and perhaps an imperative) to learn how to die.

I will insist on distinguishing between a *gift*, something that is given and demands acceptance, and an *offering*, something that can only be offered but cannot demand acceptance, reception, or even acknowledgment. A gift invites us to receive whereas an offering is simply offered, and the offering itself is sufficient regardless of the terms of its exchange or refusal.

This distinction haunts me as I consider the specific fact, which I learned along with the news of Martha's death, that Martha enrolled in this class so as to offer me the chance, not only to be her teacher in the context of this three-week period of study, but also to consider joining her doctoral committee. This offering of hers is real to me, though Martha herself is completely absent, apart from her name on my class roster and her friendship with my student, our colleague, Maryam Dalkilic.

What does one mourn when the dead are not revealed in the gift of a relationship? More importantly, *whom* does one mourn? A possibility? A ghost? A stranger? A future consigned to a recent past? Where does the object of affection live in the experience of the death of the one who never arrives and never gives but nonetheless offers a chance to feel the loss of an encounter that never took place? Where would Martha sit? What would she say to us, and how would we begin to understand the presence we were never able to observe or experience, directly or even indirectly?

These are not theoretical questions, and philosophy in this sense is equally not theoretical. In the presence of death, we struggle to find words. We are speechless. But more specifically, in the presence of *this* death, I struggle to find the import of philosophy, the "So what" of philosophical tools and skills. In philosophy today, I am afraid, I see mostly technical formality and historical records. These miss the intimacy of the empty chair and the voice silenced forever, the absent person in our midst who is not in our midst, and who could so easily slip into the oblivion of *pro forma* acknowledgement.

The challenge, then, is not simply to see what philosophy becomes in the encounter with the question of death. It is to divine what, if anything, distinguishes philosophy from the trivial things of life. Trivialities vanish at the hour of death, and good riddance to them. How does philosophy differ from the bills that will go unpaid, the tuition and registration deadlines to be ignored, the tedium of life severed so abruptly and instantly by the passing from life into death?

It is hard to defend a conception of philosophy that lacks relevance in the actual and real face of death. This notion of philosophy becomes, like all other things, no more important than the regular tedium of daily life: groceries, where is the washroom, and television. Fortunately, there is a sense of philosophy that does retain a capacity to contemplate and even plumb the abyss of death without suffering complete annihilation.

To appreciate this sense of philosophy we must first abandon all pretensions to systematically categorize it into discrete areas of study, or even into a historical narrative of past legacies and intellectual progressions. No. Philosophy as a preparation for death has no big words or -isms or clever distinctions for logic chopping and analysis. Nor is it reducible to erudition or intellectual history. It can only toil in the near-paralysis that death brings.

The word for this paralysis in Greek is *aporia*, which describes the state of being puzzled, but in this case the metaphor of the puzzle is too shallow. Philosophy does not merely puzzle over death; philosophy, like all things, is interrupted by death, and the only question is whether anything remains after that most radical rupture and interruption.

We might consider education under a similar light. If education is to be something lasting and even something capable of looking wide-eyed into the face of death without losing its significance and reality, then perhaps the education we can experience, if we allow ourselves to accept the offering of death we have been presented with here, is coextensive with what philosophy as a preparation for death is. If philosophy is a preparation for death, perhaps learning how to die is its educational outcome.

Because I cannot bear the weight of continual abstraction when facing this concrete and real instance where death has struck a shared relation, albeit a relation to whom we have little to no actual relationship, I must also mention that our classmate died alone, far from her home in Colombia. I am not sure to what degree her isolation adds to the tragedy of her death. It fills me with sorrow, but it also causes me to feel kinship with Martha. Perhaps I am grasping at anything that will justify my sense of grief, which includes a grief for the absence of my grief, my sadness over the modest scale and proportion of my sadness. I am saddened by the loss of Martha, a loss that was never a loss since there was never a finding, but this sadness seems too minuscule, so I am also sad for the insufficient lack of my sadness.

Martha was born only five days after me, on October 26, 1982. Like me she was a Latin American living in Canada. These facts make it easier for me to claim some connection with this person, whom fate has denied me the chance to meet. These factors are not so much quantities to be calculated and balanced as they are qualities that distill my sorrow into a glass of grief that remains strangely opaque.

When a loved one has died, *eros* is present for reasons anyone can understand. We remember the loved one and desire to have them once again in our midst, the grip of love is firm and strong and refuses to let go. But the *eros* present when the departed is an unknown quantity feels almost more tragic because of its mystery, or perhaps because of its pure potentiality, its sense of fiction. But this is a weaker grip, a soft and even fleeting grasping, hard to even feel or touch.

Philosophy, for me, was first a way to escape the conditions of my everyday. It was a way to hide and to defend a position of weakness and most of all material poverty. Philosophy did not so much empower as it distracted me and eventually seduced me into its trap. Even without mastering or gaining much direct knowledge of philosophy, I was able to intuit its importance. Philosophy struck me first in the heart, long before I was capable of holding it in my head. Only later did I realize that philosophy had something to say about life and humanity that was much less extravagant than the message it delivered to me about my own condition of anger and fear and constant sense of inadequacy. This something didn't advertise its importance with pompous-sounding phrases like the "the human condition," but it was closer at hand and consoled me in a more intimate way. Really, it was terrifying.

In this way, I became aware that philosophy could prepare us for death. My concern at the time was not my own mortality, but about a choice between living and dying, options that contrast more starkly than any other two. Facing yesterday's news of Martha's death as I prepared for this lecture on philosophy, I found myself lost in a similar sea of emotions, albeit emotions that came in the form of melancholy more than outright grief. I could not conceit to give anything like the lecture on philosophy a philosopher should give; I could only try to offer a meditation, a gamble, on the possibility of understanding philosophy in the light of a loss I could not properly feel, and the feelings this absence of feeling produced.

In our present age of therapeutic self-help and pop psychology, melancholy might be the definitive condition. Surely we want to know so much about what people have to say about themselves because we have so little to say or think about ourselves. Thus, we find the constant polling of opinion that, according to some, has become the new social science (even though this it is the most antisocial thing imaginable to quantify and qualify things into data and process that dead data through scientific research and fake findings). But perhaps this looming anxiety is less a condition of our times than a collective mood that defies explanation by reference to any contemporary crisis. If melancholy and anxiety were considered products of our time alone, we would miss the fact that philosophy as a preparation for death was realized 2,400 years ago by Socrates, as he stood trial for the corruption of Athenian youth.

Gathered here, in this classroom, we must bear in mind the fact that this anxious and melancholy mood is not only "out there" somewhere in the trials of geopolitics, journalism, and more. This melancholic mood is also the state that results when we are moved to think in a way that is neither reducible to pure reason nor divorced from the human faculties of thought for which reason is essential. It is aroused by death, not in the abstract, but in the actual, real loss of someone whose company most of us did not have the chance to even properly lose.

Mood motivates this kind of philosophy. It evokes a particular philosophical idiom that is unconcerned with the more technical aspects of philosophical inquiry but still expresses the most basic idea of what philosophy is, or at least should be, namely, the *love* of wisdom.

Is not my melancholy born from the sense that I cannot love Martha as she perhaps should be loved without betraying love itself? Were I to mourn her in such a way that pretended her to be my beloved, I would surely be a fraud and my sorrow would not be for her, but instead, for the melodrama of my own self-deception. So, as a coping mechanism, my mood clouds my mind and I seek wisdom through understanding, or at least through the fleeting sense of understanding I can render into the words, sentences, and paragraphs that I am reading to you now. This is a lecture. A lecture most faithfully refers to a *lectura*, a reading. In light of philosophy's claim to be the love of wisdom and a means of preparing for death, is there a more concrete way of "doing philosophy" than writing down thoughts and reading them aloud, offering them before others, during a moment of shared bereavement?

Wisdom arrives *in extremis*. It requires a certain sobriety and focus but also intoxicates through mood and other things. To love wisdom in this way is simply to acknowledge it as an offering. There is wisdom here, in the absent presence of a person we all might have known but now can know only through never having known her.

Imagine walking through breeze-ruffled curtains of translucent gray silk, seeking a human figure suggested by nothing but airy shadow and motion. Whenever the person sought seems to be within embracing distance, we reach out with both arms and find ourselves grasping silk, only silk, while the impression of a more substantial human presence lingers just out of reach. For me, this image captures the experience of loving wisdom. I am not sure if the metaphor can be generalized, but as I seek words and images that might communicate something real and true to you, as I try to convince you of something I am not sure I myself understand, and as I equally try to keep Martha's memory alive and to make sense of that desire which cannot move me to grieve, as it remains stuck between the awareness of melancholy and the neutrality of modern life, I sense that every point of emphasis is a distortion but also a glimpse of something worth inspecting.

Wisdom cannot be loved if it is unlovable. If wisdom is a car or a piece of dry skin or something that is not a true object of affection, then it goes without saying that there is no sense to philosophy, the love of wisdom. For wisdom to be a true object of affection, it must be not only *something*; it must transcend the objective state to become *someone*, to become a subject. We can like objects like cars, we can even like them a lot, but love is not a hobby and objects must become subjects to be loved. The beloved is always a who, never reducible to the what.

What philosophy requires, then, if it really means to prepare us for death, is a notion of wisdom worthy of love and capable of loving in return. Notice that love has been simply asserted, without explanation or exposition. This is because love operates in this exact way: it asserts itself without ever explaining or exposing itself in full. Wisdom, on the other hand, is easily confused and lost. When we lose a wisdom worthy of love, we lose the capacity to love wisdom. Here we find the death of philosophy that is starkly opposed to, and indeed brings an end to, philosophy as a preparation for death.

To prepare for death is to accept death, even to accept death as an event that offers the wisdom that philosophy loves. This wisdom, however, is painful and doesn't joke around. This wisdom is serious, dead serious. This means that the wisdom of death that we prepare for by loving it is essentially tragic. We do not love the comedy of death; its wit and humor are sharp but empty when the time comes to die. Death's timing is not a punchline but a punch to the gut. Anyone who has been punched in the stomach knows the symptoms of philosophical inquiry: the shortness of breath, the gasping for air, the dull and strange pain sometimes followed by nausea.

The signs of tragedy are not accidental to death, death itself is the tragedy that we all are consigned to play in, and philosophy as a preparation for death is the learning how to die that may *console* us with wisdom but cannot *change* the script. Death is the ultimate hegemon. When death comes near, and especially when it comes near so suddenly to someone we don't even know but whose absence haunts our gathering all the same, a philosopher cannot ignore or explain it away.

So this is where I am: I can either disavow philosophy as absent in the presence of death or I can attempt to show and offer a notion of philosophy that prepares us to face this presence, a presence that for us arrived yesterday and looms here now. I am unsure that these words make any argument for philosophy, or even any argument, period, but this is perhaps the most remarkable quality of philosophy. Like poetry, which Carl Leggo described as being *capacious*, philosophy is not only unafraid of death; philosophy is ultimately obsessed with it. This obsession often leads philosophy to attempt suicide. Unlike science, which advances through scientific progress, philosophers sometimes try advance the field by destroying it. The detritus that remains is often more potent than, but more or less identical to, its antecedent.

In other words, it is not that philosophy becomes useless when death arrives. It could certainly be useless; this is not saying that philosophy is good or even worthwhile, all things considered. What it is saying is that the tragedy of death gives birth to philosophy itself; whenever death arrives, philosophy is born anew. With each chance to prepare anew for death and learn how to die, I am again called by wisdom to love her and to renew myself as a lover of wisdom and, consequently, to bring renewal to the soulcraft of philosophy. The tragedy of death, and the more profound tragedy of a tragic death, is what Augustine calls a *felix culpa*, a happy fault, a dark and flawed but rich and beautiful chance for renewal and redemption. Martha's death has called me to renew my commitment to philosophy. What a sinister and wretched offering, what depths of insight and wisdom, what a wondrous and mysterious and most terrible fate!

All this means is that philosophy can be a preparation for death, but this preparation is also what it means to make philosophy a way of life. In the mutual embrace of life and death, we find a fuller view, but a view that "begins in a minor key," as William James put it. Tragedy, suffering, loss, and more: in these dark moments of wisdom we find what love is, a love more durable than the hobbies of liking, an *eros* that extends beyond enjoyment. Out of obligation to that love, I have taken the enormous liberty of asking you to suffer through these thoughts that, most of all, attempt to gather the airy, empty curtains of Martha's life here with us, a life that never actualized into a gift, but which I accept as an offering all the same.

I hope you will find some time and space to consider my own offering here under similar terms.

May the souls of the faithfully departed, through the mercy of God, rest in peace. Amen.

University of British Columbia
July 29, 2016

APPENDIX
An Interview with Sam Rocha

MAX LINDENMAN: In these writings, you express frustration with both of the major existing political parties in the United States because, despite their differences, they reject any good more transcendent than that of the autonomous individual. Can you describe what kind of political arrangement would succeed in upholding a higher good?

SAM ROCHA: The two-party system in the United States is too small a target. Even if we had five viable parties, as they do in Canada, I would bet my life that all of them, in one way or another, would buy into the mythology of Enlightenment liberalism. In some ways, this puddle-deep teleology ending with the autonomous individual illustrates a widespread modern political predicament: without a *polis,* there can be no politics.

Here's what I mean by that: The Greek city-state was the exception in its own time, and perhaps in most times. Most of the surrounding associations were not built around a *polis.* They were empires. Babylon, Assyria, Egypt, Persia, later Rome, and so on. So the choice, as I see it, is between the *polis* and the empire, between politics and imperial rule. This means that the basic unit that all modern so-called politics take for granted, the autonomous individual, is but a micro expression of a certain kind of existential imperialism. Nowadays, everyone's an emperor ruling over an empire the size of a private home, or even smaller. Why should millions of Augustuses stoop to helping manage a *polis*? What chance would any of them have against all the other Augustuses?

To return to the classical categories of government, we can have a rule by one, by the few, or by the many. To those three, I would add a fourth: rule by all. I've presumed to improve on Plato and Aristotle in this instance because rule by *many* and rule by *all* really are two different things—just ask the people not included in the "many."

In the first three classical categories we find monarchy and tyranny, aristocracy and oligarchy, democracy and ochlocracy, or mob rule. These pairings cover the rule by one, few, and many, but I think rule by all is worth exploring. Its debased form may be collectivism, just as monarchy's debased form is tyranny, but I don't think that should disqualify it straightaway. I think the political theology we find in Judaism and more fully in the writing of Paul hint at rule by all as the ideal. It is hard to outline in the concrete, but I think it requires a deeply imaginative political theology and, also, a complete dismantling of the autonomous individual of political liberalism. The "higher good" this would uphold is, to my mind, obvious.

On the subject of education, rule by all has a few implications that bear outlining in bold. First, the *polis* itself is the educational apparatus, modeled, by analogy, on the soul itself. We see this in Plato's *Republic*, Aristotle's *Politics*, and also in Augustine's *City of God*. In Aquinas we see the analogy metaphysically expressed as *analogia entis*. In an empire, by contrast, there is no need for education to take a theological approach. Aristotle tutored Alexander and a few other aristocrats in Macedonia, whereas the democratic Athens and even oligarchic Sparta had internal and general senses of universal education. So not only can there be no politics without a *polis*; lacking a *polis,* there is no room or place for real education. We see this now in the adoption of compulsory schooling, a pale substitute.

This extends back into my rejection of the autonomous individual because this miseducated imperial self lacks the analogy to the soul necessary for the theological formation of an existential *polis*. Most of us today have no idea what it means to be a divided and communal person. In his *Confessions,* when Augustine exclaims, "My inner self is a house divided against itself," he is speaking a language largely forgotten. This is but one reason why, in this book, I cannot separate politics from education any more than I can separate theology from folk culture, and so on.

Alienation, the frequent fate of the autonomous individual, may stand as modernity's most articulate and compelling critique. Emperors are lonely by strict definition, even more so than their subjects. They also suffer more stress than your average helot—"Uneasy lies the head," and all that. Paradoxically, autonomous individuals are often bored; in fact, only autonomous individuals *can* be bored, because to be an autonomous individual requires existential alienation.

MAX LINDENMAN: In many spots, you take aim at the modern political actor's determination to preserve maximal freedom. Pope Leo XIII would agree—in his encyclical *Libertas*, he defined true freedom as the freedom to pursue moral good according to the dictates of reason. He contrasted this with false freedom, or license, which permitted people to enslave themselves by sinning. Usual suspects like legalized abortion aside, in what ways do you believe our constitutional republic permits too much license?

SAM ROCHA: The confusion between positive and negative freedom is a good place to start. Positive freedom is freedom to do something, negative freedom is freedom from being made to do something. As the Bill of Rights demonstrates, our present constitutional republic does recognize the distinction. For all the fire I direct at liberalism, I have to credit liberal theorists, from Locke to Rawls, with recognizing not only positive and negative *freedom*, but also positive and negative *rights* and so on. I am less confident that United States politicians have ever been so careful as the theorists, or the framers of the Constitution, but my ungenerosity in this respect might be a cliché at this point.

More fundamentally, the problem is baked into the previously discussed autonomous individual. There was never a time when one's freedom was entirely denied, even in the wholly negative sense. Indeed, the place of conscience within the political self and community is precisely what raises the question of freedom. The problem as I see it is one of imbalance and faulty emphasis. The maximization of freedom is pursued, not as a means to an end, but as a moral end in itself. This could only make sense in a system that took the autonomous (and alienated) individual as its ideal. As I observed earlier, this makes every person into an empire of one, incapable of engaging in real politics or receiving real education.

In the United States, the folklore supporting this "maximal freedom," as you rightly call it, is revolutionary and rebellious, but also rather naïve and even pathetic. Even the Romantics, who wanted to see humanity freed from civilization and directed back to Nature, understood that this would not mean free love and weed for everyone. I think the libertarian legacy of the hippies, which was distinct from the vision of the beats and completely out of joint from the various civil rights movements of the 1960's, communicated these noxious ideas globally in an exalted way that captured everyone's imagination and has dominated it ever since.

The free-love hippie vision is essentially escapist. It sets aside no place for suffering. For that reason, it's neither free nor loving. I consider this the fatal absence in any political climate that seeks maximal freedom.

The hippies didn't appear one day in a cultural vacuum. In some ways, they're worthy heirs to the Bostonians who found a few pence tax on tea to be as intolerably oppressive as other people have found arbitrary arrest and extrajudicial killing. One must admit that the Boston Tea Party makes the Trojan Wars look downright noble. The Greeks fought for Helen, for the pagan institution of marriage even, while the American colonists threw a fit for the sake of cheaper luncheon imports. For me, the problem is not so much license as it is the sensibility that makes its extension into an overriding moral imperative.

MAX LINDENMAN: Recent polls report that Millennials are losing faith in democracy and are, increasingly, willing to criminalize certain types of speech. Do you see these trends in any way as vindicating your own indictment of the liberal order?

SAM ROCHA: Generational demographic polling strikes me as being a major part of the problems of this liberal order. Besides, Methuselah, I am myself dated a Millennial, technically speaking. So perhaps my defensiveness to the question is a self-parody.

On the other hand, I cannot deny that part of what drove me to publish this book was a sense that I have been vindicated by current events. I mean, I did call the Trump phenomenon as far back 2011, and my political critique of the Catholic Right predated the Age of Francis by a crucial couple of years.

Nonetheless, I think the disatisfaction with democracy is completely understandable, unless you're so blinded by ideals of American exceptionalism that you can't recognize a pattern when one recurs right before your eyes. Look at the turns against democracy of the past century. Lenin was hardly a Millennial, and the rejection of democracy in the Middle East is surely not a generational effect. No, I think that democracy will always find critics because it is ultimately self-defeating. Where majorities rule, an anti-democratic majority is always a live option.

In the American experiment, we find a more quixotic empire than the categories I drew earlier: the *polis* that is not political. We might call this the placebo *polis*. Interestingly enough, many of the features of polling (another etymological relative of the word *polis*) that create these demographic assessments were classically understood to be anti-democratic. For instance, elections were seen as oligarchic to the Greeks, especially during the Periclean Age, since they so obviously lean in favor of a certain social class, as we can see today in the United States—and as I try to point out in my writing on a radical presidency in Part Two. Democratic representation in the direct democracies of classical antiquity relied on lottery, not election. Only the autonomous individual would see modernity's so-called free and democratic elections as guarantors of maximal freedom. Past a certain point, common sense is bound to re-assert itself. When that happens, malfunctioning institutions come in for criticism.

Now, the question of censoring speech shows how, deep down, the maximal freedom we claim to seek is as empty as our imperial farce of democracy. I am deviating here a bit because I am not sure how, exactly, dissatisfaction with democracy leads to suppression of speech. In my mind I see them more as multiples of the same phenomenon. Here, in the move to police language, we actually see freedom of speech and expression pressed to their natural limits and observe the convoluted madness that has become the logic of modern democratic nation-states: We can say anything which means there is nothing we can say. Now we find out that, in reality, there are real things we cannot say.

What it calls for, of course, is not a regime of schooling that criminalizes forms of speech (schools of all kinds are the places where much of this censorship is happening) but, instead, a robust return to the political education of rhetoric, public speech, and all forms of truly political speech. I doubt Millennials will do this en masse, but I do think that every generation will find a voice to express its own crisis of faith in the secular religion of modernity, especially its version of democracy, which has never lived up to its hype.

MAX LINDENMAN: Your ideal seems to be the creation of an *ordo amoris*, a social order based on love. I understand St. Augustine coined the term. What, exactly, did he mean by it? Are you using it in exactly the same way?

SAM ROCHA: The expression come from Augustine's *City of God* XV.22: ". . . it seems to me that it is a brief but true definition of virtue to say, it is the order of love." He means something similar to Plato and Aristotle's "order of the soul," which refers to the political order of the city. In other words, for Augustine, virtue is manifest through the ordered analogy to God that we find in love, and this order is the basis for a just and good city.

Augustine, like his predecessors, had in mind a *social* order of love, to be sure, but when we consider the *theological* footing he envisions for this social order, we find that the *ordo amoris* is not a legal framework like the U.S. Constitution or even the Ten Commandments. It is first and foremost a deep mystery in which we find a Trinitarian expression of politics—the sort of "rule by all" I gestured toward in my response to your first question.

In Augustine's *Sermon 24* we find an equally succinct articulation of love in his famous saying "*nemo est qui non amet*," "no one is who does not love" or "without love, no one is." Here the order of love is not merely moralistic or axiological, related solely to virtue and the just structure of social relations; it is nothing short of the Trinitarian order of creation to which the alternative is nihilism. To call for an order of love as a basis for political association is not an innovation. It is a call to revive the classical ideal that matter must follow form. The form in this case is love and this demands a theological reply before it results in a social or political one.

So I hope I am using the *ordo amoris* in an Augustinian way, which does not reduce the *ordo amoris* to the order of virtue or even the city. This order must begin in a theological exploration that drives down to the very dawn of creation—the depths where we are faced with a choice between something or nothing. The metaphysics we'd find at these depths would be radical indeed. They would not resolve into the sort of order we might expect in these days of technocratic economy.

The *order* of the *ordo amoris* draws us into the depths of mystery, where we find that the order of love is love itself, a love that cannot be totalized nor extracted. It can only be loved in return. The amorous basis for this order is mystical, to be sure, but I think that mysticism may prove more tenable in the long run than the alternatives, which rest upon a false metaphysics or simple bad faith.

MAX LINDENMAN: You express a great deal of sympathy for the theology of Jean-Luc Marion, who argues that Descartes was wrong about man's being a rational animal, first and foremost. In Marion's view, man loves before he thinks. How would internalizing that concept, as we seem to have done with Descartes', change the way we relate to one another? (It's a big question, I know, but work with me.)

SAM ROCHA: This *is* a huge question, but I think I can answer it more or less directly. Marion has exercised an enormous influence on my thought; in fact I wrote a lot of the material in this book during my first encounter with his ideas—love's first blush, you might say. I took a theological entry into his thought, but today I think there are other routes as well. The one I will use in reply to your question is psychological, foundational to his phenomenology.

Marion actually defends and upholds the Cartesian tradition with this one exception you mention. Marion arrives at that exception through his reading of Descartes' third meditation of his *Meditations*. Marion's objection shows how Descartes' *ego cogito*—who is really just Descartes himself—cannot think or reason without the first spark of intuition, which is none other than an amorous spark. The *ego amans,* as Marion calls the person who loves her way into existence, does not so much replace the *ego cogito* as correct and perfect her. We humans aren't other than rational, but our reason presupposes passion.

Without our gut feelings we would have absolutely no psychology. No ideas or judgements or sense impressions come to us through pure reason, without a prerequisite layer of feelings, emotions, and vague impressions of that intuitional sort. William James had the same dynamic in mind when he wrote of a "sentiment of rationality."

To me, phenomenologically speaking, this is simply the state of affairs. It is how thinking works and how the soul, mind, brain, and body function. We can still remain rational animals, a coinage more Aristotelian than Cartesian, so long as we don't forget that we are rational *animals*. That is, we do our reasoning with the help of an *anima*, or soul. This is a matter of emphasis and, as always, order.

So what would change if we were to restore the emphasis to its proper place? I tend to think that it would change everything by reattaching us to the real; in other words, it would change everything by refusing to change anything. In the same way, the Christian idea of conversion, *metanoia*, turns or transforms us into who we truly and most fully are. The deepest change does not actually *change* us or anything else; it remains faithful, fiercely so, to the real. Revolution in this sense is metaphysically conservative. Now, I should warn you that the real comes with no obvious consolations; instead, it entails numerous risks and dangers. But I believe that contact with the real is the first step toward abandoning the fantasies, projections, ideologies, etc. that bind us. And nothing confines us more snugly than the empty promises of licentious freedom. Love liberates by returning us to our own psychology, to the primacy of intuition by reasserting the proper route from the heart to the head.

Now, when we move from the psychological to the real itself, we return to theology. One might say that this route from psychology to theology is Marion's crowning jewel as a phenomenologist. Marion's theology begins with his book *God Without Being,* but I think his more recent study of Augustine, *In The Self's Place*, rounds out a better overall picture, especially when understood through the lens of the book that came right before it, *The Erotic Phenomenon.*

In Marion's usage of Augustine—"*nemo est qui non amet*," is the epigraph to *The Erotic Phenomenon*—we find the options resituated from nothing versus something to nothing versus love. Love then replaces the more generic being of something. Marion's view would have a more profound effect than simply changing our relations to each other, or even to ourselves. It would change our very relation to reality. No longer could we find the real in the raw matter of *Something;* the real would only appear to us incarnate as *Love* itself.

Today I am very interested in presenting a more robust articulation of what I mean by love, which I have consistently referred to as *eros*. The source I find most illuminating for this task is another Augustinian, Benedict XVI, our emeritus pope. In terms of my present concerns and sources, I would say that Benedict XVI has in many ways extended Marion's analysis for me. Right now I find Benedict XVI's recovery of *eros* for Christianity to be perhaps even more radical and revolutionary than Marion's similar suggestion of an *ego amans* to complete Descartes' *ego cogito*.

MAX LINDENMAN: You seem to have found a pet peeve in the tendency of some modern forms of discourse to either condemn or attempt to perfume away the harsher side of human existence. For example, you look down on catch-and-release fishermen for insulating their consciences against the predation inherent in fishing. You write of ethnic pride as a reality that should not so quickly be cast overboard in favor of some utopian sense of shared humanity. At one point, you write, "Hatred, in its purest form, can be a kind of reverence." How, in your view, can reserving a place at the table for pride, for the will to dominate, even for cruelty, serve the cause of creating the *ordo amoris*?

SAM ROCHA: Your questions are becoming more and more difficult to answer because they expose and even irritate the tension that runs through this book and that perhaps holds it together. This tension is something I often feel in my work, and sometimes it is an experience on the verge of tearing my mind apart. But I do not dare loosen it, except to try and tune it as I might do to a guitar string; there are times when the tension needs to be adjusted for the sake of making it productive.

I say all of this because it is a meta description of the sort of answer I want to give to your question. Another example might be in the poetic fact that antonyms, like light and dark, can be used at exact odds from their literal meanings. Our language possesses a wit that prevents it from narrowing onto itself, it can escape and transform itself through complete artistic inversion. Instead of paired opposites pulling on either end of the rope, this wit is the *tension itself* that binds the two poles together in a subtle relation of unity and opposition.

Some people might call this dialectics. I am fine with that so long as we are clear that a true dialectic is absolutely negative. In this sense I am a Hegelian, although Hegel's wit is surely neoplatonic. Thesis and antithesis are not reconciled; they are both wholly negated, giving way to a new creation. If you look at the political problems I've tried to outline, you will see how they are really problems of a positive anti-dialectical approach that works through addition and misses the revolutionary wit of total subtraction.

In theology, you can find this double-edged negation in all forms of apophasis, kenosis, sacrifice, ascesis, and other related things. Fasting and all that. The danger here comes in the form of distraction; we are tempted to fetishize these practices and forget what we're supposed to be creating in the first place. We miss the tense poetics of the relation.

So when I assert, "Hatred, in its purest form, can be a kind of reverence," I am of course referring to love. After all, true hatred is impossible without loving to hate just as true love is always built on the trial of hating to love. This, again, puts us in touch with the metaphysical abyss between nothing and love. This may sound like empty cleverness or slippery rhetoric, but if we look closely enough at the wit built into language, we can see the blueprint for a worldview that cannot afford to be anesthetic.

When we think of a story like Shelley's *Frankenstein*, subtitled "A Modern Prometheus," we see the failure even more clearly—and the gothic wit of that very failure. Literature is really the best microscope we have for this kind of research. In our attempt to protect the imperial self, we have entered into peril previously unimaginable. We moved from an apocalyptic imagination to an actual potential for planetary apocalypse. What a time to be alive! Things have never been so good as they are now in this respect. We lost the idea and now have to live with its reality. Sci-fi cannot keep up with reality.

But beneath it all remains the potential for re-enchantment. However bad things are, their wretchedness makes them interesting. One shallow but accurate way to square this sense of tragedy with my conception of the *ordo amoris* is to insist that whatever the *ordo amoris* is, it can never settle for being good or true if those qualities make it uninteresting. Beauty, in this sense, is the fundamental tension that measures against the dull extremes of moralism and logic-chopping truths. It is either this or a bullet to the head, which is a graphic and extreme way to assert the same morbid notion of beauty I opened the book with.

Encountering the possibility of death, which can happen when hatred is let loose, prods us to choose love over nothing. Awful as this might sound to most people, replacing *that* choice with other forms of the beautiful sounds infantilizing to me. Some, like Solzhenitsyn, are unlucky enough to face this choice in an actual gulag; I see in at the shopping mall.

MAX LINDENMAN: Ivan Illich, the Catholic priest and educator turned social critic, has obviously exerted a major influence on your intellectual development. In your essays, you've made many references to his book *Deschooling Society*, where he attacks modern schooling on the grounds that it "objectifies" the human person. Can you provide us with a few examples, either from Illich's work or from your own experience, how schooling transforms people into objects?

SAM ROCHA: For the most part, I had a great time in school, despite the hardships of moving all the time and matriculating into one school after another after another. The game of school is very much my thing. Too many critics of schooling are just mad over some spilled milk—personal pain or things gone wrong at a petty level. I do not share disdain for schooling at this anecdotal level. I don't think Illich does either. After all, Illich wrote the essays that would comprise *Deschooling Society* while running a language school of his own in Cuernavaca, Mexico. By all accounts, it was an excellent language school and Illich was a demanding and strict teacher.

I mention this because when we think of the objectification of the human person, we can very easily substitute lesser harms in place of objectification. To be objectified is to be dehumanized, depersonalized, to be treated as something entirely other than what and who one is. To be objectified is to be reduced from an end to a means. Objectification is not just this nasty thing Teacher X said that caused me to doubt my abilities. Objectification is the slavery that operates at such a sophisticated level that one becomes accustomed to it, even enamored with it. Those objectified do not resist their own personal demise. If anything, the objectified ask politely to be further and totally objectified. The best objectification is the kind that feels good and makes it all seem worth it, which happens to be a wonderful description of the modern day school.

In *Deschooling Society*, Illich shows how the modern compulsory school most thoroughly objectifies the poor by making them despise their way of life to the point where they effectively desire their own destruction. It is congruent with what Frantz Fanon wrote about in *Black Skin, White Masks*, and what Carter G. Woodson described in *The Miseducation of the Negro*, or even what Francis writes about in *Laudato Si*. But for Illich the fundamental confusion results from the creation of a new order of "needs" sold as the modern, developmental narrative of schooling.

The best evidence of this is what in many ways built the ideas for Illich which was not only poverty, but the specific poverty of Latin America, from Puerto Rico to Cuernavaca, and also the *favelas* of Brazil. When Illich sees the poor starving, he questions whether they can be best saved from starvation by being schooled into an alien way of life, one in which they compete in the marketplace on its own terms. In this sense, the object of Illich's critique is the entire poverty-industrial complex, which seeks to save the poor not simply from their poverty but from their very selves and convivial ways of life.

There is a small bit of Romantic "noble savage" built into this view. But having lived in Latin America, I have to say Illich doesn't romanticize anything out of recognition. We see the same dynamic at work in the United States, which sells its commercial values, along with its own image of itself, through the school institution, just as it penalizes through the prison and pathologizes through the hospital and the pharmacy. All of this selling, penalizing, and pathologizing is not hard to see or find, and the school is teeming with evidence of it. If I gave you one or seven good examples I would still be understating its effects. I would instead ask anyone to give one positive counterexample.

MAX LINDENMAN: You're a university professor, and I happen to know that you take the teaching side of your job very seriously. Do you find yourself at all able to deschool your students? If so, how? For that matter, how do they like being deschooled?

SAM ROCHA: I can't take full credit for this, but I always have been proud that not a few of my students have chosen to leave the profession on principle. While studying in my classes, several student-teachers have decided not to teach in schools. Some of these still believed they were called to teach, they just saw fit to do it elsewhere. Two that come to mind immediately pursued religious vocations—one to the Catholic priesthood, the other to the rabbinate. You can bet they'll be doing plenty of teaching from the pulpit, among other places.

But if you really want to see deschooling in action, at least as I practice it, I offer my track record as a father to three children—a subject I touch on from time to time in my writing. All three of my children seem to like being deschooled, some more than they should. Should they ever be enrolled in a school—which for me is not incompatible to deschooling—I think they will always find it difficult to equate what goes on there with education. That basic distinction between schooling and education is one I try to impress on all my students, and I think many of them understand it. In fact, some try to deschool me by challenging that distinction in a way that forces me to make it in a more sophisticated way.

MAX LINDENMAN: It's my understanding that Illich proposed, as an alternative to schooling, the creation of "learning webs," in which people interested in acquiring a particular skill would use modern technology to seek out those who could teach it. He made this recommendation in 1971, long before the development of the Internet. To what extent do you believe that the Internet has realized its potential as a facilitator of learning? I ask because you've also written about the ways in which the Internet serves to objectify us even more than other media have done. It encourages morbid curiosity regarding death and disaster, it plays to our tribal instincts and encourages us to think in simplistic binaries. Is there any way that the plugged-in person of today can use his critical judgment to find or build some facsimile of the *ordo amoris* online?

SAM ROCHA: Illich spends a chapter on learning webs in *Deschooling Society,* and in many ways it is the least inspiring of his ideas in that book. I find the chapter that immediately follows it, "Rebirth of Epimethean Man," much more fascinating. But his learning webs do *resemble* the World Wide Web, it's true. Unlike most Illichian scholars, I find it hard to read much into this relation for all the reasons you point out. Illich lived into the years of the internet (he only died in 2002) and by all accounts was agnostic about it. Plus, all digital repositories work on an analogy to analog forms of library archiving (that is why we use the terms folder and document and mail). If learning webs have any promise, we shouldn't expect technological innovation alone to fulfill it.

Illich comes much closer to the *ordo amoris* when he talks about conviviality, which he does in his aptly-titled book *Tools for Conviviality.* Learning webs would be a tool, but they could never replace conviviality, which fills a theological need. Many who take learning webs on their own miss this. Add to this my sense that learning needs to be qualified, i.e., surely there are better and worse forms of learning, and I won't be quick to get excited about Illich's learning webs.

But I also think that the total separation of digital and analog forms of social relations is overstated. Deceptions equivalent to "catfishing"—creating a false online identity—go back ages, and have always piqued the literary imagination. Shakespeare was obsessed with them. Read *The Merry Wives of Windsor.* I tend to read in buses and I even walk and read, which is dangerous. How is this different from being on a phone? The whole "real person" idea is for me more dangerous today than the conspiracy theorists. This attitude I have is, of course, built on a philosopher's conceit: I don't really think that fundamentals ever change. The idea that big data or supercomputers are going to reveal the nature of consciousness or bring about a new world order leaves me cold and agnostic. I think Illich has this same blood in his veins. So his criticism, and my own, should not be reduced to problems that are at least mostly made up.

Now if I were to recommend a critic of the internet and digital culture it would without question be Jaron Lanier. I refer to him in my essay on Catholics hating Catholic stuff. He really understands what this thing we call "digital" is, as an analog object. He is able to show, for instance, how binary code can be saved through music in ancient instruments that rely on on/off, ones and zero switches and controls. So I'd say skip Illich and go to Lanier for technology commentary, but for the *ordo amoris* stick with Illich's conviviality.

MAX LINDENMAN: The title of this anthology, and of the essay introducing it, is "Tell Them Something Beautiful." You speak of truth with beauty as superior to plain truth. Later on, you supply many examples of beauty in the forms of art and music, and well-executed liturgy. You're a musician and a wordsmith—not to mention someone who, in the words of one of your early pastors, "knows how to move at the altar." How can ordinary schlubs with none of these talents infuse their truth-telling with beauty?

SAM ROCHA: I need to insist on a very particular idea of beauty. Otherwise, as you justly note, beauty can be limited according to elite ability, intelligence, or technical skill. For me beauty is not going to save the world, as Dostoevsky thinks, nor is beauty an axiological or normative quality. Sure, there is something *beautiful* about beauty, but this quality is not the end of the story. Otherwise, beauty is nothing more than an affectation or something precious but inessential.

A qualitative or messianic beauty comes about through accident. My sense of beauty is as a substance. In the concrete flesh of beauty, I think we encounter a paradox: the paradox of art. This paradox conceals the true rigor of art. This rigor, as any artist can attest, is not technical or analytical or even therapeutic. The rigor of art is simple and total. The artist's first and last work of art is her life, which always operates in the shadow of death. Without a sense of one's life as the primal work of art, the medium of artistic expression becomes a distraction. One might find this a bit harsh, but again I am not speaking of art as a critic would; I am asserting that what I mean by beauty can be found in art precisely because art's demands are rigorous.

But the raw materials for this primary practice of art are not the exclusive property of a caste of trained specialists. They exist as a fundamental part of the human condition. This is a condition we all share, a transcendent condition that extends even beyond the human person and into the world itself. The evidence can be found in love and suffering. The fashioning of a self, a life, a society, a *polis*, a dress, a family, a party, a soul, a song, a story, a painting, a garden, a shudder, a eulogy, a memory set to prose. All of this is working from the same excessive resources that cannot be relegated, I think, to specialization. *Amor mundi*, as Hannah Arendt put it. Sure, there is room here for better and worse and all sorts of qualification, but the terms and criteria are, I think, impossible to lay out as a rubric or system of beauty. Beauty is more than that, infinitely more.

What this means for truth-telling is that everything that bears witness to the truth has a potential for beauty—even those things that bear witness to the truth of a lie, deception, or perversity itself. I could yell "1+1=2!" to people all day long and I would, mathematically speaking, be telling the truth. But of course there is something untrue about what I am doing. I am merely expressing an obvious logical statement in an annoying arithmetic way. There is nothing inspiring about it; there is nothing true about it below the surface of the simplistic calculation.

This so-called truth is what I feel many defenders of "the truth" today have reduced truth to. It is an ugly, wretched truth. The performance belies the content. Beauty here, for me, does not save or redeem what is true. It is not a mere supplement or balance. Beauty, in this formulation, is the form that the content of truth needs if it is to express and reveal itself. Without form, matter is contingent and cold. Bloodless. Absent.

As this book shows, I've listened to countless homilies, lectures, sermons, and speeches. My dad is an evangelist, and I was raised going to churches, retreats, and so on. I heard some amazing homilists along the way. Fr. Joseph Goetz, at evening Mass at St. Joseph's Cathedral in Columbus, Ohio set the bar really high. As I wrote in "Liturgy as Mystagogy," he had a Ph.D. from Cambridge in philosophical theology, yet his homiletic formula was simple and accessible. He opened and ended with the sign of the Cross and always read a short meditation he had prepared in advance where he drew on observations from his daily life. Those homilies fed and sustained me during a time when I was running on spiritual fumes.

Imagine the contrast when I arrived in Crawfordsville, Indiana, at the local parish, St. Bernard's. The priest there had just arrived, he had a military background. He was shy and seemed somewhat aloof. I didn't see or hear him regularly because I ran the choir for the Spanish Mass, celebrated by priests who drove in from nearby Lafayette. When I did hear his homilies, they were bad enough to be exquisite. They relied on spiritual platitudes and canned jokes and were delivered in a way that felt forced, but not in bad faith. Just forced.

As I got to know my pastor better, I came to believe he had a mild case of Asperger's. Occasionally I would attend the Masses he celebrated on campus, for the College. One week I heard him give the same annual diocesan appeal homily he had delivered at the parish to the College. In the context of parish life, this homily suffered from its usual faults; at the college, it failed to make the slightest sense. After Mass, I don't recall how, I happened to see a copy of his homily manuscript. It was highlighted and bolded in a way that made clear that he relied on textual clues to tell him when express emotion.

Only a man of true humility would have taken that trouble, I realized. Father's awareness of his own limits was obviously the product of deep reflection. It showed a kind of brilliance. He had always been in the habit of referring to himself as an idiot, but now I realized he wasn't fishing for compliments; he was describing himself in terms he thought accurate.

Now this priest happened to have gifts unrelated to preaching. He was generous to everyone around him. By all accounts, he had brought that small parish's finances under control. Knowing all this about him, I began to find his homilies fascinating and deeply beautiful. This man was a schlub's schlub, just doing his job. I won't say I miss his homilies in the same way I miss Fr. Goetz's, but I do miss *him*. His words might have sounded clumsy in a vacuum, but the beauty of his person bled into them. In his notable weakness, he showed and taught me something profoundly beautiful. If you ask me today who was my favorite homilist, it would be him.

I could go on and on, but the point in this case is very simply laid out in the distinction between the two wonderful priests and their beautiful homilies. The former shows a sort of beauty that is exclusive and rare; the latter shows the universal form and substance of the beautiful. This notion of beauty requires no ability or skill in the technical sense, but it can grow and thicken and even deform in its manifestation or concealment. We see it perhaps most strikingly in struggles and failures, just as the human person is uniquely beautiful in her first and last moments, moments that are developmentally opposite but also identical in fragility and grace. Our mortality, our weakness, our fear, the burdens and the atrocities, the bitter, tragic side of beauty is what we can all reach for without needing any special training.

It is this side that I find absent today, but in its absence can be found a deep longing and a real hope. This hope is perhaps best expressed by Monica, in book nine of Augustine's *Confessions*, when on her deathbed she proclaims, "Nothing is distant from God, and there is no ground for fear that he may not acknowledge me at the end of the world and raise me up."

Amen.

Bibliography

Aristotle. *Politics*. Translated by C. D. C. Reeve. Indianapolis, IN: Hackett, 1998.

Augustine. *The City of God*. New York: Random, 1950.

———. *Confessions*. Translated by Phillip Burton. New York: Alfred A. Knopf, 2001.

Benedict XVI. *Caritas in veritate*. Encyclical Letter. June 29, 2009. Online: http://w2.vatican.va/content/benedict-xvi/en/encyclicals/documents/hf_ben-xvi_enc_20090629_caritas-in-veritate.html.

———. *Deus caritas est*. Encyclical Letter. December 25, 2005. Online: https://w2.vatican.va/content/benedict-xvi/en/encyclicals/documents/hf_ben-xvi_enc_20051225_deus-caritas-est.html.

Cavanaugh, William T. *The Myth of Religious Violence and the Roots of Modern Conflict*. Oxford and New York: Oxford University Press, 2009.

Collins, Suzanne. *The Hunger Games*. New York: Scholastic, 2008.

Descartes, Rene. *Meditations on First Philosophy with Selections from the Objections and Replies*. Translated by Michael Moriarty. Oxford: Oxford University Press, 2008.

Doyle, Brian. *The Thorny Grace of It and Other Essays for Imperfect Catholics*. Chicago: Loyola, 2013.

Ellison, Ralph. *Invisible Man*. New York: Vintage, 1995.

Foucault, Michel. *The History of Sexuality*. Translated by Robert Hurley. New York: Pantheon, 1978–1988.

Francis. *Evangelii gaudium*. Apostolic Exhortation. November 24, 2013. Online: http://w2.vatican.va/content/francesco/en/apost_exhortations/documents/papa-francesco_esortazione-ap_20131124_evangelii-gaudium.html

Illich, Ivan. *Deschooling Society*. New York: Harper and Row, 1971.

Jackson, Shirley. "The Lottery." In *Novels and Stories: The Lottery, The Haunting of Hill House, We Have Always Lived in the Castle and Other Stories and Sketches*. New York: Library of America, 2010.

James, William. "What Makes A Life Significant?" In *Talks to Teachers on Psychology and to Students on Some of Life's Ideals*. New York: Henry Holt, 1910.

———. *The Will to Believe and Other Essays on Popular Philosophy, and Human Immortality*. New York: Dovers, 1956.

Lanier, Jaron. You Are Not A Gadget: A Manifesto. New York: Alfred A. Knopf, 2010.

Marion, Jean-Luc. *The Erotic Phenomenon*. Translated by Stephen E. Lewis. Chicago: University of Chicago Press, 2007.

———. *God Without Being*. Translated by Thomas A. Carlson. Chicago: University of Chicago Press, 1995.

Meinong, Alexius. "The Theory of Objects." In *Realism and the Background of Phenomenology*, edited by Roderick Chisholm, and translated by Isaac Levi, D. B. Terrell, and Roderick Chisholm, 76–117. Atascadero, CA: Ridgeview, 1981.

Okin, Susan Moller. "Is Multiculturalism Bad for Women?" In *Is Multiculturalism Bad for Women?* Edited by Joshua Cohen, Matthew Howard, and Martha C. Nussbaum. Princeton, New Jersey: Princeton University Press, 1999.

Plato. *The Republic.* Edited by G. R. F. Ferrari. Translated by Tom Griffith. Cambridge; New York: Cambridge University Press, 2000.

Ravitch, Diane. *Death and Life of the Great American School System: How Testing and Choice are Undermining Education.* New York: Basic Books, 2016.

Rawls, John. *A Theory of Justice.* Oxford: Clarendon, 1972.

Rocha, Samuel D. *Folk Phenomenology: Education, Study and the Human Person.* Eugene, OR: Pickwick, 2015.

Rorty, Richard. *Philosophy and Social Hope.* New York: Penguin, 1999.

Taylor, Charles. *A Secular Age.* Cambridge, MA: Harvard University Press, 2007.

Tolstoy, Leo. *The Death of Ivan Ilyich.* Translated by Richard Pavear and Larissa Volonkhosky. New York: Vintage, 2009.

Webb, Stephen H. *Blessed Excess: Religion and the Hyperbolic Imagination.* Albany: State University of New York Press, 1993.

———. *The Gifting God: A Trinitarian Ethics of Excess.* New York: Oxford University Press, 1996.

West, Cornel. *Democracy Matters: Winning the Fight Against Imperialism.* New York: Penguin, 2004.

Woodson, Carter Godwin. *The Mis-education of the Negro.* Trenton, NJ: Africa World, 1990.

Zizek, Slavoj, and John Millbank. *The Monstrosity of Christ: Paradox or Dialectic?* Edited by Creston Davis. Cambridge, MA: MIT Press, 2009.

Index